READING LUKE-ACTS IN ITS MEDITERRANEAN MILIEU

SUPPLEMENTS TO
NOVUM TESTAMENTUM

EDITORIAL BOARD

C.K. Barrett, Durham - P. Borgen, Trondheim
J.K. Elliott, Leeds - H.J. de Jonge, Leiden
A.J. Malherbe, New Haven
M.J.J. Menken, Utrecht - J. Smit Sibinga, Amsterdam

Executive Editors
M.M. Mitchell, Chicago & D.P. Moessner, Dubuque

VOLUME CVII

READING LUKE-ACTS
IN ITS MEDITERRANEAN MILIEU

by

CHARLES H. TALBERT

BRILL
LEIDEN · BOSTON
2003

This book is printed on acid-free paper.

Library of Congress Cataloging-in-Publication Data

Talbert, Charles H.
   Reading Luke-Acts in the Mediterranean milieu / by Charles H. Talbert.
      p. cm. -- (Supplements to Novum Testamentum, ISSN 0167-9732 ; v. 107)
   Includes bibliographical references and index.
   ISBN 90-04-12964-2 (hb : alk. paper)
   1. Bible. N.T. Luke--Criticism, interpretation, etc. 2. Bible. N.T. Acts--Criticism, interpretation, etc. I. Title. II. Series.

BS2589.T345 2003
226.4'06--dc21

2002033037

BS
2589
.T345
2003

ISSN   0167-9732
ISBN   90 04 12964 2

© Copyright 2003 by Koninklijke Brill NV, Leiden, The Netherlands

All rights reserved. No part of this publication may be reproduced, translated, stored in a retrieval system, or transmitted in any form or by any means, electronic, mechanical, photocopying, recording or otherwise, without prior written permission from the publisher.

Authorization to photocopy items for internal or personal use is granted by Brill provided that the appropriate fees are paid directly to The Copyright Clearance Center, 222 Rosewood Drive, Suite 910 Danvers, MA 01923, USA. Fees are subject to change.

PRINTED IN THE NETHERLANDS

To
Donna Orsuto and the Lay Center
and
The Pontifical Biblical Institute
in Rome

TABLE OF CONTENTS

Preface	ix
Acknowledgements	xi
1. On Reading Luke and Acts	1
2. Succession in Luke-Acts and in the Lukan Milieu	19
3. Reading Aune's Reading of Talbert	57
4. Prophecies of Future Greatness: The Contributions of Greco-Roman Biographies to an Understanding of Luke 1:5–4:1	65
5. Jesus' Birth in Luke and the Nature of Religious Language	79
6. The Way of the Lukan Jesus: Dimensions of Lukan Spirituality	91
7. Martyrdom in Luke-Acts and the Lukan Social Ethic	105
8. The Place of the Resurrection in the Theology of Luke	121
9. Conversion in the Acts of the Apostles: Ancient Auditors' Perceptions	135
10. Acts 20:7–12 as Early Christian Apologetic	149
11. Once Again: The Gentile Mission in Luke-Acts	161
12. The Theology of Sea Storms in Luke-Acts	175
13. What is Meant By the Historicity of Acts?	197
Bibliography	219
Index of Modern Authors	233
Index of Subjects	237
Index o Ancient Sources	239

PREFACE

The essays published herein reflect a selection of my work on Luke-Acts done since the late 1970's as I was gaining clarity about my method: reading as a participant in the authorial audience. They originally appeared as scattered items, often in out of the way places like *Festschriften*. Being pulled together between two covers allows them to be seen as a coherent reading of the Lukan writings.

That these essays appear in print in this form is because of the services of a number of people. This volume appears in the *Novum Testamentum* Supplement Series due to its gracious acceptance by the editors, David Moessner and Margaret Mitchell. It appears at all because of the painstaking copy-editing of my graduate assistant, Michael W. Martin, who has transformed a variety of editorial styles into one, following *The SBL Handbook of Style*, edited by Patrick H. Alexander and others (Peabody, Mass.: Henrickson Publishers, 1999). It is to that Handbook that the reader is referred for abbreviations used in this book. This study was supported in part by funds from the Baylor University Research Committee that underwrote Mr. Martin's expenses during the summer 2002. The generous permission given by the original publishers to use these essays in a new form is gratefully recognized in the Acknowledgments. As always, any productive work on my part would not have been possible without the stimulating and supportive relationship over the years with my wife, Dr. Betty W. Talbert. To these loved ones and friends I say, thank you.

Charles H. Talbert

ACKNOWLEDGEMENTS

Grateful acknowledgment is made for permission to use previously published material of mine.

'Luke, Gospel of,' *Dictionary of Biblical Interpretation* (ed. John H. Hayes; Nashville: Abingdon Press, 1999), 2:91–96.

'Succession in Mediterranean Antiquity Part 1: The Lukan Milieu,' and 'Succession in Mediterranean Antiquity Part 2: Luke-Acts,' *Society of Biblical Literature Seminar Papers, 1998* (2 vols.; SBLSP 37; Atlanta, Georgia: Scholars Press, 1998), 1:148–68, 169–179.

'Prophecies of Future Greatness: The Contribution of Greco-Roman Biographies to an Understanding of Luke 1:5–4:15,' *The Divine Helmsman: Studies on God's Control of Human Events, Presented to Lou H. Silberman* (ed. James L. Crenshaw and Samuel Sandmel; New York: KTAV, c. Vanderbilt University Divinity School, 1980), 129–42.

'Jesus' Birth in Luke and the Nature of Religious Language,' *The Heythrop Journal* 35 (1994): 391–400. (c. The Editor/Basil Blackwell Ltd, Oxford, UK)

'The Way of the Lukan Jesus: Dimensions of Lukan Spirituality,' *Perspectives in Religious Studies* 9 (1982): 237–50.

'Martyrdom in Luke-Acts and the Lukan Social Ethic,' *Political Issues in Luke-Acts* (ed. Richard J. Cassidy and Philip J. Scharper; Maryknoll, New York: Orbis Books, 1983), 99–110.

'The Place of the Resurrection in the Theology of Luke,' *Interpretation* 46 (1992): 19–30.

'Conversion in the Acts of the Apostles: Ancient Auditors' Perceptions,' *Literary Studies in Luke-Acts: Essays in Honor of Joseph B. Tyson* (ed. Richard P. Thompson and Thomas E. Phillips; Macon, Georgia: Mercer University Press, 1998), 141–154.

'Once Again: The Gentile Mission in Luke-Acts,' *Der Treue Gottes Trauen: Beiträge zum Werk des Lukas, Für Gerhard Schneider* (ed. Claus Bussmann and Walter Radl; Freiburg: Herder, 1991), 99–110.

'Acts 20:7–12 as Early Christian Apologetic,' *I Must Speak to You Plainly: Essays in Honor of Robert G. Bratcher* (ed. Roger L. Omanson; Carlisle, UK: Paternoster Press, 2000), 83–96.

'A Theology of Sea Storms in Luke-Acts,' *Jesus and the Heritage of Israel: Luke's Claim upon Israel's Legacy* (ed. David P. Moessner; Harrisburg, Penn.: Trinity Press International, 1999), 267–83; *Society of Biblical Literature Seminar Papers, 1995* (SBLSP 34; Atlanta, Georgia: Scholars Press, 1995), 321–36.

'What Is Meant by the Historicity of Acts?' *Reading Acts: A Literary and Theological Commentary on the Acts of the Apostles* (Macon, Georgia: Smyth & Helwys, 1997), 237–54.

CHAPTER ONE

ON READING LUKE AND ACTS

This volume contains a selection of my essays on Luke and Acts produced since the late 70's. They reflect a certain method and yield a coherent reading of the Lukan writings. The essays can best be understood if the approaches employed in them are seen within their context in the history of interpretation. Because of the availability of sources, Luke will be the focus of this survey, with Acts discussed as appropriate.

The Interpretation of Luke in Early Christianity

The interpretation of Luke has generally followed the cultural and religious currents of the times. In the early period the context for interpretation was the church. The occasions were two: the demand for a defense against heresy within the church and the need for an apology directed toward the world outside the church. Tertullian and Cyril of Alexandria represent the former, Augustine the latter.

Luke was early on the object of Gnostic and Marcionite interpretation. Irenaeus complained that Valentinians disregarded the order and connection of the Scriptures and adapted the Gospels to their own positions.[1] For example, there are, they said, three kinds of people: material (Luke 9:57–58), animal (Luke 9:61–62), and spiritual (Luke 9:60; 19:5); Achamoth wandered beyond the pleroma and was sought by the Savior (Luke 15:4, 8); Simeon (Luke 2:28) is a type of the Demiurge, Anna (Luke 2:36) a type of Achamoth (*Haer.* 1.8.3–4). Marcosians, Irenaeus claimed, also misinterpreted the Gospels, e.g., for them Luke 2:49 speaks of Jesus' announcement of the Unknown God (*Haer.* 1.20.2). Clement of Alexandria further charged that Heracleon, a leading Valentinian, interpreted Luke 12:11–12 in a way that allowed a Gnostic to avoid martyrdom (*Strom.* 4.9).[2] Marcion dispensed with the Law and the Prophets and in their place substituted an abbreviated version of

---
[1] *ANF* 1.
[2] *ANF* 2.

the Gospel of Luke and an expurgated collection of Paul's letters, supporting thereby his understanding of Christ as one who stood in antithesis to the creator God of the Jews.

Tertullian's *Adversus Marcionem*, book 4, may be regarded as his commentary on Luke.[3] The work's form is to take up a position of Marcion and then refute it by appeal to the Third Gospel. Its focus is that Jesus is the Christ of the Creator, with proof being derived from Luke's Gospel, since that is the narrative portion of the New Testament accepted, at least in part, by Marcion. At the end, Tertullian concluded: "Marcion, I pity you; your labor has been in vain. For the Jesus Christ who appears in your Gospel is mine" (4.43). The first full-scale orthodox interpretation of Luke, then, was by an early third century anti-heretical Latin writer of North Africa who used the Third Gospel to refute Marcion's *Antitheses*.

The commentary on Luke by Cyril, patriarch of Alexandria from A.D. 412 to 444, is a collection of 150 extemporaneous sermons.[4] The opening sentence of Homily Three betrays the sermonic form: "Very numerous indeed is the assembly, and earnest the hearer—for we see the church full." The focus of the commentary is Cyril's opposition to Nestorius amid the christological controversies leading up to Chalcedon (A.D. 451). For example, in Homily One on Luke 2:4, "because he was of the house and lineage of David," he says: "The natures, however, which combined unto this real union were different, but from the two together is one God the Son, without the diversity of the natures being destroyed by the union." Homily Twelve on Luke 5:14 reads: "Yes, verily, as both to think and say, that the Word of God the Father is one Christ separately by himself, and He who is of the seed of David is another." From the Greek church this early interpretation of Luke, like Tertullian's from the Latin church, had an antiheretical aim.

Augustine's *De consensu evangelistarum*, written ca. A.D. 400, employs the form of the harmony, a literary type previously produced by Tatian in the second century, Ammonius of Alexandria in the third, and Eusebius in the fourth.[5] The focus of *De consensu evangelistarum* is to vindicate the Gospel against the critical assaults of the heathen who attacked the veracity of the Gospel writers, claiming that the Gospels

---

[3] *ANF* 3.

[4] Cyril of Alexandria, *Commentary on the Gospel of Luke* (ed. and trans. R. P. Smith; 2 vols.; Oxford: Oxford University Press, 1859).

[5] *NPNF¹* 6.

contradict each other, contradict the Hebrew Bible, and add to Christ's teaching (1.7.10). Using a Latin translation older than the Vulgate, in book 1 Augustine denied that the Gospels go beyond what Jesus taught; in book 2 he examined Matthew, comparing it with Mark, Luke, and John and exhibiting the perfect harmony between them in the narrative down to the Last Supper; in book 3 he completed the project of book 2, dealing with the narrative from the Supper to its end; in book 4 he dealt with passages in Mark, Luke, and John that have no parallel in Matthew. One way Augustine sought to avoid difficulties was by supposing different instances of the same circumstances or repeated utterances of the same words. For example, the different versions of the voice from heaven at Jesus' baptism mean that both voices were heard from heaven (2.14.31); if Matt 20:29–34 has two blind men and Luke 18:35–43 has only one, it is explained by the fact that Luke is narrating a miracle wrought on a blind man as Jesus came near Jericho while Matthew tells of a similar miracle as he was leaving Jericho; Luke 5:4, although similar to John 21:1–11, refers to another, similar incident. Augustine's interpretation of Luke, then, had the practical, churchly aim of displaying the unity and harmony of all Scripture in order to refute the pagans' charges.

The Interpretation of Luke in Medieval Christianity

Early medieval exegesis, designed to move its audience, was cast in two forms: that of the sermon, if it was meant to move the hearer, and that of the commentary to be read by monks as part of their ascetic discipline, if it was meant to move the reader. The Venerable Bede's impact is from the latter.[6] This eighth century monk's exegetical writings were much in demand in later centuries and were studied and copied in monastic centers all over Europe, with the result that his authority grew to be little inferior to that of the four doctors of the Latin church. His *Commentarius in Lucam* is a good example of his exegetical work. In Bede's time to be a scholar meant digesting the learning of earlier thinkers and passing it down in a simpler and

---

[6] Bedae Venerabilis, *Corpus Christianorum. Series Latina 120, 121* (Turnholti: Typographi Brepols, 1953–); M. L. W. Laistner, ed., *Bedae Venerabilis Expositio Actuum Apostolorum et Retractatio* (MAAP 35; Cambridge, Mass.: Medieval Academy of America, 1939); idem, *Venerable Bede: Commentary on the Acts of the Apostles* (trans. L. T. Martin; Kalamazoo: Cistercian Publications, 1989).

more intelligible form. What this meant for exegetical work was that, after the fifth century, for more than one thousand years the task of a biblical commentary was that of compiling and ordering extracts from the exegetical literature of the patristic age. This Bede did. In his commentary on Luke he initiated a system of marginal source marks to indicate which passages he borrowed from Ambrose, Augustine, Jerome, or Gregory the Great, "lest I be accused of stealing from my elders, and of proposing their views as if they were my own." The focus of his exegetical work was eminently practical. In his *Historia ecclesiastica* 5.24, Bede wrote of himself:

> I have spent all my life in this monastery, applying myself entirely to the study of the Scriptures. ... From the time I became a priest until [this] the fifty ninth year of my life, I have made it my business, *for my own benefit and that of my brothers*, to make brief extracts from the works of the venerable fathers on the holy Scripture, or to add notes of my own to clarify their sense and interpretation.

The same point is made in the preface to his *Commentarius in Actus*, where he wrote that the author is Luke the physician and that "all of his words are ... medicine for the ailing soul." Bede's exegesis tended to be, like monastic exegesis in general, devotional, concerned with living the Christian life and attaining salvation.

The Interpretation of Luke in the Renaissance and the Protestant Reformation

Erasmus produced not only the first printed Greek New Testament (1516) but also paraphrases and annotations on biblical books.[7] His paraphrase of Luke (*In Evangelium Lucae Paraphrasis* [1523]) was not a translation but a freer kind of continuous commentary that nevertheless maintained the integrity of the persons speaking. The *Annotationes*, which went through five expanding editions in Erasmus's lifetime, are characterized by two principal features: Textual Criticism (his primary concern) and consideration of the opinions of the fathers (like the medieval exegetes but with greater freedom). Thus he reported the opinions of the fathers who agreed with him, pointed out differences among them to justify his own departures from commonly held views,

---

[7] A. Rabil, Jr., *Erasmus and the New Testament* (TUMSR 1; San Antonio: Trinity University Press, 1972); Erika Rummel, *Erasmus' Annotations on the New Testament: From Philologist to Theologian* (Erasmus Studies 8; Toronto: Toronto University Press, 1986).

and criticized their errors. The focus of his interpretation was the moral meaning of Scripture. Humanists like Erasmus used Luke, as they used other Scripture, to expose the folly and corruption of the church. Erasmus's favorite subjects were the tragedy of the institutionalization of religion, the sophistical nature of scholastic theology, and the worldly aspirations of the clergy. Beyond his specific moral interpretation of Luke and other NT documents, he gave the Protestant Reformation a Greek text and a philological method to use in its theological exegesis.

If humanists like Erasmus used Scripture to expose the church's corruption, Reformers like Calvin employed Scripture as a theological weapon. In his *Harmonia ex tribus Evangelistis* (1555) Calvin reclaimed an ancient form.[8] Maintaining that no one can comment intelligently or aptly on one of the three synoptic Gospels without comparing it with the other two, he treated Luke in connection with the other synoptic writers, focusing on Reformation theology. For example, when Luke 1:6 says, "They [Zachariah and Elizabeth] were both righteous before God" (RSV), does it mean that they had no need of Christ? No! They were not perfect. They needed forgiveness. Their righteousness depended on the free kindness of God whereby God did not lay their unrighteousness to their charge because of the covenant God had made with them. On this point Calvin fought against both those who read justification by faith into the passage and those Roman Catholics who claimed to be justified by works. In Luke 1:46–50, did Mary say, "Henceforth all generations shall call me blessed" (RSV) because she sought renown through her own virtue and efforts? No! She was celebrating God's work alone. Calvin held that this shows how completely Roman Catholics were mistaken in giving her titles like 'Queen of Heaven' and in conferring on her the royalty that belongs to Christ, saying, "Ask the Father, bid the Son." The holy Virgin rejects them all, fixing her glory on the grace of God. "It follows that the praises of Mary, where the might and sheer glory of God are not entirely set forth, are perverse and counterfeit." Although Calvin, like Augustine, dealt with such difficulties as the different genealogies of Matthew and Luke, his major concern remained theological; and Luke served as a tool for his aim of the theological reformation of the church.

---

[8] John Calvin, *A Commentary on a Harmony of the Evangelists* (3 vols.; Grand Rapids: Eerdmans, 1949).

Calvin's treatment of Acts was more historical than theological.[9] Nevertheless, it still functioned in the interests of reformation. Operating out of the assumption that history teaches what people ought to do and what they ought to eschew, Calvin focused on how Acts is concerned to show how God cared and still cares for the church and directed its life through the Spirit, how Satan and his hosts oppose the church, and how the apostles are examples of patience in the midst of reproach, sorrow, and calamity, trusting in God to deliver the church.

The Interpretation of Luke in the Enlightenment

H. S. Reimarus (1694–1768), professor of oriental languages at the Hamburg academic gymnasium, worked in the context of developments in the German Enlightenment's understanding of the relation between revelation and reason.[10] The leading German philosopher of the period, C. Wolff (1679–1754), held that (a) revelation may be above reason but not contrary to reason, and (b) reason establishes the criteria by which revelation may be judged. The Wolffian synthesis was attacked from two directions. Neology, the middle phase of the Enlightenment, contended that (a) revelation is real, but its content is not different from that of natural religion in general and that (b) reason may eliminate those doctrines of Christian revelation that are not identical with reason. Rationalism, however, (a) agreed that reason establishes the criteria to judge revelation but (b) contended that reason's criteria prove revelation to be false, leaving reason to exist alone. Publicly Reimarus followed Wolff in saying that natural religion prepares for Christianity; privately he joined rationalism in saying that natural religion replaces Christianity. Wolff held that there are certain criteria by which any alleged revelation must be tested: First, revelation must be necessary, containing knowledge available only by miraculous means. Second, it must be free from contradictions. Privately Reimarus took Wolff's criteria and applied them to Christian origins, as set forth in the four Gospels and Acts, to show that it is possible to trace the natural

---

[9] John Calvin, *A Commentary upon the Acts of the Apostles* (2 vols.; Grand Rapids: Eerdmans, 1949).

[10] Charles H. Talbert, ed., *Reimarus: Fragments* (Lives of Jesus Series; Philadelphia: Fortress, 1970).

origins of Christianity and that the supposed revelation is filled with contradictions. Reason's criteria thereby undermine the claims of the alleged Christian revelation.

Reimarus accepted the traditional view that Matthew and John were written by eyewitnesses, while Mark and Luke were not. He claimed that the evangelists constructed their own picture of Jesus after his death, but that they left, unintentionally and through sheer carelessness, traces of the historical reality of Jesus. From these traces one can see that Jesus did not espouse the three central doctrines of Christianity: spiritual deliverance through the suffering and death of Christ (atonement), Christ's bodily resurrection from the dead, and Christ's speedy return for reward and punishment. Jesus saw himself as a worldly Messiah, but his disciples turned him into a spiritual Savior after his death for economic reasons. It requires no miracles to explain the development of Christian origins; furthermore, the historical facts of Jesus' career contradict the claims made for him by his disciples after his death. Other contradictions are everywhere apparent, e.g., Matthew and John make no mention of the appearance on the road to Emmaus as Luke 24:13–32 does; Matthew knows nothing of the appearance in Jerusalem that is found in Luke 24:36–49; John and Matthew do not report Jesus' ascension as Luke 24:51 does; Mark 16:1 says the women buy spices when the feast day is past, whereas Luke 23:56 has them buy the spices in the evening before the feast day; Matthew and Mark report only one angel at the tomb, while Luke 24:4 says there were two. Reimarus used Luke only to illustrate contradictions in the Gospel accounts, contradictions that he believed show the falsity of the alleged Christian revelation.

Reimarus wrote as an academic, not a cleric, expressing his personal doubts in the form of an apology focused, not at the enemies of the church, but at Christianity itself. He sought to disprove its claims to have received truth through revelation. His interpretation of Luke, the other Gospels, and Acts both denied their essential historicity and exposed their creation by Jesus' disciples after his death. Reimarus is so important for biblical interpretation because on these two points his work set the stage for the subsequent interpretation of Luke and the other Gospels up to our day.

The Interpretation of Luke in the Modern World

Since 1800, interpretation of the Gospels, including Luke, has followed two very different lines. On the one hand, in response to Reimarus's denial of the essential historicity of the Gospel accounts (later reinforced by D. F. Strauss), there has been a drive to establish the historical basis of the tradition by means of source analysis and by appeals to authorship and archaeology: the quest of the historians' Jesus. On the other hand, there has also been an attempt to interpret the meaning of the Gospels in their final form by relating the tendency of each to its historical context or occasion: the quest of the evangelists' theology. The different ways Luke and Acts have been interpreted since 1800 have depended on which of these two approaches has been applied to them at any given time.

The impetus to establish the historical basis of the tradition about Jesus was sometimes undertaken on behalf of the aims of orthodox Christianity in the belief that, if the historicity of the tradition was validated, it would confirm the picture of Jesus in the Gospels. Sometimes the impetus came from the desire to overthrow Chalcedonian christology in the belief that the historical tradition behind the Gospels would reveal a Jesus more intelligible to modern times, a Jesus of obvious moral superiority to all others and, therefore, self-validating to the modern conscience. Exponents of this general approach to scholarship as it applies to Luke and Acts include A. von Harnack,[11] W. Ramsay,[12] B. H. Streeter,[13] and V. Taylor.[14]

In order to reestablish the value of the Lukan writings as historical authorities, von Harnack (1907) sought to prove that the Third Gospel and Acts were written by a fellow worker of Paul, Luke the physician. Von Harnack then (1908) reconstructed Q from Matthew and

---

[11] Adolf von Harnack, *Luke the Physician: The Author of the Third Gospel and the Acts of the Apostles* (ed. W.D. Morrison; trans. J. R. Wilkinson; NT Studies 1; New York: G. P. Putnam's Sons, 1907); idem, *The Sayings of Jesus: The Second Source of St. Matthew and St. Luke* (trans. J. R. Wilkinson; NT Studies 2; New York: G. P. Putnam's Sons, 1908).

[12] William M. Ramsay, *Was Christ Born at Bethlehem? A Study of the Credibility of St. Luke* (London: Hodder and Stoughton, 1905); idem, *The Bearing of Recent Discovery on the Trustworthiness of the New Testament* (London: Hodder and Stoughton, 1915).

[13] B. H. Streeter, *The Four Gospels: A Study of Origins, Treating of the Manuscript Tradition, Sources, Authorship, and Date* (New York: Macmillan, 1925).

[14] Vincent Taylor, *Behind the Third Gospel: A Study of the Proto-Luke Hypothesis* (Oxford: Oxford University Press, 1926); idem, *The Passion Narrative of St. Luke: A Critical and Historical Investigation* (Cambridge: Cambridge University Press, 1972).

Luke, concluding that Q was a document of the apostolic epoch, more ancient than Mark and composed in Palestine. Ramsay took what is perhaps the most historically dubious passage in the New Testament, Luke 2:1–4, and attempted to establish its essential historicity on the basis of contemporary discoveries in Egypt that seemed to indicate a system of periodic enrollments in Syria and the East generally. Streeter, assuming the two source theory, argued for the existence of Proto-Luke, a synthesis of Q+L that was, in fact, a complete Gospel prior to the composition of the Third Gospel. Proto-Luke appears to have been a document independent of Mark and approximately of the same date—a conclusion Streeter believed to be of considerable moment to the historian. Taylor contended that behind the Third Gospel's passion narrative was a special source, an authority as old as Mark but independent of the Second Gospel. Such an independent pre-Lukan passion narrative would assist the historian in reconstructing the events of Jesus' final days.

The focus of all these efforts was to use the Third Gospel as a window through which to view something other than the Lukan text; interpretation consisted of treating Luke as a mine from which one could dig the ore of pre-Lukan historical tradition. This concern persists—in part at least—in I. H. Marshall[15] and J. Nolland,[16] doubtless due to the authors' evangelical Christian conviction that "faith follows not feeling but fact." Since Luke was regarded as a secondary source by this line of interpretation, moreover, the Third Gospel received considerably less attention from scholars pursuing the quest of the historical Jesus than did Mark.

The attempt to interpret each of the Gospels in its final form was, initially at least, based on the assumption that the true meaning of a Gospel is determined by discerning its place in the historical development of early Christianity, as opposed to its canonical context. Interpretation, therefore, took the form of a history of early Christianity. F. C. Baur, in the first half of the nineteenth century, is the epitome of this approach.[17] Assuming J. J. Griesbach's order of the Gospels, with Matthew first, then Luke, and finally Mark, Baur read Luke as a reinterpretation of Matthew from a Pauline perspective. The Gospel of

---

[15] I. H. Marshall, *The Gospel of Luke* (NIGTC; Grand Rapids: Eerdmans, 1978).
[16] John Nolland, *Luke* (3 vols.; WBC 35A, 35B, 35C; Dallas: Word, 1989–93).
[17] F. C. Baur, *Kritische Untersuchungen über die kanonischen Evangelien ihr Verhaltnis zu einander ihren Charakter und Ursprung* (Tübingen: LF Fues, 1847).

Luke arose in its final form after A.D. 70, motivated by the party relationships of that period. Luke's universalistic tendency was a Pauline antithesis to the particularism of the Jewish Christian Matthew; it was related to an alleged occasion in the historical development of early Christianity. Thus interpretation of Luke consists of the act of bringing tendency and occasion together. For Baur, such interpretive activity must be accompanied by indifference to result and freedom from subjectivity, the shining goal toward which every true scholar presses. It never occurred to the university-based Baur that his Hegelian presuppositions were a significant component of his own subjectivity.

R. Bultmann's view of Luke in his *Theology of the NT*[18] represents both continuity and discontinuity with the interpretive scheme of Baur. Like Baur, Bultmann was concerned to set the Third Gospel in its historical context. The tendency of Luke and its companion volume, Acts, is to substitute a history of salvation for the primitive Christian imminent eschatology. The occasion is the delay of the parousia in early Christianity at the end of the first century. Faced with disappointments arising from the delay, the Third Evangelist told the story of Jesus as part of a history of salvation in which the gift of the Holy Spirit replaces the imminent end. Unlike Baur, Bultmann then engaged in content criticism: The NT contains two strata, the first embodying the early eschatological *kerygma*, the second reflecting an early Catholic fall away from the truth. Paul and John's Gospel represent the authentic stratum; Luke, among others, belongs to the early Catholic distortion of the original Gospel and as such does not have the same normative quality for the church that Paul and the Fourth Gospel have. Interpretation for Bultmann began with discerning Luke's alleged tendency and setting it in connection with an alleged occasion; it finished with a critical appraisal of the value of Luke's tendency for Christian faith.

H. Conzelmann further developed Bultmann's view of Luke as an account of Jesus that eliminates imminent eschatology in response to the delayed parousia,[19] although he refused to relegate Luke to early Catholicism.[20] Conzelmann's contribution lies in the methodology pro-

---

[18] Rudolf Bultmann, *Theologie des Neuen Testaments* (Tübingen: Mohr, 1948–53); idem, *Theology of the New Testament* (New York: Scribner, 1951–55).

[19] Hans Conzelmann, *Die Mitte der Zeit: Studien zur Theologie des Lukas* (BHT 17; Tübingen: Mohr-Siebeck, 1954); idem, *The Theology of St. Luke* (New York: Harper & Brothers, 1960).

[20] Hans Conzelmann, *An Outline of the Theology of the New Testament* (New York: Harper & Row, 1969), 298–99.

posed to discern the Lukan tendency. By noting Luke's departures from his primary source, Mark, and by paying special attention to the overall narrative framework or pattern of arrangement, one can discern the Lukan tendency. This became, with some fine-tuning, the method of Redaction Criticism that dominated Lukan studies for more than a generation. Even where the overall Bultmannian picture of Lukan theology is resisted, as in the commentaries by Marshall,[21] J. Fitzmyer,[22] Nolland,[23] and Bovon,[24] the German redaction-critical method is assumed. F. Bovon[25] summarizes the results of such redaction-critical study of Luke under the headings plan of God, the interpretation of the OT, christology, Holy Spirit, salvation, reception of salvation, and church.

At the end of the twentieth century, interpretation of Luke reflected a multiplicity of methods and approaches. In addition to those carried over from the past, five interpretive options may be mentioned in a logical, not chronological, order.

1) *Interpreting Luke in light of Mediterranean parallels.* From 1973 to 1983 the Society of Biblical Literature's Luke-Acts Group (1973–78) and Seminar (1979–83) broke with the construct of Conzelmann and developed an approach to Luke more akin to that of H. Cadbury.[26] Like Conzelmann, Cadbury assumed the two source theory and viewed Luke as a reinterpretation of Mark. Unlike Conzelmann, he did not believe it possible to detect a single dominating occasion for Luke's Gospel or a singular purpose formulated consciously in response to it; he was concerned to set Luke's literary techniques, no less than his theology, in relation to parallels from the Mediterranean world. The Luke-Acts working groups likewise eschewed an approach that depended on a dominant conception of the development of early Christianity and opted for a method of interpretation that depended heavily on paral-

---

[21] I. H. Marshall, *The Gospel of Luke* (NIGTC; Grand Rapids: Eerdmans, 1978)

[22] Joseph A. Fitzmyer, *The Gospel According to Luke* (2 vols.; WBC 28, 28a; Dallas: Word, 1981–85). See my critical review in *CBQ* 48 (1986): 336–38.

[23] John Nolland, *Luke* (WBC 35A, 35B, 35C; Dallas: Word, 1989–93). See my review in *CRBR 1995*, 270–73.

[24] Francois Bovon, *L'Evangile selon Saint Luc 9:51–14:35* (CNT IIIb; Geneve: Labor et Fides, 1996). See my critical review in *Biblica* 78 (1997): 425–28.

[25] Francois Bovon, *Luke the Theologian: Thirty Three Years of Research (1950–1983)* (Allison Park, Pa.: Pickwick, 1987); idem, *Luc le Theologien: Vingt-Cinq Ans de Recherches (1950–1975)* (Neuchatel: Delachaux & Niestle, 1978).

[26] Henry J. Cadbury, *The Making of Luke-Acts* (New York: Macmillan, 1927).

lels, especially literary ones, from the Mediterranean world. *Perspectives on Luke Acts*[27] and *Luke-Acts: New Perspectives from the Society of Biblical Literature Seminar*,[28] reflect an approach that sees interpretation primarily as setting what is said in Luke and how it is said by Luke in its immediate context in Mediterranean antiquity. The Mediterranean milieu allows one to determine how Luke would have been heard by an ancient auditor and, therefore, to discern what it would have meant to him or her. The focus is on what Luke meant in the context of his own time. This stream of interpretation has yielded monographs like that of S. Garrett[29] and a commentary by Talbert.[30]

2) *Interpreting Luke in light of non-biblical literary criticism.* The older New Criticism has been supplanted by a Narrative Criticism based on a communications model like that of R. Jakobson, which regards texts as mirrors rather than windows. This way of reading focuses on the final form of the text and concentrates on such matters as plot, characters, and type of narration by an implied author. Something of the method was presented to historically oriented New Testament scholars by N. Petersen.[31] This type of literary study is devoid of references to the Mediterranean environment just as was that of the New Criticism; thus the narrative world of the Gospel text is abstracted from its time and place. This type of reading has borne fruit in monographs like that of D. Gowler,[32] which deals with the matter of characterization, and in the commentary by R. Tannehill,[33] a combination of New Criticism and modern narrative criticism in which there is an almost total lack of references to Mediterranean sources outside the Bible. Tannehill's thesis is that the author of Luke-Acts consciously understood the story of

---

[27] Charles H. Talbert, ed., *Perspectives on Luke-Acts* (Edinburgh: T. & T. Clark, 1978).

[28] Charles H. Talbert, ed., *Luke-Acts: New Perspectives from the Society of Biblical Literature Seminar* (New York: Crossroad, 1984).

[29] Susan R. Garrett, *The Demise of the Devil: Magic and the Demonic in Luke's Writings* (Minneapolis: Fortress, 1989).

[30] Charles H. Talbert, *Reading Luke: A Literary and Theological Commentary on the Third Gospel* (New York: Crossroad, 1982); idem, *Reading Luke* (rewritten ed.; Macon, Ga.: Smyth & Helwys, 2002).

[31] Norman R. Petersen, *Literary Criticism for New Testament Critics* (Philadelphia: Fortress, 1978).

[32] David B. Gowler, *Host, Guest, Enemy and Friend: Portraits of the Pharisees in Luke and Acts* (New York: Peter Lang, 1991).

[33] Robert C. Tannehill, *The Narrative Unity of Luke-Acts: A Literary Interpretation* (2 vols.; Philadelphia: Fortress, 1986–90).

Jesus and his followers as unified by the controlling purpose of God.[34] A less insular example of a commentary written from this perspective is that of Joel Green.[35]

3) *Interpreting Luke in light of anthropological and sociological models.* J. Neyrey's edited collection is concerned with the question, What is the social system assumed by Luke?[36] Issues addressed include: What is the typical economic system in a peasant society? What are the features of patron/client relations? What is the relation between city and countryside? Who benefits from labeling another as deviant? How do honor and shame operate in Mediterranean society? Given these questions and their answers, where does Luke fit and how does he react?

4) *Interpreting Luke in the context of ancient liturgical practices.* M. Goulder contends that Luke wrote his Gospel as a cycle of liturgical/Gospel readings to be used throughout the year in Christian worship as fulfillments of the Hebrew Bible lections then existent in the synagogues.[37]

5) *Interpreting Luke in the context of the canon.* B. Childs reflects what has come to be called Canonical Criticism.[38] This approach tries to take account of the fact that as a result of the canonization process a new and larger context has been effected for originally independent material. Luke, for example, cannot be read canonically if it is interpreted in isolation from the other three Gospels. Read in connection with them, Luke can neither become part of a complete harmony of the Gospels (as with Tatian) nor be sifted to discover the real Jesus behind the levels of accretion (as with the quest of the historical Jesus). The plural form remains constitutive for the canonical critic, so the Lukan Gospel must be read as part of the canonical four. A large segment of Childs's book

---

[34] See my critical review of volume 1 in *Biblica* 69 (1988): 135–38.

[35] Joel B. Green, *The Gospel of Luke* (NICNT; Grand Rapids: Eerdmans, 1997). See my review in *Biblica* 79 (1998): 579–82.

[36] Jerome H. Neyrey, ed., *The Social World of Luke-Acts: Models for Interpretation* (Peabody, Mass.: Hendrickson, 1991).

[37] Michael D. Goulder, *The Evangelists' Calendar: A Lectionary Explanation of the Development of Scripture* (London: SPCK, 1978); idem, *Luke: A New Paradigm* (2 vols.; JSNTSup 20; Sheffield: Sheffield Academic Press, 1989). See the evaluation of Goulder's work by Mark S. Goodacre, *Goulder and the Gospels: An Examination of a New Paradigm* (JSNTSup 133; Sheffield: Sheffield Academic Press, 1996).

[38] Brevard S. Childs, *The New Testament as Canon: An Introduction* (Philadelphia: Fortress, 1985).

is given over to 'A Canonical Harmony of the Gospels,' in which he treats the final form of the text of Luke in its individuality but alongside the other Gospels read in the same way. Childs refuses either to harmonize or to attempt to establish the historical events behind the Lukan text.

In large measure the diversity of methods proposed for interpreting Luke today is rooted in biblical scholars' openness to currents in fields outside biblical studies. Their inability to choose among the multiplicity of methods derives largely from the confusion over which community they represent: church or academy. What may be appropriate for the one may not always be appropriate for the other, as F. Dreyfus has convincingly shown.[39] One's community determines what questions are deemed appropriate to ask of the text; methods of interpretation are chosen and/or developed in order to answer such questions. If there is anything the history of interpretation of Luke teaches us, it is this.

The Method(s) Employed by Essays in This Volume

The essays in this volume reflect both lines of interpretation characteristic of scholarship since 1800: theological and historical. All but the last are concerned with the theological perspectives of Luke and Acts. The last focuses on the possible historicity of Acts.

The essays devoted to the theology of Luke-Acts reflect methodological continuity with the work of Cadbury, Dibelius,[40] and the SBL Group and Seminar (1973–83) in that the Lukan milieu is deemed critical for understanding the New Testament writings. They are more particularly aligned with the work of modern non-biblical literary critics Peter J. Rabinowitz[41] and Hans Robert Jauss,[42] although the roots of such a way of reading are found in the German New Testament tradition of scholarship at least as early as Walter Bauer.[43] The essays that follow,

---

[39] F. Dreyfus, 'Exegese en Sorbonne, Exegese en Eglise,' *RevBib* 81 (1975): 321–59.

[40] Martin Dibelius, *Aufsätze zur Apostelgeschichte* (ed. H. Greeven; Göttingen: Vandenhoeck & Ruprecht, 1951).

[41] Peter J. Rabinowitz, 'Truth in Fiction: A Reexamination of Audiences,' *Critical Inquiry* 4 (1977): 121–41; idem, *Before Reading: Narrative Conventions and the Politics of Interpretation* (Ithaca, N.Y.: Cornell University Press, 1987); idem, 'Whirl Without End: Audience Oriented Criticism,' in *Contemporary Literary Theory* (ed. G. Douglas Atkins; Amherst: University of Massachusetts Press, 1989), 81–100.

[42] Hans Robert Jauss, 'Literary History as a Challenge to Literary Theory,' *New Literary History* 2 (1970): 7–37.

[43] J. Louis Martyn, *The Gospel of John in History* (New York: Paulist, 1978), 105–6,

save two, reflect a concern for the authorial audience. They join a concern for a synchronic reading of the final form of the text with a focus on the milieu within which Luke and Acts were written. Explanation is in order.

Rabinowitz distinguishes between the 'actual audience' (the flesh-and-blood folks who listen to a text), the 'authorial audience' (those for whom the author thought he was writing, who possessed the background knowledge presumed by the text), the 'narrative audience' (those with whom the narrator communicates, who have a particular understanding of reality that would not be consistent in all ways with the actual or authorial audience), and the 'ideal narrative audience' (who embrace the perspective of the narrator even when neither the narrative nor authorial audience does).

The 'authorial audience' is different from W. Iser's 'implied reader' (an idealized hypothetical reader who must be extracted from the text itself, which text is viewed as a closed, autonomous object).[44] By contrast, the 'authorial audience' is presupposed by the text. Identifying it involves a careful analysis of both the text itself and the context in which the text was produced. The authorial audience equals the contextualized implied readers.

Reading in light of the authorial audience builds also on the work of H. R. Jauss whose *Rezeptionsgeschichte* attempts to determine the horizon of expectations (= the set of cultural, ethical, and literary expectations) that would have been current at the time the work appeared.

To read as authorial audience is to attempt to answer the question: If the literary work fell into the hands of an audience that closely matched the author's target audience in terms of knowledge brought to the text, how would they have understood the work? This type of reading involves trying to adopt the perspectives of the authorial audience so that one may become a member of the author's original audience's conceptual community. To do this, modern readers must gain an understanding of the values of the authorial audience and the presuppositions upon which the original text was built. We must reconstruct the conceptual world that was used in the creation and

---

n. 169, refers to a hermeneutical rule attributed orally by E. Käsemann to W. Bauer: "Before one inquires into the author's intention, he must first ask how the first readers are likely to have understood the text."

[44] Wolfgang Iser, *The Implied Reader: Patterns in Communication in Prose Fiction from Bunyan to Beckett* (Baltimore: Johns Hopkins University Press, 1974).

original reception of the text. This approach focuses on how members of a particular culture communicate with one another.

This approach to reading yields a very different use of comparative materials from that characteristic of the old *Religionsgeschichtliche Schule*. Whereas the History of Religions School saw comparative material as evidence of Christian borrowing from non-Christian sources with the result that Christianity was perceived as a syncretistic religion, reading in terms of the authorial audience sees material from the milieu as data for reconstructing the reader who would have heard the text in a certain way. Christianity is assumed to have its own integrity as a religion. Not borrowing but understanding is the focus.

Jauss proposes a similar tack. He says:

> Whenever a writer of a work is unknown, his intent not recorded, or his relationship to sources and models only indirectly accessible, the philological question of how the text is "properly" to be understood, that is according to its intention and time, can best be answered if the text is considered in contrast to the background of the works which the author could expect his contemporary public to know either explicitly or implicitly.[45]

In reading this way, one is not claiming that the ancient readers were consciously aware of these particular texts. Rather these texts help to establish the most likely conceptual world of the readers, the authorial audience. This conceptual world is similar to what Wolfgang Iser calls "the readers' repertoire," the broader societal ways of looking at the world.[46]

The question of how the authorial audience would have understood the text is not a novel notion of recent non-biblical literary critics. Although these critics have developed the theoretical framework for such a way of reading, the awareness of the correctness of this type of approach is found in earlier New Testament scholarship. A hermeneutical rule attributed orally by E. Käsemann to W. Bauer runs: "Before one inquires into an author's intention, he must first ask how the first readers are likely to have understood the text." Quite apart from Jauss, Iser, and Rabinowitz, this stream from New Testament studies has continued into the present, as witnessed by the following: "A likely (reasonable) interpretation by an original audience ... is ... part of the social or

---

[45] Jauss, 19.
[46] Wolfgang Iser, *The Acts of Reading* (Baltimore: Johns Hopkins University Press, 1978).

public meaning of the discourse in its original moment."[47] Ultimately, this way of reading rests on the reality that authors share with their intended audience a set of background information and presuppositions that make communication possible.[48]

This approach to reading does not rule out all attempts to discern authorial intent. Richard B. Hays' comments are on target.

> Often overlooked in the discussion of authorial intention is the fact that W. K. Wimsatt, Jr. and Monroe C. Beardsley, in their landmark essay, 'The Intentional Fallacy,' *The Verbal Icon: Studies in the Meaning of Poetry* (Lexington: University of Kentucky Press, 1954), did not exclude in principle the possibility of gaining information about the author's intention in all texts. Indeed, they asserted that "practical messages"—as distinguished from "poetry"—"are successful if and only if we correctly infer the intention" (5). Their primary point was that "the design or intention of the author is neither available nor desirable *as a standard for judging the success of a work of literary art*" (3, emphasis mine). This is a proposal about aesthetics, not a skeptical stricture on historical knowledge.[49]

Sometimes, starting with the question, "How would the authorial audience have heard this text," leads to a conclusion about what the author of the text probably intended.

By authorial audience one is not necessarily referring to a particular, localized community from which and for which a text is alleged to have originated. Rather the authorial audience refers to the larger cultural milieu within which a document was read/heard. So when R. Bauckham argues that a Gospel was expected to circulate widely among the churches with no particular Christian audience in mind,[50]

---

[47] Charles H. Cosgrove, 'The Justification of the Other: An Interpretation of Romans 1:18–4:25,' *SBL Seminar Papers, 1992* (SBSLP 31; Missoula: Scholars Press, 1992), 613, says: "A likely (reasonable) interpretation by an original audience … is … part of the social or public meaning of the discourse in its original moment."

[48] Selected examples of scholars who use this method in their work include: Warren Carter, 'The Crowds in Matthew's Gospel,' *CBQ* 55 (1993): 54–67; idem, 'Recalling the Lord's prayer: The Authorial Audience and Matthew's Prayer as Familiar Liturgical experience,' *CBQ* 57 (1995): 514–30; idem, 'Matthew 4:18–22 and Matthean Discipleship: An Audience-Oriented Perspective,' *CBQ* 59 (1997): 58–75; Warren Carter and John Paul Heil, *Matthew's Parables: Audience-Oriented Perspectives* (Monograph Series; Washington, D.C.: Catholic Biblical Association, 1998); Stanley D. Harstine, *Moses as a Character in the Fourth Gospel* (JSNTSup 229; Sheffield: Sheffield Academic Press, 2002).

[49] Richard B. Hays, *Echoes of Scripture in the Letters of Paul* (New Haven: Yale University Press, 1989), 201, n. 90.

[50] Richard Bauckham, 'For Whom Were Gospels Written?' in *The Gospel for All Christians: Rethinking Gospel Audiences* (Grand Rapids: Eerdmans, 1998), 13–26.

he is critiquing the redaction critical assumption that the Gospels were produced in and for specific churches with specific problems to be addressed, by analogy with the occasional letters of Paul. His critique, however, is entirely compatible with a reading in terms of the authorial audience. When, moreover, C. R. Koester argues that the original readers of the (Fourth) Gospel came from a variety of backgrounds,[51] this poses no problem for a reading in terms of the authorial audience. Although the original readers were not entirely homogeneous, they would have nevertheless shared in the conceptual repertoire of the popular culture of the day.

Readers of this volume will be aware immediately that, even when not explicitly stated, the method used when discussing Lukan theology is a reading in terms of the authorial audience. The question is: How would ancient auditors have heard this text?

When perusing the final essay on the historicity of Acts, the reader will quickly recognize that the old handles of authorship and sources are not criteria employed. The final essay is more in tune methodologically with Dibelius than Ramsay. Like Dibelius it assumes that the historicity of Acts will be established in the sifting of the Lukan sands one grain at a time.[52]

---

[51] Craig Koester, 'The Spectrum of Johannine Readers,' in *What Is John?* (ed. F. F. Segovia; SBLSymS 53; Atlanta: Scholars Press, 1996), 5–19.

[52] Martin Dibelius, 'Zur Formsgeschichte des Neuen Testament (ausserhalb der Evangelien),' *TRu* 3 (1931): 207–42.

CHAPTER TWO

SUCCESSION IN LUKE-ACTS AND IN THE LUKAN MILIEU

The question addressed in this essay is: How would ancient auditors have heard the sections of Luke-Acts that deal with succession? Pursuit of an answer to this question requires a focus on two topics: succession in the Lukan milieu and succession in Luke-Acts. We may take up these two topics in order.

Succession In Mediterranean Antiquity, Part 1: The Lukan Milieu

The purpose of this essay, in Part 1, is to describe the concept of succession in Mediterranean Antiquity, to delineate its semantic field, to identify extant texts in which succession plays a key role, and to define the conventional form of a succession story. The authors[1] do not claim that their work is exhaustive, only that it is as exhaustive as their time constraints allowed.

The Concept of Succession in Antiquity

In the Greco-Roman world the concept of succession was widespread. It was used above all for *rulers* (e.g., Phoenician kings [Porphyry, *Christ. acc.* to Eusebius, *Praep. ev.* 10.9]; succession to the Lydian throne [Oenomaus, Γοήτων φωρά, acc. to Eusebius, *Praep. ev.* 5.20]; kings of Athens, Macedon, Ptolemies, and Seleucids [Tatian, acc. to Eusebius, *Praep. ev.* 10.11]; Alexander the Great's successors [Diodorus Siculus 17ff.]; Druid chiefs [Caesar, *Bell. gall.* 6.13]; Assyrian kings [Vellius Paterculus 2.93.1]; kings of Tyre [Josephus, *Ag. Ap.* 1.18 §121–25]; governors [Livy 36.31.12; Cicero, *Fam.* 2.17.5; Josephus, *A.J.* 18.2.2 §31–35]; a ruler in Syria [Josephus, *A.J.* 19.6.4 §316]; pagan rulers [Athenagoras, *Leg.* 37.2]; Roman emperors [Josephus, *A.J.* 18.2.2 §32; Dio Cassius 2.11.12; 44.34.5; 48.15.4; 49.17.6]). It was also used widely for *philoso-*

---

[1] This essay was jointly authored with my graduate student, Perry Stepp, and is used with his permission.

phers (e.g., generally [Cicero, *Nat. d.* 1.10.25–1.15.41]; of the Stoic succession [*Div.* 1.3.6]; of the Platonic succession [*Acad.* 1.34–35]; cf. also Plutarch, *Exil.* 14; Athenaeus 546d; Clement of Alexandria, *Strom.* 1.14; Diogenes Laertius, *Vit. phil.* and his predecessors; Origen, *Cels.* 3.67). Writers also employed the concept when referring to such figures as *jurists* (Pomponius Sextus, *Ench.* [acc. to a fragment contained in Justinian's *Dig.*, Book 1, authority 2, sections 35–53]), *magi* (Lucian, *Men.* 6; Xanthus of Lydia, acc. to Diogenes Laertius, 1.2.10), *rhetoricians* (Aristotle, *Soph. elench.* 34.27–35 §183b; Cicero, *Div.* 1.3.6; *Brut.* 1.37), *temple wardens* (Lucian, *Alex.* 60), *priests* (Athenagoras, *Leg.* 28.5), *admirals* (Dio Cassius 41.48.1), and *generals* (Livy 23.27.12; 43.4.8). It could also be used of a succession in a *craft* (Ovid, *Metam.* 3.587). The concept of succession was so integral to Greco-Roman thinking that Pliny, *Naturalis historia* 30.4–5, notes that the survival of magic is surprising because there is "no line of ... continuous successors" in it.

In the Jewish world the concept of succession was related to *leaders* or *rulers of the people* (e.g., the patriarchs [Josephus, *A.J.* 1.4 §85]; Joshua as successor to Moses [LXX Num 27:12–23; LXX Deut 1:37–38; 3:21–22, 28; 31:2–6, 7–8, 14–15, 23; LXX Josh 1:2–9; Josephus, *A.J.* 4.7.2 §165; Sir 46:1; *L.A.B.* 25.3; *T. Mos.* 1:6 and 10:15; Clement Alex, *Strom.* 1.21.109] ; kings of Israel [LXX 3 Kgs 1–2; 11:43, etc.; Josephus, *A.J.* 8.15.6 §420; 9.2.2 §27, etc.; Clement Alex, *Strom.* 1.21.119]; Edomite kings [Gen 36:33–39//1 Chr 1:44–50]; Maccabean rulers [Josephus, *B.J.* 1.2.1 §48; 12.6.4 §285; LXX 1 Macc 3:1]). It was also used for *prophets* (e.g., LXX 3 Kgs 2; Eupolemos, acc. to Eusebius, *Praep. ev.* 9.30; Sir 48:8; Josephus, *Ag. Ap.* 1.8 §41; Justin, *Dial.* 52.3), and for *priests* (e.g., Aaron is succeeded by Eleazar who is succeeded by Phinehas [LXX Num 20:23–28; 25:10–13; Josephus, *A.J.* 5.11.5 §361]; the succession in the high priesthood under the kings [Josephus, *A.J.* 10.8.6 §151–53]; the succession of high priests from Aaron [Josephus, *A.J.* 20.10 §224–51]; the succession of priests under the Herods [Josephus, *A.J.* 20.5.2 §104] the discontinued authoritative succession of the Jewish high priesthood [Eusebius, *Hist. eccl.* 5.17.4]). The concept of succession was furthermore used in discussions about the passing on of both *rabbinic tradition* (Josephus, *A.J.* 13.10.6 §297; Acts 6:14 when read in terms of 2 Macc 11:25 and 4 Macc 18:5; *m. Avot* 1; *Avot of Rabbi Nathan* 1; Letter of Peter to James in *Pre. Pet.* 1.2; Ps-Hippolytus, Fragment [*ANF* 5.194–95]) and the *mystical tradition* (*3 En.* 48D.10).

Christian writers also made use of the concept. It was used for *bishops* (e.g., Irenaeus, *Haer.* 3.3.3; Tertullian, *Praescr.* 32; Pseudo-Clement,

Hom., Ep. Clem. Jac. 2; Eusebius, *Hist. eccl.* 3.11.1; 6.29.4; 7.14.1; 7.32.1–6; Ennodius, *Vit. Epiph.*; Paulinus, *Vit. Ambr.* 46, 49; Hegesippus, acc. to Eusebius, *Hist. eccl.* 4.22.3). It was also employed for *monastic founders* (e.g., *Vit. Pachom.*; *Serm. vit. Hon.*) and for *teachers/elders* (e.g., Irenaeus, *Haer.* 3.2.2; 3.3.1). The idea of succession was furthermore related to the notion of the passing on of tradition, whether the *apostolic tradition* (Pastoral epistles; Polycarp, *Phil* 7:2; Clement Alex, *Strom.* 1.1; Letter of Peter to James in *Pre. Pet.* 1.2) or the *Gnostic tradition* (Hippolytus, *Haer.* 5.2; Irenaeus, *Haer.* 3, preface; *Ep. Ptol. Flor.*; *Gos. Phil.* 122.16–18).

The Semantic Field of Succession Thinking

Certain expressions were characteristic of ancient references to succession when a phenomenological description of the fact was given.

1. The one after him/me/you (μετά or *post/ab hoc/deinde*) in

   Aristotle, *Soph. elench.* 34.32–33 §183b
   LXX 3 Kgs 1:13 [David said Solomon will reign after me]
   Sir 47:12 [Solomon was the one raised up after David]
   L.A.B. 25:3 [Joshua who was ruler after Moses]
   Josephus, *A.J.* 18.2.2 §32 [after Marcus Ambivius came Annius Rufus]
   Plutarch, *Vit. X orat.* 835C [Philocles was the one after ...]
   Pomponius Sextus, *Ench.* [acc. to Justinian, *Dig.* 1.2.37, 38, 39, 44, 46; 1.2.36, 44; 1.2.37, 38]
   Hegesippus [acc. to Eusebius, *Hist. eccl.* 4.22.3]
   Diogenes Laertius 7.36 [Sphaerus and Cleanthes are said to be after Zeno]

2. The one in his stead//instead of him/me/you (ἀντί)

   LXX Gen 36:33–39 [Edomite kings rule instead of their predecessors]
   LXX 3 Kgs 1:35 [David says Solomon will rule in his stead]
   LXX 3 Kgs 15:8 [Asa, his son, reigns in his stead]
   LXX 3 Kgs 19:16 [Elijah is to anoint Elisha as prophet in his stead]
   LXX 1 Macc 3:1 [Judas rules in his father's place]

3. To be successor/to succeed/be succeeded by/by succession/to spring from (διάδοχος/ *successit*/ διέρχομαι ἀπο)

   Eusebius, *Praep. ev.* 11.14
   Pomponius Sextus, *Ench.* [acc. to Justinian, *Dig.* 1.2.48, 51, 53]
   Josephus, *A.J.* 13.10.6 §297
   Diogenes Laertius 2.47; 2.85–86

4. His/their disciples included/were (*ab ... profecti*/ μαθητής + verb to be/ to be a hearer of [using ἀκούω or διακούω])

Pomponius Sextus, *Ench.* [Justinian, *Dig.* 1.2.40-these men's pupils included] Diogenes Laertius 2.46; 7.36; 10.22 [his disciples were] Diogenes Laertius 2.3.1; 1.6.2 [he was a hearer of]

When speaking of the one who passes something on to a successor, certain expressions are conventional.

1. To give/deliver/commit (παραδίδωμι)

   P.Hercul. 1021 [X.17; XX.7; XXII.36]
   Josephus, *A.J.* 1.4 §85; 5.11.5 §362
   Luke 1:2
   Diogenes Laertius 4.60

2. To bequeath (διατίθημι/διαθήκη + διάδοχον//*relinquere testatur*)

   Isocrates, *Aegin.* 43 [διέθετο an inheritance to διαδόχους]
   Josephus, *A.J.* 13.16.1 §407 [Alexander left behind him two sons but bequeathed his kingdom to Alexandria]
   Josephus, *B.J.* 1.23.2 §451; 1.30.7 §600; 1.33.7 §664; 2.1.1 §2; 2.2.5–7 §31–38 [διαθήκη + successor]
   Josephus, *A.J.* 17.3.2 §53 [διαθήκη + successor]
   Luke 22:39
   Tacitus, *Ann.* 15.62 [Seneca bequeathed to his friends the image of his life]

3. To leave to (ἀπολείπω)

   P.Hercul. 1021 [X.6]
   Diodorus Siculus 18.1.4; 17.117.4; 20.78.3
   Arrian, *Alex.* 7.26.3

   (καταλείπω)

   P.Hercul. 1021 [XVI.3; XXV.43]
   Diodorus Siculus 4.47.5; 11.66.4; 30.9.2 Dionysius of Hal 1.53.4
   Josephus, *A.J.* 1.4 §85; 5.11.5 §361; 9.2.2 §28
   Dio Chrysostom 11.124.6
   Diogenes Laertius 5.68.5

4. To appoint (καθίστημι)

   P.Hercul. 1018 [VIII.7]
   LXX 1 Macc 6:14, 55
   Josephus, *A.J.* 4.7.2 §165; *B.J.* 2.12.1 §223
   1 Clem. 42:4; 44:2
   Titus 1:5
   Acts 6:3

   (συνίστημι)

   LXX Num 17:23

(χειροτονέω)

P.Hercul. 1018 (VII.7)
P.Hercul. 1021 (VIII. 10)
Josephus, *A.J.* 13.2.2 §45
Acts 14:23

(ἀναδείκνυμι)

2 Macc 9:23; 14:26

(ἀποδείκνυμι)

Josephus, *A.J.* 17.3.2 §53

5. To entrust to (παρατίθημι)

P.Hercul. 1021 [V.12; VIII.39; XI.3]
2 Tim 2:2

(πιστεύω)

Dio Cassius 53.31.3

(ἐγχειρίζω)

Josephus, *A.J.* 18.6.9 §219

6. To cast (something) upon him (ἐπ' αὐτόν)

LXX 3 Kgs 19:16 [God tells Elijah to anoint Elisha to be prophet after him]

so

LXX 3 Kgs 19:19 [Elijah casts his mantle upon him]

The language used for the one who receives something passed on is also reasonably stable.

1. To receive (διαδέχομαι)

Aristotle, *Soph. elench.* 34.30 §183b
P.Hercul. 1021 [VI.29; IV.16; XXXV.4]
P.Hercul. 1018 [XLV.1]
Diodorus Siculus 18.1.6
Dio Chrysostom 37.5.2; 64.22.1
Josephus, *A.J.* 1.4 §85; 7.14.2 §337; 5.11.5 §361
1 Clem. 44:2
Lucian, *Alex.* 60
Appian, *Hist. rom.* 1.1.1
Athenagoras, *Leg.* 28.5 and 37:2

Diogenes Laertius 7.37
Eusebius, *Hist. eccl.* 6.29.4

(ἐκδέχομαι)

Appian, *Hist. rom.* 1.1.1
Numenius, Περὶ τῆς τῶν ἀκαδημαϊκῶν πρὸς Πλάτωνα διαστάσεως [acc. to Eusebius, *Praep. ev.* 14.9]

(παραλαμβάνω)

P.Hercul. 1018 [X.4]
P.Hercul. 1021 [XXVIII.36; XXIX.40] Dionysius of Halicamassus 4.34.3
Josephus, *A.J.* 5.11.5 §361

(λαμβάνω)

LXX 4 Kgs 2:13
P.Hercul. 1018 [1.5; XV.7]
P.Hercul. 1021 [II.10; III.7; VIII.46]
Acts 24:27

2. To be upon me/him (ἐπ' ἐμέ/ἐπ' αὐτόν/ἐπάνωθεν αὐτόν)

LXX 4 Kgs 2:9 [a double portion of Elijah's spirit upon Elijah]
LXX 4 Kgs 2:13 [Elijah's mantle fell off him upon Elisha]
LXX 4 Kgs 2:16 [the spirit of Elijah has rested upon Elisha]

The language used for what is passed on varies widely because what is passed on is so diverse.

1. A kingdom (βασιλεία)

Diodorus Siculus 18.1.6; 11.66.4; 30.9.2
Alexander Polyhistor [acc. to Eusebius, *Praep. ev.* 9.31; 9.32; 9.33]
Dionysius of Halicamassus 1.53.4
Josephus, *A.J.* 7.14.2 §337; 13.16.1 §407
Athenagoras, *Leg.* 37.2

2. Rule/authority/leadership (ἀρχή)

Diodorus Siculus 15.60.4
Dio Chrysostom 11.124.6
Dio Cassius 49.17.6
Josephus, *A.J.* 1.3.4 §83–87

(ἡγεμονία)

Diodorus Siculus 18.2.1
Dionysus of Halicarnassus 4.34.3
Josephus, *A.J.* 18.6.9 §219

(μοναρχία)

Dio Cassius 53.31.3

(δυναστεία)

Dio Cassius 44.34.5

(ναυαρχία)

Dio Cassius 41.48.1

3. The succession (διαδοχή)

Aristotle, *Soph. elench.* 34.30–31 §183b
P.Hercul. 1021 [XXXVI.19]
Plutarch, *Exil.* 14

4. The school (*scholia*)

P.Hercul. 1021 [XII.22; XX.44] Athenaeus 5464
Diogenes Laertius 7.37; 5.68
Iamblichus, *Vit. Pythag.* 36
Numenius, Περὶ τῆς τῶν ἀκαδημαϊκῶν πρὸς Πλάτωνα διαστάσεως [acc. to Eusebius, *Praep. ev.* 14.5]

(*diatribe*)

P.Hercul. 1021 [VI.29; VII.9; XXXV.4]
Plutarch, *Vit. X orat.* 850C
Lucian, *Alex.* 5
Diogenes Laertius 5.62
Numenius, Περὶ τῆς τῶν ἀκαδημαϊκῶν πρὸς Πλάτωνα διαστάσεως [acc. to Eusebius, *Praep. ev.* 14.8, 9]
Ammonius Saccus [acc. to Porphyry, *Isag.* 46.10]

5. The disciples (μαθητής/*profecti*)

P.Hercul. 1021 [X.6; IV.7; X.12; XX.35]
P.Hercul. 1018 [XII.4; XVI.8]
Josephus, *A.J.* 9.2.2 §28
Pomponius Sextus, *Ench.* [acc. to Justinian, *Dig.* 1.2.40]

6. The instruction/true teaching (*disciplinam*/παραθήκη)

Cicero, *Nat. d.* 1.10.25–26
1 Tim 6:20; 2 Tim 1:12

7. The ministry (λειτουργία)

1 Clem. 44:2

8. The chair (καθέδρα)

Pseudo-Clement, *Hom., Ep. Clem. Jac.* 2, 19
Pre. Pet., Letter of Peter to James 1

9. The role of prophet

LXX 2 Kgs 19:16 [anoint Elisha to be prophet after you]

10. An oracle shrine (μαντεῖον)

Lucian, *Alex.* 60

11. The priesthood (ἱεροσύνη)

Josephus, *A.J.* 5.11.5 §362

12. βίος / *vita*

P.Hercul. 1021 [XXVII.3]
Tacitus, *Ann.* 15.62
Diogenes Laertius 9.110

Extant Texts from Antiquity in Which Succession Plays a Key Role

A surprising number of extant texts from Mediterranean Antiquity employ the succession motif in significant ways (in references to succession; in succession lists; in stories of succession). They are related to at least seven different types of figures.

1. *Rulers.* Texts that reflect a significant influence of the succession concept in relation to rulers include:

LXX Num 27:12–23 ; LXX Deut 1:37–38; 3:21–22, 28; 31:2–6, 7–8, 14–15, 23; LXX Josh 1:2–9; Josephus, *A.J.* 4.7.2 §165; *L.A.B.* 25:3 [Moses to Joshua]
LXX 1 Kgs 16–18 [Saul to David]
LXX 3 Kgs 1; Josephus, *A.J.* 7.14 §335–82 [David to Solomon]
Diodorus Siculus 17ff. [Alexander the Great's successors]
Josephus, *A.J.* 18.6.9–10 §211–37 [Tiberius to Caligula]
Josephus, *A.J.* 19.3–4 §212–73; *B.J.* 2.11.1–5 §204–17 [Caligula to Claudius]
Josephus, *A.J.* 20.8.1–2 §148–53 [Claudius to Nero]

2. *Priests.* Texts that relate priests to succession include:

LXX Num 20:23–28
Lucian, *Alex.* 60

3. *Prophets.* Texts that speak about prophets in terms of succession include:

LXX 3 Kgs 19:16–21; 4 Kgs 2; Josephus, *A.J.* 9.2.2 §28
Lucian, *Alex.* 60

4. *Philosophers*. Texts that employ succession in descriptions of philosophers include:

Philodemus, Σύνταξις τῶν φιλοσόφων
Aulus Gellius, *Noct. att.* 13.5
Diogenes Laertius, *Vit. phil.*
Iamblichus, *Vit. Pythag.*

EXCURSUS

The four documents that contain succession information
about philosophers require further explanation

Philodemus's Σύνταξις τῶν φιλοσόφων comes from the first century B.C. It is extant in fragments from the Herculaneum papyri: (a) on the Eleatic and Abderite schools (P.Hercul. 327); (b) on the Pythagorean school (P.Hercul. 1508); (c) on the Epicurean school (P.Hercul. 1780); (d) on the Socratics (P.Hercul. 495 and 558); (e) on the Academics (P.Hercul. 1021 and 164); and (f) on the Stoics (P.Hercul. 1018). Of these the ones most studied and most accessible are P.Hercul. 1018 and 1021. On P.Hercul. 1018, see Domenico Camparetti, 'Papro ercolanese inedito';[2] Augusta Traversa, *Index Stoicorum Herculanensis*;[3] and Titiano Dorandi, *Storia dei Filosofi: La Stoa da Zenone a Panezio (P Herc 1018)*.[4] On P.Hercul. 1021, see Segofredus Mekler, *Academicorum Philosophorum Index Herculanensis*;[5] Konrad Gaiser, *Philodems Academica: Die Berichte uber Platon and die Alte Akademie in zwei herkulanensischen Papyri*;[6] and Tiziano Dorandi, *Storia dei Filosofi: Platone e L'Academia (P Herc 1021 e 164)*.[7] Much of the recent work on the Herculaneum papyri has come as the result of the founding of the 'Centro Internazionale per lo Studio dei Papiri ercolanesi' in 1969 by Marcello Gigante. A survey of the studies to the early 1980's is given by Gigante in his article 'Les Papyrus d'Herculanum aujourd'hui.'[8]

---

[2] *Rivista di Fililogia* 3 (1875): 449–555.
[3] Genoa: Istituto di Filologia Classica, 1952.
[4] Leiden: Brill, 1994.
[5] Berlin: Weidmannos, 1902, repr. 1958.
[6] Stuttgart: Frommann-Holzboog, 1988.
[7] Naples: Bibliopolis, 1991.
[8] *BullSocFrPhil* 78 (1984): 1–30.

The Σύνταξις is constructed in the style of a large 'institutional' manual.[9] This describes its function, not its genre. What is its genre? First, it is not a history as the ancients defined history near the beginning of our era. In Antiquity, history claimed completeness (Cicero, *De or.* 34.120). History dealt with grand events (Herodotus 1.177; Xenophon, *Hell.* 5.1.4; Polybius 10.21.5–8; Dionysius of Halicarnassus 5.56.1; Statius, *Silv.* 1.2.96–97). In history there was an attempt to discern causes (Polybius 3.32; 12:25b.1; Cicero, *De or.* 2.15.63). As Dionysius of Halicarnassus put it: "The readers of histories do not derive sufficient profit from learning the bare outcome of events, but ... everyone demands that the causes of the events be related." Much of history was designed as instruction for political figures as political figures. Dionysius of Halicarnassus 5.56.1 is to the point. "For statesmen I perceive that the knowledge of these things is absolutely necessary, to the end that they have precedents for their use in the various situations that arise." The subject matter of history was states, that is, political and military events. The Σύνταξις does not satisfy these criteria. This conclusion is supported by the fact that our search of P.Hercul. 1018 and 1021 finds no evidence of ἱστορία used self-referentially. Second, Walter Scott, *Fragmenta Herculanensia*[10] spoke of these fragments as Lives. Dorandi calls the pieces of it that he has studied *bios, vita,* and *biografia*.[11] Furthermore, the closest analogies to the Σύνταξις are the collections like the *Vitae prophetarum*, Diogenes Laertius and his numerous predecessors, Philostratus's *Vitae sophistarum,* and Jerome's and Gennadius's *De viris illustribus*. These either call themselves, or are called by others, Lives (βίοι). Their brevity (some sketches in such documents are no more than one sentence while others are a long paragraph) raises the question in what sense these sketches convey character, individuality, distinctiveness. For that matter, the same may be said of the first century biography of Aristotle that served to introduce his works, and its later derivatives. Can anything this sketchy be said to be βίος? They can, we think, be said to be βίοι in the same way that biography in the modern world covers not only a long, fully developed treatment of an individual personality but also the sketches of people that appear in volumes like

---

[9] Marcello Gigante, *Philodemus in Italy: The Books from Herculaneum* (trans. Dirk Obbink; Ann Arbor: University of Michigan Press, 1990), 21.

[10] Oxford: Clarendon Press, 1885.

[11] Titiano Dorandi, *Storia dei Filosofi: La Stoa da Zenone a Panezio (P Herc 1018)* (Leiden: Brill, 1994), 9, 13, 14, 17, etc.; idem, *Storia dei Filosofi: Platone e L'Academia (P Herc 1021 e 164)* (Naples: Bibliopolis, 1991), 25, 27, 29–30, 39, etc.

that of the *Dictionary of International Biography*. Even the sketches convey something of an individual's uniqueness. So also in antiquity. The Σύνταξις, taken as a whole, however, is not a biography. There is no certain place in P.Hercul. 1018 and 1021 where βίος is used self-referentially. Although the pieces are biographical, the whole is not. It would not be too great a stretch to translate Σύνταξις as 'Dictionary' and to complete the title Σύνταξισ τῶν φιλοσόφων with a translation like 'Dictionary of Philosophical Biography.' It contains biographical material but is itself something else.

The Σύνταξις is not polemical but is fundamentally descriptive. Its substance is faithful to the principle of the successions. There is disagreement about whether its function was esoteric (so Dorandi) or exoteric (so Gigante). The forms of the individual sections, 1021 and 1018, may be described. P.Hercul. 1021 gives a fairly full Life of Plato followed by much briefer sketches of his successors. P.Hercul. 1018 gives an outline of the Stoic succession which is filled in at least four points by anecdotal material about the successors. The absence of more anecdotal material elsewhere is often due to the fragmentary nature of the papyri.

Aulus Gellius's *Noctes atticae* is a second century A.D. collection of notes on grammar, public and private antiquities, history and biography, philosophy, law, textual criticism, literary criticism, and more. It consists mainly of extracts from a great number of Greek and Roman authors (275 are mentioned by name), many of whom are otherwise lost. It is not at all clear from whom Gellius derived his story of the Aristotelian succession.

Diogenes Laertius's *Vitae philosophorum* is a third century collection of successions whose thesis is that philosophy had its origin wholly within Greek culture. His succession lists establish the coherence of Hellenistic civilization in terms of a common philosophic culture. (An analogy might be Irenaeus who used the successions of Christian bishops as a guarantee of the coherence of a common Christian doctrine untainted by pagan culture.)

Iamblichus's *De vita Pythagorica* (Περὶ τοῦ πυθαγορείου βίου) is the first volume of a ten volume encyclopedia of Pythagorean thought. The latest editors, John Dillon and Jackson Hershbell, *Iamblichus, On the Pythagorean Way of Life*,[12] claim that the work is not merely a biography

---

[12] Atlanta: Scholars Press, 1991.

of Pythagoras. The reason is that, although it contains the founder's Life, it also contains additional material about the school, including a succession narrative in chapter 36. Actually this work is a βίος, not of an individual but of a community, the Pythagoreans. It tells what is the essence of the Pythagorean school by including a Life of the founder who defines the Way and adds to it other school traditions as well. In this regard, it is analogous to the ancient biographies of peoples which attempted to depict the character of the group: e.g., Dikaiarchus's 4th century B.C. Βίος τῆς Ἑλλάδος, a life of the Greek people from the Golden Age to his own time, and Varro's 1st century B.C. *De vita populi Romani*, a social treatment of the Roman people.

In order to evaluate this evidence, especially the biographical parts, it is necessary to have some perspective on the data.

The collections of successions such as are evidenced by Philodemus and Diogenes Laertius are part of a large stream of such writings: e.g., Antigonus of Carystus, Διαδοκὴ τῶν φιλοσόφων (3rd century B.C.); Hermippus of Smyrna, Βίοι (3rd century B.C.); Sotion, Διαδοκαί (200–175 B.C.); Heraclides of Lembus, Ἐπιτομὴ Σωτίωνος (175–150 B.C.); Sosicrates of Rhodes, Διαδοκαί (2d century B.C.); Alexander Polyhistor, Διαδοκή τῶν φιλοσόφων (75–50 B.C.); Iason (50 B.C.); Antisthenes of Rhodes (1st century B.C.); Nicias of Nicaea, Διαδοκαί (1st century B.C. or 1st Century A.D.). There may be others as well.[13]

There were also histories (?) of single schools: e.g., Phaenias of Eresus, Περὶ τῶν Σωκρατικῶν (4th century B.C.); Idomeneus of Lampsacus, Περὶ τῶν Σωκρατικῶν; Sphaerus of Borysthenes, Περὶ τῶν Ἐρετριακῶν φιλοσόφων (3rd century B.C.); Stratocles, a history of the Stoics; Plutarch, Περὶ τῶν πρώτου φιλοσοφησάντων καὶ τῶν ἀπ' αὐτῶν and Περὶ Κυρηναϊκῶν; and Galen, Περὶ τῆς Πλάτωνος αἱρέσεως and Περὶ τῶν Ἡδονικοὶ αἱρέσεως.[14]

There were biographies of individual philosophers as well. Most of these Lives seem to have been written between approximately 350 and 200 B.C.: e.g., Xenocrates, Βίος Πλάτωνος; Hermodorus, Περὶ Πλάτωνος; Philippus, Περὶ Πλάτωνος; Aristoxenos, Βίος Σωκράτους; Βίος Πλάτωνος; Βίος Πυθαγόρου; Βίος Ἀρχύτους; Zeno the Stoic, Βίος Κράτους; Aeschines Socraticus, *Alcibiades* (P Oxy 1608); from the 3rd

---

[13] Jorgen Mejer, *Diogenes Laertius and His Hellenistic Background* (Wiesbaden: Franz Steiner, 1978), 62–73.
[14] Ibid., 74–75.

century B.C. a biography of Socrates (P Hibeh 182); Eratosthenes, Περὶ Ἀρίστωνος; Apollophanes, Περὶ Ἀρίστωνος; Ariston the Peripatetic, Περὶ Ἡράκλειτος; Βίος Ἐπικούρος; etc.[15] Biographies of individual philosophers were far less numerous between 200 B.C. and A.D. 200: e.g., P.Hercul. 1044's *Vita Philonidis* and Lucian's *Demonax*.[16] Although the boundaries are not exact, it is fair to say that in general terms the Lives of individual philosophers dominated from 350–200 B.C. and collections of biographies of philosophers dominated from 200 B.C. to the beginning of our era. In our era, there was a renewed interest in both individual Lives and collections in the 3rd and 4th centuries. Often later Christian and pagan biographies give a clue about earlier Lives that we know only by name or in fragments. Palladius's *Dialogus de vita Joannis Chrysostomi* (A.D. 408) and Sulpicius Severus's *Vita Sancti Martini* (A.D. 397) offer two late Christian biographies in the form of a dialogue. There is only one such pre-Christian biography, Satyrus's *Vita Euripidis* from the 3rd century B.C. (P Oxy 1176). The question is: were the late Christian biographies modeling themselves on Satyrus's work in particular or are they but examples of a form that was widespread in pre-Christian Antiquity but whose examples have now been lost? To us at least, the latter is more plausible than the former.

The context also comes into play in matters of biographies of founders of communities whose Lives contain a succession list or narrative that is integral to the founder's biography. The *Vita Pachomii* and Hilary of Arles's *Sermo de vita Honorati* offer 4th and 5th century Christian examples. Diogenes Laertius includes at least six such lives, the fullest of which is his *Vita Epicuri* in Book 10. The various Lives of Aristotle collected by Ingemar During from Medieval times go back, he claims, to a fourth century biography by Ptolemy.[17] Certain of these contain a succession component. Arnaldo Momigliano contends that the *Vita Marciana* of Aristotle, one of During's collection with a succession note, is likely to reproduce the substance of the biography Andronicus wrote about 70 B.C. to introduce his epoch-making edition of Aristotle.[18] Is there other evidence of individual Lives with succession components from pre-Christian times? The clearest evidence is that of Aristoxenos's

---

[15] Ibid., 90.
[16] Ibid., 91.
[17] Ingemar During, *Aristotle in the Ancient Biographical Tradition* (Goteborg: Goteborg Universitet Arsskrift, 1957), 469–70, 475.
[18] Arnaldo Momigliano, *The Development of Greek Biography* (Cambridge: Harvard University Press, 1971), 86–87.

Βίος Πυθαγόρου.[19] Of Aristoxenos's work Clement of Alexandria says in *Stromata* 1.14: "Aristoxenos, in his Life of Pythagoras, and Aristarchos and Theopompos (Ἀριστόξενος ἐν τῷ Πυθαγόρου βίῳ καὶ Ἀρίσταρχος καὶ Θεόπομπος)." Are we to suppose that there were one or maybe two pre-Christian biographies of individual founders of philosophical schools that were used as models by later authors in the 3rd and 4th centuries A.D. or are we to think that what is evident in the later Lives is representative of a whole range of pre-Christian Lives that are now lost? Either way, there is evidence for the existence of individual biographies of founders of philosophical schools with a succession component integral to the Life, as well as collections of successions, from pre-Christian times.[20]

5. *Jurists*. A text that records the succession of jurists is:

Pomponius Sextus, *Ench.*

6. *Monastic founders*. Sources that employ succession thinking in accounts of founders of monastic communities include:

Vit. Pachom.
Hilary of Arles, *Serm. vit. Honor.*

7. *Bishops*. Texts that utilize the succession concept in the treatment of Christian bishops include:

1 Clem. 42:4; 44:2
Pseudo-Clement, *Ep. Clem. Jac.*

---

[19] F. Wehrli, *Die Schule des Aristoteles* (8 vols.; Basel: Schwabe, 1967), 2:10–15, frgs. 11–25.

[20] This answers Loveday Alexander's question about the alleged missing middle stage of biographical development ('Acts and Ancient Intellectual Biography,' in *The Book of Acts in Its Ancient Literary Setting* [ed. Bruce W. Winter and Andrew D. Clarke; Grand Rapids: Eerdmans, 1993], 31–64, esp. 55). A further argument derives from an observation about Diogenes Laertius' sources. Take the case of the *Vita Epicuri* in Book 10. In the section of this Life which deals with Epicurus' career and his successors, Laertius mentions as his sources: Heraclides, Ἐπιτομή Σωτίωνος, Apollodorus the Epicurean's multi-volume Βίος Ἐπικούρος and Ariston's Βίος Ἐπικούρος. The first is a collection of Lives like that of the later Laertius. The second and third are individual Lives. Thus Laertius drew not only on collections but also on individual bioi. If he did the latter, then they existed and apparently included succession motifs. In the section on Epicurean teaching, Laertius draws on a different set of sources: e.g., Κανών, Περὶ φύσεως, Περὶ Βίων, and Περὶ τέλους. In other words, the materials for Epicurus' Life and Succession come from one set of sources and the materials for the teaching of Epicureans from another.

Paulinus, *Vit. Ambr.*
Ennodius, *Vit. Epiph.*

8. *Tradition.* Sources that use the concept of succession with reference to the passing on of tradition are:

Pastoral Epistles
Clement of Alexandria, *Strom.* 1.1
m. *Avot* and *Avot of Rabbi Nathan*
3 Enoch[21]

A Conventional Form of a Succession Story?

Was there such a thing as a conventional form of a story of a succession? In order to answer this question, one must do two things: first, separate the accounts into three groups (Jewish, Greco-Roman, and Christian), and second, analyze the individual sources.

The Jewish sources that employ succession thinking to a significant degree may be divided according to what is passed on: rule, priesthood, prophet's role, and tradition.

1) *Rule.* Here one must examine accounts of three successions: that from Moses to Joshua, that from Saul to David, and that from David to Solomon.

(a) *The succession from Moses to Joshua.* There are two separate stories of the succession from Moses to Joshua in the Bible. The first, LXX Num 27:12–23, says that a leader of the congregation was needed for the time after Moses. The act of passing the torch was accompanied by certain symbolic rites: Joshua was set before Eleazar the priest (vv. 19, 22); Moses laid his hands on him (vv. 18, 23), gave a charge to him before the congregation (v. 19) and the congregation a charge concerning him (v. 19), and put his glory upon him (v. 20), and appointed him (συνέστησεν, v. 23). The second, LXX Deut 1:37–38; 3:21–22, 28; 31:2–6, 7–8, 14–15, 23, involves the passing on of the role of field general or head of the army (Deut 1:38; 3:21–22, 28; 31:7, 23).[22] This succession

---

[21] James H. Charlesworth, *The Old Testament Pseudepigrapha* (2 vols.; Garden City, N.Y.: Doubleday, 1983, 1985), 1:315: This is a chain of mystical tradition similar to the chains of tradents of the oral law. Cf. L.I. Levine, 'R. Abbahu of Caesarea,' in *Christianity Judaism and Other Greco-Roman Cults, Part Four* (ed. J. Neusner; Leiden: Brill, 1975), 56–76.

[22] Norbert Lohfink, 'The Deuteronomy Picture of the Transfer of Authority from Moses to Joshua,' in *Theology of the Pentateuch* (trans. Linda M. Maloney; Minneapolis:

involved Moses' exhortation to Joshua in the presence of the people (Deut 31:7–8), a theophany in which Yahweh charges Joshua with his new task (Deut 31:14–15, 23), and Moses' laying his hands on Joshua (Deut 34:9). It was confirmed by Joshua's being filled with the spirit of wisdom (Deut 34:9) and by the people's listening to him (Deut 34:9). Both succession accounts lead to the book of Joshua where further evidence is given of the transfer. This confirmation involves the people's acknowledging Joshua as leader (Josh 1:16–18) and Yahweh's exalting him through success in his ventures (Josh 3:7; 4:14). One of the most striking strands of evidence for the transfer's having taken place is the correspondence between Moses' and Joshua's careers (e.g., the Lord says to both, "I will be with you" [Exod 3:12//Josh 1:5, 9; 3:7]; both send out spies [Num 13//Josh 2:1]; both are involved in the parting of the waters [Exod 14//Josh 3–4]; both have the people circumcised [Josh 5:5; Lev 12:3; Exod 12:44, 48//Josh 5:2–8]; both celebrate the Passover [Exod 12//Josh 5:10–12]; both are involved with the manna [its gift, Exod 16//its cessation, Josh 5:12]). At the same time that Joshua's career is like that of Moses, it is also unlike his (e.g., Moses is the giver of the law [Exod 20] while Joshua is to do all the law which Moses commanded [Josh 1:7–8]). Moses is a foundational figure in a way that Joshua could never be, even if he were Moses' successor.

Later Jewish writings address the same succession. *Liber antiquitatum biblicarum* 25:3 merely says that Joshua was ruler "after him" (Moses). In 20:2–5, God says to Joshua after Moses' death:

> Take his garments of wisdom and clothe yourself, and with his belt of knowledge gird your loins, and you will be changed and become another man. Did I not speak on your behalf to Moses, my servant, saying, "This one will lead my people after you"? (v. 2)

When Joshua does so, "his mind was afire and his spirit was moved" (v. 3). The people then say to Joshua: "Behold we know today ... 'After Moses goes to rest, the leadership ... will be given over to Joshua.'" From then on, the people believe and acknowledge him as ruler in Israel (v. 5). The *Testament of Moses* 1:6–9 says Moses called to himself

---

Fortress, 1994), 234–47, contends that the succession involves two offices: field general and distributor of the land. Our reading of Deuteronomy indicates that therein the only succession is that of leader of the army. One must wait until Josh 13:1, 7 to hear about Joshua's appointment by God to be the distributor of the land. That, in turn, is not something passed on from Moses as is the role of field general.

Joshua, a man approved by the Lord, "that Joshua might become the minister (successor) for the people in the tent of testimony and that he might lead the people into the land promised to their fathers." Josephus, *Antiquitates judaicae* 4.7.2 §165, says Moses appointed (καθίστησιν) Joshua as his successor (διάδοχον). Joshua had been instructed in all learning concerning the law and God. Moses had been his instructor.

(b) *The succession from Saul to David.* The LXX 1 Kgs 16–18 deals with the passing of kingship from Saul to David (16:1). In obedience to Yahweh, Samuel anoints David (16:13a) and the Spirit of the Lord comes upon (ἐπί) him from that time (16:13b). (The MT, 18:4, has Jonathan give David his clothing and weapons. This is not in the LXX or Josephus.) In 18:12, 28 we hear that the Lord was with David; in verse 14 that David had success; and in verses 16, 28 that all Israel loved David. Josephus, *Antiquitates judaicae* 6.8.1–6.10.2 §156–196 tells a similar story of Samuel's anointing David as king, of the Divine Power's coming upon David so that he began to prophesy, of David's successes in battle, and of the women's celebrations of David's prowess. Josephus says that David had God going along with him wherever he went and so prospered in his undertakings.

(c) *The succession from David to Solomon.* The LXX 3 Kgs 1 has David say that Solomon would sit upon his throne "after me" (μετ' ἐμέ, v. 30) and "in my stead" (ἀντ' ἐμοῦ, v. 30). The succession is accompanied by certain symbolic acts: Solomon is set on David's mule (vv. 33, 38), he is anointed by Zadok the priest (vv. 34, 39) and Nathan the prophet (v. 34), and the trumpet is blown (vv. 34, 39). The succession is confirmed by the people's acclamation: "Let king Solomon live" (v. 39). Josephus, *Antiquitates judaicae* 7.14.5 §351–58, tells essentially the same story about the passing of the kingship to Solomon: the ride on the mule, the anointing by Zadok and Nathan, and the people's acclamation. The people's acclamation is expanded in Josephus to include the people's celebrating a festival after Solomon was set upon the throne.

2) *Priesthood.* The LXX Num 20:23–28 tells of the succession of the priesthood from Aaron to his son, Eleazar. The act was accompanied by certain symbolic acts. God told Moses to take Aaron's apparel off him and to put it on (ἔνδυσον) his son, Eleazar, before all the congregation. The succession is confirmed by Eleazar's being associated with Moses in leadership (e.g., 26:1, 3) as Aaron had been (e.g., 20:2, 6).

3) *Prophet's role*. The LXX 3 Kgs 19 has God command Elijah to anoint Elisha prophet in his place (ἀντὶ σου). Elijah does so by casting his mantle upon him (ἐπ' αὐτόν). The succession is confirmed by Elisha's being willing to "follow after you" (ἀκολουθήσω ὀπίσο σου). The LXX 4 Kgs 2 tells of Elishah's succeeding Elijah as prophet. A certain symbolic act accompanies the succession: Elijah's mantle falls from off Elijah and upon Elisha. "He received (ἔλαβε) the mantle of Elijah which fell upon (ἐπάνωθεν) him" (v. 13). The confirmation that Elisha is the true successor is that he divides the water and goes over (v. 14, an act like that of Moses and Joshua and Elijah) and that the sons of the prophets acclaim him ("The spirit of Elijah has rested upon Elisha," v. 15), and do obeisance to him (v. 15), and that he performs deeds reminiscent of those of Elijah: aiding a widow (3 Kgs 17//4 Kgs 4), a water miracle (3 Kgs 18//4 Kgs 3), and the resuscitation of a dead child (3 Kgs 17//4 Kgs 4). Josephus, *Antiquitates judaicae* 9.2.2 §28, speaks of Elijah disappearing from among men but leaving behind him his disciple (μαθητήν), Elisha.

4) *Tradition*. Jewish writers used the concept of succession to refer to the passing on of two very different kinds of tradition.

(a) The Mishnaic tractate *m. Avot* begins with the well known words:

> Moses received the Law from Sinai and committed it to Joshua, and Joshua to the elders, and the elders to the Prophets, and the Prophets to the men of the Great Synagogue. ... Simeon the Just was of the remnants of the Great Synagogue. ... Antigonus of Soko received the Law from Simeon the Just.

A similar account of the succession of the Pharisaic/rabbinic oral law is also given in *Avot of Rabbi Nathan* chapter 1.[23]

(b) *Third Enoch* 48D.10 gives a succession of mystical tradition. It says that Metatron committed to Moses a secret (7)

> and Moses to Joshua, Joshua to the elders, the elders to the prophets, the Prophets to the men of the Great Synagogue, the Men of the Great Synagogue to Ezra the scribe, Ezra the scribe to Hillel the Elder, Hillel the Elder to R. Abbahu, R. Abbahu to R. Zira, R. Zira to the Men of Faith, and the Men of Faith to the Faithful—so that they should use it to admonish men and to heal the diseases that befall the world. ...[24]

---

[23] Judah Goldin, *The Fathers According to Rabbi Nathan* (New Haven: Yale University Press, 1955), 4–5.

[24] Charlesworth, *The Old Testament Pseudepigrapha*, 1:315.

In these Jewish sources, a full-fledged succession story has three main components: (1) naming what is to be passed on (e.g., rule, priesthood, prophet's role); (2) giving the symbolic acts which accompany the succession (e.g., transfer of clothing or other possessions; transfer of glory, spirit, authority/role; laying on of hands; anointing); and (3) confirming that the succession has taken place (e.g., the people's acclamation; repetition by the successor of acts that replicate the type of thing performed by his predecessor). A succession story is different from a succession list such as one finds in Gen 36:33–39, *m. Avot*, or *3 En.* 48 in that components 2 and 3 are missing in the list.

The sources that speak about succession in the Greco-Roman world may also be divided according to what is passed on.

1) *Rule.* Two sources provide evidence for the succession of rule.

(a) Diodorus Siculus 17ff. presents a narrative of the succession from Alexander the Great. In 17.117.4, when Alexander is asked, "To whom do you leave (ἀπολείπεις) the kingdom (βασιλείαν)?" he replies, "To the strongest." In 17.118.4 Diodorus says that in the next book (18) he will "narrate the actions of the successors" (τὸν διαδεξάμενον). This is repeated in summary form in 18.1.4. Then Alexander's words are added: "for I foresee that a great combat of my friends will be my funeral games." In 18.1.6, we are told: "The preceding Book included all the acts of Alexander up to his death; this one, containing the deeds of those who succeeded to his kingdom. ..." (τοῖς διαδεξαμένοις τὴν τούτου Βασιλείαν). In 18.2.1 we hear that great contention arose over the leadership (ἡγεμονίας).

(b) Josephus, *Antiquitates judaicae* 18.6.9–10 §211–37, offers a narrative of the succession of the ἡγεμονία from Tiberius to Gaius Caligula. Tiberius's speech, giving the Roman empire into Gaius's hand, is the lad's appointment as successor. Gaius confirms the transfer by three acts: he has Tiberius's grandson killed, he sends letters to the Senate announcing his elevation, and he sets Agrippa free and makes him king of the tetrarchy of Philip.

2) *Temple guardianship/priesthood and prophet's role.* Lucian's *Alexander* 60 says that around the time of Alexander's death

> the foremost of his fellow-conspirators and impostors referred it to Rutilianus to decide which of them should be given the preference, should succeed (διαδέχασθαι) to the shrine (τὸ μαντεῖον, the oracle), and should

be crowned with the fillet of priest and prophet (τὸ ἱεροφάντικο καὶ προφήτικο στέμματι, the priestly and prophetic wreaths). Rutilianus, the umpire, sent them off unfilleted, keeping the post of prophet for the Master after his departure from this life. (LCL)

3) *Philosophic succession.* (a) Philodemus's Σύνταξισ τῶν φιλοσόφων (in 10 books) is preserved in fragments among the Herculaneum papyri. In P.Hercul. 1018 the Stoic succession is preserved. At a number of points the list is interrupted by anecdotes about the teachers mentioned. P.Hercul. 164 and 1021 present the succession in the Academy. P.Hercul. 327 contains sections of the Eleatic and Abderite schools; P.Hercul. 1508, the Pythagorean; P.Hercul. 1780, the Epicurean; and P.Hercul. 495 and 558, the Socratic successions. This institutional manual is closer to a list with anecdotes than to a story of an actual succession.

(b) Diogenes Laertius, *Vitae philosophorum* (in 10 books), is heir to a long tradition of such collections of philosophic successions. At about half a dozen places, Laertius includes individual Lives that give the life of a founder followed by a list of his successors: Socrates, Aristippus, Plato, Zeno, Pythagoras, Epicurus. In some of these six, the list contains anecdotes about the successors' words and/or deeds.

(c) Iamblichus, *De vita Pythagorica*, the first volume of a ten volume encyclopedia of Pythagorean thought, is a combination of a Life of Pythagoras and a collection of Pythagorean traditions that define the way of life of this philosophical school. In chapter 36 the Pythagorean succession is given. Pythagoras's acknowledged successor was Aristaeus. He carried on the school. Then when he grew old, he relinquished the school to Pythagoras's son, Mnesarchus. He was followed by Bulagoras, etc. There then follows a list of other famous Pythagoreans. This again is more a list than a story of succession.

(d) Aulus Gellius, *Noctes atticae* 13.5, provides a full description of a philosophic succession. When Aristotle was old and near his death, his disciples asked him to choose a "successor to his position and office" (*loci sui et magristerii successorem*). He agreed. The two best men in his school were Theophrastus of Lesbos and Eudemus of Rhodes. A little later, he asked his disciples to bring him a foreign wine, either from Rhodes or Lesbos. He would use the one he liked better. They did so. Aristotle tasted the Rhodian and said: "This is truly a sound and pleasant wine." Then he tasted the Lesbian. He said: "Both are very good indeed, but the Lesbian is the sweeter." When he said this, no one doubted that he had by those words chosen his successor (*successorem*

... *delegisset*), Theophrastus of Lesbos. So when Aristotle died not long after, they all became followers of Theophrastus.

4) *Study of the law*. There is a long fragment from Pomponius Sextus's *Enchiridion* quoted in Justinian's *Digesta*, Book 1, section 2, authority 2. In 1.2.2.1–34, this second century A.D. author deals with the origins and development of law. In 1.2.2.35–53, Pomponius gives the succession of jurists. The section dealing with succession is more a list than a story of a succession, even when it gives information about the accomplishments of the individual jurists.[25]

It may be noted that when a succession event is described in detail by a Greco-Roman author, it possesses the same three components as the Jewish stories: (1) naming what is being transferred (emperor's role; headship of a school); (2) specifying the symbolic acts that are associated with the act of transfer (speech of some type); and (3) indicating what confirms that the succession has taken place (decisive acts by the new emperor, recognition by Aristotle's followers of the new leader).

The early Christian sources that deal with succession will also be divided according to what is being transferred.

1) *The episcopacy*. (a) *First Clement* 42 speaks of a succession that runs from God to Christ to the apostles to their appointees as bishops and deacons. The key sentence is in verse 4: "they appointed (καθιστάνων) their first converts, testing them by the Spirit, to be bishops and deacons of the future believers." In 44:2, the apostles who knew there would be strife for the title of bishop, "appointed (κατέστησαν) those who have been already mentioned, and afterwards added the codicil that if they should fall asleep, other approved men should succeed (διαδέξονται) to their ministry (λειτουργίαν)."

(b) The Pseudo-Clementine *Homiliae* is a narrative about Clement's boyhood and association with Peter. It is introduced by a succession narrative in the form of the Epistle of Clement to James. When Peter was about to die, he told the church: "I lay hands upon this Clement as your bishop; and to him I entrust my chair of discourse. ... I communicate to him the power and the binding and loosing" (2). Peter

---

[25] Theodor Mommsen, Paul Kruger, Alan Watson, *The Digest of Justinian* (Philadelphia: University of Pennsylvania Press, 1985), 1:3–11. This volume gives the Latin text on the left and an English translation on the right.

then reminds Clement in the presence of all about the things belonging to the administration (5). "Having thus spoken, he laid his hands upon me in the presence of all, and compelled me to sit in his chair" (19).[26] The Pseudo-Clementine *Recognitiones*, in the preface, refers to the letter from Clement to James which informs him of the death of Peter and that Peter had left Clement his (Peter's) successor in his chair and teaching.

(c) Paulinus's *Vita Ambrosii* says that Simplicianus is Ambrose's successor (49). In chapter 46 we hear how this occurred. The deacons, Castus, Polemius, Venerius, and Felix, when Ambrose was near death, were talking about who should be ordained bishop after Ambrose's death. Ambrose heard, and when they spoke the name of Simplicianus, he exclaimed three times: "Old but good." So when Ambrose died, none other succeeded him in the episcopacy except him whom the bishop had designated.[27]

(d) Ennodius's *Vita Epiphanii* tells that Bishop Crispinus knew he was about to die. He then commends his young cleric, Epiphanius. Then the people agree on Epiphanius as the bishop's successor and lead him away to be consecrated.

2) *Rule in a monastic order.* (a) *Vita Pachomii*[28] tells about the life of this founder of cenobitic monasticism and includes toward the end accounts of the appointment of his successors: Petronius (114), Orsisius (διάδοχον, 117), and Theodore (διάδοχον, 130).

(b) St. Hilary's *Sermo de vita Honorati* was given on the anniversary of the death of Honoratus, the founder of a monastery on the Island of Lerinson in the early fifth century. The encomium not only celebrates the life of Honoratus but also tells how Hilary was elected as Honoratus's successor.

3) *Tradition.* (a) The Pastoral Epistles reflect a succession of true tradition. In 1 Tim 6:20, Timothy is exhorted to "guard what has been entrusted (τὴν παραθήκην) to you" (RSV). In 2 Timothy we hear that Paul has been entrusted with the tradition παραθήκην, 1:12). Timothy

---

[26] *ANF* 8:218–22.
[27] *The Fathers of the Church. Vol 15: Early Christian Biographies* (ed. Roy J. Deferrari; New York: Fathers of the Church, Inc., 1952). This volume contains translations of Ennodius, Hilary, and Paulinus.
[28] Apostolos A. Athanasskis, *The Life of Pachomius* (Atlanta: Scholars Press, 1975).

has been entrusted with the tradition (παραθήκη, 1:14) by Paul (2:2). He is exhorted to guard what has been entrusted to him (1:14). He is also to entrust this tradition that he heard from Paul to faithful men who will be able to teach others also (2:2). Here there is a line that runs from God to Paul to Timothy to the faithful men who will be teachers also. The succession is first of all a succession of tradition.

(b) Clement of Alexandria, *Stromata* 1.1, refers probably to Pantaenus, master of the catechetical school in Alexandria and Clement's teacher, as "the true Sicilian bee, gathering the spoil of the flowers of the prophetic and apostolic meadow, engendered in the souls of his hearers a deathless element of knowledge." He preserved "the tradition of the blessed doctrine derived directly from the holy apostles, Peter, James, John, and Paul, the sons receiving it from the father ... came by God's will to us also to deposit those ancestral and apostolic seeds."[29]

Here again in the Christian stories of succession the same three components are found: (1) naming what is being passed on (either the role of bishop or ruler of a monastery); (2) giving the symbolic acts that accompany the transfer (e.g., laying on of hands, commendation by authority, transfer of possessions); and (3) confirming that the succession has been completed (usually recognition by the community involved; sometimes repetition of key actions like teaching, binding and loosing). Since these same three components are found in all the stories of succession, whether they be Jewish, Greco-Roman, or Christian, it seems reasonable to conclude that there was a conventional form of a succession story in Mediterranean antiquity.

The survey so far yields certain conclusions.

1) The notion of succession is a cross-cultural phenomenon. It is found in Greco-Roman, Jewish, and early Christian cultures.

2) It is not limited to any one social context. It is associated with rulers, priests, prophets, philosophers, jurists, etc.

3) It is not genre specific. Succession material has been found in histories, biographies, institutional manuals, novels, letters, Israelite scrip-

---

[29] *ANF* 2:301.

tural narratives, sermons, collections of anecdotes, halakhic collections, and mystical sources.

4) It serves a variety of goals but is usually associated with the desire to show continuity in a given area, to guarantee preservation of something, to legitimate or authenticate. (a) The LXX stories of succession function to show the true line of leadership in salvation history. It is often not the line that would have been expected but the one God wills: e.g., it is not Moses' son but Joshua who succeeds him; it is not Saul's son but David who succeeds; it is not David's eldest son but Solomon who comes after him. (b) A similar theme runs through the successions of Roman emperors. The successions often reflect unexpected turns and twists: e.g., it is not Tiberius's grandson who succeeds him but a more distant relative because of Tiberius's perception of divine intervention in the matter. Nevertheless the succession provides the continuity in rule that is needed. (c) The same emphasis on continuity is seen in Pomponius Sextus's succession of Roman jurists. (d) Perhaps in Pliny's comment about how surprising it is that magic has survived because it had no continuous line of succession, we hear that succession functioned in the interests of preservation (*Nat.* 30.4). (e) The philosophical successions show the true line of leadership in the schools. It is often based on outstanding performance, as Aullus Gellius shows. (f) *M. Avot*'s succession of tradition serves clearly to legitimate. This rabbinic mindset is made explicit by *y. Pesahim* 6.1.33a. There one hears about Hillel who discoursed on a matter all day only to have his interpretation rejected until he said: "Thus I heard from Shemaiah and Abtalion."

5) The use of the concept of succession is found, at least, from the 5–4th centuries B.C. to the 4–5th centuries A.D. During that time span, the language and form of succession thinking is remarkably consistent.

6) What is passed on varies: sometimes a role or office, sometimes a tradition or lifestyle, and sometimes a combination of the previous two.

7) The centrality of the concept of succession to a document may be determined by whether or not it seriously affects the form of the document. When a source is seriously influenced by succession thinking, it manifests a form that is [a+b] or [a+b+b'+b''+b'''+b''''], etc.]. Information about the founder of an empire, a school, a monastic community, an oracle, or the originator of a tradition or profession is given

first and then comes matter about his successor(s). This form may shape the entire document or it may merely shape the part of the document in which it is located.

Succession in Mediterranean Antiquity, Part 2: Luke-Acts

The purpose of this essay, in Part 2, is to explore, on the basis of the data base from Part 1, what affinities, if any, the Lukan narrative might have with the succession material in Mediterranean antiquity.

The Concept of Succession and Luke-Acts

Succession thinking was a part of the Lukan narrative world. Acts 6:14 ("the customs which Moses delivered to us," RSV) echoes the Pharisaic succession of the oral law. Acts 24:27 ("Felix was succeeded by Porcius Festus," RSV) reflects the succession of Roman procurators. The issue for this paper is: Does succession play a part in the Messianists' story as it is depicted in Luke and Acts? How would the 'authorial audience,'[30] sensitized by the thinking about succession in Mediterranean antiquity, have heard the Lukan narrative's depiction of Jesus and the church? Would they have encountered any parts of the semantic field involved with succession?

In the prologue to the Gospel of Luke the Evangelist speaks about a succession of tradition. Luke 1:2 mentions the matters fulfilled among believers that were delivered (παρέδοσαν) by eyewitnesses (1st generation?) and ministers of the word (2nd generation?) to the Evangelist's own time (3rd generation?). Moreover, at three points they would have heard succession terminology used of the Messianist movement: Luke 22:28–30, especially verse 29 (διατίθημι + βασιλείαν) Acts 6:1–6, especially at verse 3 (καθίστημι); and Acts 14:23 (χειροτονέω). Would the Lukan authorial audience have recognized a story about a succession at any of these three points in the narrative?

The first passage with succession terminology, Luke 22:28–30, seems to be related to material with the requisite three components. (A) Luke 22:28–30 is a logion in the mouth of the Lukan Jesus at his last meal with his disciples and in the midst of a farewell speech.

---

[30] P. J. Rabinowitz, 'Whirl Without End: Audience-Oriented Criticism,' *Contemporary Literary Theory* (ed. G.D. Atkins and L. Morrow; Amherst: University of Massachusetts Press, 1989), 81–100; 'Truth in Fiction: A Reexamination of Audiences,' *Critical Inquiry* 4 (1977): 121–42.

> You are those who have continued with me in my trials. And I bequeath (διατίθεμαι) to you, since/just as my Father has bequeathed (διέθετο) a reign (βασιλείαν) to me, that you should eat and drink at my table in my reign (βασιλείαν) and sit upon thrones judging (κρίνοντες) the twelve tribes of Israel.

The only significant textual variant, the insertion of "covenant" after "I bequeath to you" in verse 29 (so A, Θ, 579, and a few others) is most likely to be explained as a copyist's following of LXX patterns of speech (cf. LXX Gen 15:18; 21:27, 32; 26:28; 31:44; Deut 5:2, 3; 7:2; 29:14; Josh 9:6; 24:25; Judg 2:2; 1 Kgs 11:1–2; 2 Kgs 3:21; 3 Kgs 5:12; 4 Kgs 17:38, etc.). It is not original. What is bequeathed to the disciples? Regardless of how one takes the syntax, Jesus bequeaths to the disciples/apostles some kind of position of authority.

This logion has a parallel in Matthew 19:28.

> Truly, I say to you, in the new world, when the Son of Man shall sit on his glorious throne, you who have followed me will also sit on twelve thrones, judging the twelve tribes of Israel. (RSV)

In its Matthean form, the logion is clearly eschatological. It refers to the apostles' participation in the judgment of the Last Day. Interpreters who work with a diachronic method usually read Matthew's meaning into the Lukan form (e.g., Fitzmyer[31], Nolland[32]). The reference is then to the apostles' rule at the Last Day. Interpreters who work with a more synchronic method are more sensitive to the distinctively Lukan point of the passage (e.g., Jervell[33], Johnson[34]).

A correct reading requires an understanding of the distinctive Lukan language. (a) What is Jesus' reign according to Luke-Acts? Acts 2:34–36 indicates that it is his session at God's right hand, beginning with the resurrection-ascension-exaltation (cf. Luke 22:69). The logion, then, does not refer to the time of the Last Day but to the period beginning with Jesus' exaltation. (b) What does it mean to eat and drink at his table in Jesus' reign? The image is that of the king's closest associates sitting at privileged places at the very table of the ruler himself (cf. LXX 1 Kgs 20:29b; 2 Kgs 9:7, 9, 11; 19:28; 3 Kgs 2:7; 4:27; 18:19). It

---

[31] Joseph A. Fitzmyer, *The Gospel According to Luke X–XXIV* (Garden City: Doubleday, 1985), 1418–19.
[32] John Nolland, *Luke 18:35–24:53* (Dallas: Word, 1993), 1066–67.
[33] Jacob Jervell, *Luke and the People of God* (Minneapolis: Augsburg, 1972), 75–112.
[34] Luke T. Johnson, *The Gospel of Luke* (Collegeville, Minn.: Liturgical Press, 1991), 345–46.

means to be accorded a place of honor and intimacy with the king in his house. (c) What does it mean to judge the tribes of Israel? Again the expression comes from the Jewish scriptures (e.g., Exod 2:14; 18:22; LXX 2 Kgs 15:4—Absolom said: "Oh that I were judge in the land! Then every man with a suit or cause might come to me, and I would give him justice"; 3 Kgs 3:16–28; Mic 7:3). It refers to the role of rendering decisions that were right and just. Sometimes such judges were kings' sons. Taking these three expressions together yields a reading that sees Luke 22:29–30 as referring to the apostles' role in Jesus' reign from the time of his exaltation. It is one of honor. They are sons of the king in that they eat and drink at his table and function as judges among the people within and under the reign of Christ. So Luke 22:29–30 is not about the parousia and last judgment but about the period after Jesus' ascension and about the apostles' role of judging in that period.

What does it mean for the apostles to judge? In Acts they are portrayed as witnesses of the resurrection (e.g., Acts 1:8, 22). How is judging Israel tied to being witnesses of the resurrection of Jesus? The apostles deliver God's right and just verdict to Israel about Jesus' status (Acts 3:15; 5:32). By raising Jesus, God vindicated him (Acts 3:13, 15; 5:31). Israel's earlier ignorance that allowed her to kill God's servant is now dispelled (Acts 3:17). Israel should, in light of this divine verdict, repent (3:19; 5:31). If any do not, they are cut off from the people (3:27). From this point of view, the rulers who have yet once more rejected Jesus are cut off from the people. They no longer are the rulers in the reconstituted Israel (Luke 20:9–16, 17–19). The apostles now hold that role (Luke 22:29–30; Acts 1:15–26). In other words, to bear witness to Jesus' resurrection is to render God's righteous verdict in Israel. Their being witnesses to Jesus' resurrection is at the core of their being judges. It does not exhaust their role, however. For example, in Acts 15 Paul and Barnabas go up to Jerusalem to the apostles to settle a policy issue (v. 2). The apostles and others gather together to consider the matter (v. 6). At the end of the discussion, James concludes: "I judge (κρίνω) that" + his decision (v. 19). It is a decision with which the apostles concur (vv. 28–29). When Paul goes back to south Galatia, he delivers to the churches there the matters decided (κεκριμένα) by the apostles in Jerusalem (16:4). Here the apostles are judges within the restored Israel.

The same point is born out by the role of Jerusalem in Acts. Jerusalem has a central role in the missionary enterprise in Acts (1:4, 8; 8:14–15; 11:1–2; 11:22; 15:2). This includes the Jerusalem frame of reference for Paul's entire ministry in Acts (9:27–29; 11:25–26; 13:1–3; 15:2; 16:5; 18:22; 21:17). Jerusalem's control of missions in Acts is closely tied to the fact that, for Luke, Jerusalem is the place where the twelve apostles reside (8:1; 9:28; 11:1–2; 15:2, 4; 16:4). The twelve apostles function as appointed people of honor who make key decisions within the early church under the reign of Christ.

If one assumes this reading of Luke 22:29–30, then on the basis of God's bequeathing a reign to Jesus, Jesus subsequently bequeaths to his apostles a position of honor and authority within his reign and under his authority. In this sense, a transfer of authority is involved. The first component of a story about a succession is present. What about the second?

(B) Are there any symbolic acts that accompany the transfer? Yes. Jesus' words of promise in Luke 22:29–30 are analogous to the speech Tiberius used to convey the reign to Caligula (so Josephus, *A.J.* 18.6.9–10 §211–37). Furthermore, the Spirit comes upon (ἐφ' Acts 1:8; ἐπί, 2:17) the apostles, just as it did in the case of David (LXX 1 Kgs 16:13) and Elisha (LXX 4 Kgs 2:9, 16). They are clothed (ἐνδύσησθε, Luke 24:49) with the Spirit (cf. *L.A.B.* 20:2–5; LXX Num 20:23–28). This happens in connection with Jesus' being taken up (ἀναλημφθείς, Acts 1:11) into heaven, just as in the case of Elijah and Elisha. The echoes of the Elijah-Elisha transfer are unmistakable. Why would such echoes be present? Luke's succession from Jesus to the apostles, like that from Elijah to Elisha, involves a foundation figure who, though absent from the earth, is still alive in heaven. The second component is present. What about the third?

(C) Is there any confirmation that the transfer has taken place? In some of the LXX stories of a succession the transfer is confirmed by the successor's replication of the type of actions performed by his predecessor (e.g., Joshua and Elisha). The Lukan narrative uses this technique. Just as the Lukan Jesus made a lame man walk (Luke 5:17–26), so the apostles (Acts 3:1–10; 9:32–35); just as Jesus had power come forth from himself so that people were healed (Luke 6:19), so does Peter (Acts 5:15); just as Jesus resuscitated the dead (Luke 7:11–17; 8:40–42, 49–56), so does Peter (Acts 9:36–43); just as Jesus cast out demons (Luke 4:31–37), so do the apostles (Acts 5:16). The third component is indeed present in the Lukan narrative.

Given the presence of the three requisite components and the presence of a number of linguistic signs of the semantic field related to succession, one must conclude that whatever distinctive nuances the Lukan succession from Jesus to the apostles might have, the authorial audience would have almost certainly regarded this as a conventional story of a succession.

The second text in Luke-Acts with a semantic marker denoting succession, Acts 6:3, now needs attention. Are the three requisite components of a story of succession present in Acts 6:1-6?

(a) What is being transferred? It is the function of διακονία (vv. 1, 2), here, meaning serving tables. The transfer is described with a frequently used term of succession: appoint (καταστήσομεν). The first component is present.

(b) Are there symbolic signs accompanying the transfer? "They prayed and laid their hands on them" (v. 6, RSV), just as Moses did on Joshua (LXX Num 27:18, 23; Deut 34:9). The second component is here.

(c) Are there any confirming acts to indicate a transfer has taken place? One of the strangest aspects of the plot of Acts is that, after the Seven have been appointed to the role of διακονία, the subsequent stories about Stephen (6:8–7:60) and Philip (8:5–40) show them active not in διακονία but in powerful preaching! This apparent awkwardness can be understood if one remembers that in the LXX a major sign that the succession has taken place was the replication in the life of the successor of acts characteristic of the predecessor. Since the apostles were mighty preachers, a replication of their actions would require members of the Seven to so act as well (even if they were appointed for διακονία). If this reading be accepted, then the third component is present as well.

Given the presence of the requisite three components of a story of a succession and the use of a key term from the semantic field related to succession in antiquity, the authorial audience would most likely have regarded this as a second story of a succession in Luke-Acts. What about the third possibility?

The third possibility, signaled by Acts 14:23, may also be part of an ancient story of a succession involving the Pauline appointment of elders in his churches.

(a) What is being transferred? The context is Paul's concern for the care and nurture of his churches (14:21b-22). When Paul and Barnabas appoint (χειροτονήσαντες) elders for them in every church, it is the function of nurturing and caring for believers that is primary. It is this function that is being transferred to others, the elders. In the other text in Acts that deals with elders in the Pauline churches, the function is described as shepherding (ποιμαίνειν) and the role as that of ἐπισκόπους (guardians, Acts 20:28).

(b) Are there any symbolic acts associated with the succession? In 14:23 the transfer involves prayer, fasting, and committing them to the Lord. In the other text dealing with elders in Pauline churches (Acts 20:17–38), we hear that elders (presumably appointed by Paul) have been fully instructed (vv. 20, 27) as Joshua had been (LXX Num 27:19; especially Josephus, *A.J.* 4.7.2 §165). They are also entrusted to the Lord (v. 27). The second component is present in the Lukan narrative.

(c) Are there signs that the succession has been completed? Since there are no narratives telling of the behavior of either the elders of 14:23 or those of 20:17–38, there are no explicit confirming signs of the succession (just as there had been none in LXX Num 27:12–23's account of the succession from Moses to Joshua). The auditors of the narrative most likely knew whether or not the Ephesian elder-bishops had, in fact, been faithful to Paul's charge to defend the church against the grievous wolves. If Luke-Acts represents their response to the charge, then the very existence of the Lukan narrative would complete the form.

Given the succession vocabulary and the presence of at least two of the requisite components of a story of a succession (as in the case of Joshua in LXX Num 27:12–23), it is likely that the authorial audience would have heard, in this instance as well as in the case of the former two, a Lukan adaptation of succession, as it was understood in antiquity, for the Messianists' story.

Would the authorial audience of the Lukan narrative have regarded Paul as a successor of the twelve apostles? The answer to this question is clearly NO. Why? (a) Thrice it is said in Acts that Paul's appointment is of divine origin. Acts 9:15 has the risen Jesus speak about Paul as "a chosen (ἐκλογῆς) instrument of mine" just as the Twelve were (Luke 6:13, ἐκλεξάμενος; Acts 1:2, ἐξελέξατο; 1:24, ἐξελέξω). Acts 22:14 says Paul was appointed by God (προχειρίζομαι just as the Twelve were (προχειροτονέω, Acts 10:41). Acts 26:16 says Paul was appointed by the risen Jesus (προχειρίζομαι). The agreement with Gal 1:11–12 is striking. (b) When Paul is converted on the road to Damascus, he does come to the apostles in Jerusalem. When he does, however, it is not to receive any appointment from them but rather to have his divine conversion/-call/commission declared to them by one of their own congregation (Acts 9:27). There is, moreover, no evidence of the semantic field of succession in Paul's relation to the Twelve. (c) Acts 13:1–3 does portray Paul as an apostle (14:4, 14) of the church in Antioch of Syria, a Jerusalem approved congregation. This status is limited only to Acts 13–14. In Acts 15:36ff. the focus is back on Paul's direct commission by the heavenly world (cf. 16:6–10).[35]

At no point in the narrative of Acts is there a story of Paul's succession from the Twelve. At the same time, however, Paul's career replicates that of the Lukan Jesus, just as did the careers of Peter and others of the Twelve. For example, as Jesus (Luke 5:17–26) and Peter (Acts 3:1–10) heal a lame man, so does Paul (Acts 14:8–18); as Jesus (Luke 6:19) and Peter (Acts 5:15) have power come forth from their persons to heal people, so does Paul (Acts 19:11–12); as Jesus (Luke 7:11–17) and Peter (Acts 9:36–43) resuscitate the dead, so does Paul (Acts 20:7–12); as Jesus (Luke 4:31–37) and Peter (Acts 5:16) perform exorcisms, so does Paul (Acts 16:16–18). Indeed, the replication of the pattern of Jesus' life in that of the Paul of Acts goes even further. In the narrative at the end of Acts, there are also correspondences between the life of Jesus and that of Paul: e.g., (1) both Jesus (19:45–48) and Paul (Acts 21:26) enter the temple upon their entry into Jerusalem; both Jesus (Luke 22:54) and Paul (Acts 21:30) are seized by a mob; both Jesus (Luke 22:63–64) and Paul (Acts 23:2) are slapped by the priest's assistants; both Jesus (22:26; 23:1; 23:8; 23:13) and Paul (Acts 23; 24; 25; 26) are involved in four trials; both Jesus (Luke 23:6–12) and Paul (Acts 25:13–26:32) have a Herod involved in their trials; both Jesus (Luke 23:47) and Paul (Acts 27:3, 43) have a centurion act positively towards them; both Jesus (Luke 24) and Paul (Acts 28) have their ministries end on the positive note of the fulfillment of scripture. If such replication of a predecessor's life confirms that a succession has taken place, then Luke believes that Jesus' emissaries are *both* those who came to their position by means of a horizontal, historical process of succession (the Twelve) *and* those whose appointment was a vertical, experiential event (so Paul). The validation of both is the replication of the life of the founder in their own.

Would Luke's authorial audience have considered any of the transfers to involve multiple generations? (a) *First Clement* 44:2 speaks of the apostles' appointing (κατέστησαν) bishops and deacons and then afterwards adding a codicil "that if they [the first appointees] should fall

---

[35] Charles H. Talbert, *Reading Acts* (New York: Crossroad, 1997), 33–35.

asleep, other approved men should succeed (διαδέξονται) to their ministry" (LCL). In *1 Clement* the succession is multigenerational: apostles-first appointees-the appointees of the first appointees, etc. (b) In Luke 1:2 there is a succession of tradition that conceivably could be seen as running through three generations. In Acts, however, the successions explicitly run only one generation: from Jesus to the Twelve; from the Twelve to the Seven; from Paul to the elders. This, of course, could be taken in either of two ways. On the one hand, it could be taken to mean that Acts envisioned no succession beyond the first generation. Why? An eschatological explanation might run: because of Luke's belief in an imminent End,[36] he would not have thought of later generations. A non-eschatological explanation would contend that Luke understood the writing of Luke-Acts to fulfill at least the teaching function assigned to the elders. On the other hand, it could be taken to mean that Acts assumes what *1 Clement* states. Why? If Acts is an etiological narrative indicating the origins of the offices existent in his day, then a multiple generational transfer could be assumed. The issue is moot.

Implications of Succession Thinking in the Lukan Narrative

Three literary implications may be noted. First, given the centrality of the succession from Jesus to the Twelve in the Lukan plot, the source of Lukan duality has likely been found. The narrative naturally reflects the pattern of a foundational figure and his successors (a+b). This supports the designation Luke-Acts rather than Luke and Acts.

Second, for the first time we have an explanation for the remarkable correspondences between the career of Jesus in the Third Gospel and that of the apostles in Acts. It is part of a story of a succession in the LXX to have the successors replicate in their own lives the actions of their predecessors. The correspondences are part of component three of a succession story. The employment of such correspondences, moreover, explains the expanded scale of the part of the succession story in Acts.

Third, Luke-Acts' being shaped by the succession principle raises the question of genre. Unfortunately, it does not automatically answer the question. Various genres were shaped by the succession principle.[37] Further discussion is required.

---

[36] Charles H. Talbert, *Reading Luke* (New York: Crossroad, 1984), 204.
[37] Hubert Cancik, 'The History of Culture, Religion, and Institutions in Ancient

Any discussion of genre must begin with the reminder that genres are not prescriptive. "Genres do not resemble some kind of eternally immutable Platonic Ideal Forms. ..."[38] If one, therefore, asks to what genre Luke-Acts belongs, what is meant is: with what group of writings in its cultural setting does Luke-Acts have the greatest affinity? To say that Luke-Acts belongs to this or that genre does not mean that its author imitated this or that other document. It means rather that the author of Luke-Acts reflects affinities with a stream of literature that in turn possesses affinities among its participants. Such affinities would be picked up by the authorial audience and would condition the way the document was heard and understood.

If one asks where one would look for possible genre analogies to Luke-Acts, it seems to us that one would need to search for literature possessing (1) similarities of contents, in the sense that an analogous writing would contain more than one type of succession story; (2) formal similarities, in the sense that an analogous writing would be a prose narrative whose duality of form is derived from a controlling story of a succession from a foundation figure to his successor(s), (3) similarities of details like terminology, ritual acts accompanying the succession, and evidences of the transfer, and (4) similarity of function, in the sense of what roles the stories of succession play in the plot.

1) The LXX offers the closest analogy of contents, in the sense that it includes several different types of succession in one narrative. There are stories of successions from Aaron to Eleazar (priestly), from Moses to Joshua (leader of the army, etc), from Saul to David and from David to Solomon (kingly), and from Elijah to Elisha (prophetic).

2) There are loose formal similarities with a number of surviving documents from antiquity, in the sense that the narrative is shaped by one controlling story of succession. (a) The LXX's stories of the succession from Moses to Joshua, from David to Solomon, and from Elijah to Elisha possess in themselves the necessary duality of form that is

---

Historiography: Philological Observations Concerning Luke's History,' *JBL* 116 (1997): 673–95, contends that Acts is an 'institutional history.' His analogies show that accounts of the origin and development of an institution are not genre specific. They may be found in manuals (Pomponius Sextus) and biographies (Lucian's *Alexander* and Dikaiarchus' Βίος τῆς Ἑλλάδος as well as in histories [e.g. Herodotus]).

[38] Richard A. Burridge, *What Are the Gospels* (Cambridge: Cambridge University Press, 1992), 45.

derived from a story of a succession, even if the narrative about the predecessor is not fully a Life. (b) Diodorus Siculus's account of the transfer of rule from Alexander to his successors also possesses a certain duality of form at the break between Books 17 and 18. (c) If one considers only the individual parts of Philodemus's Σύνταξισ, then there is some similarity in form here also. The life of the founder of a particular school is followed by an expanded list of his successors, giving the document a certain duality of form. (d) Iamblichus's *De vita Pythagorica* possesses some of the same duality by its following the Life of Pythagoras with a succession list in chapter 36. (e) The six Lives of philosophers with a subsequent succession list in Diogenes Laertius also reflect the duality of form. (f) That there was a pre-Christian exemplar of a single life of a philosophic founder followed by material about his successors is proved by Aristoxenos's Βίος Πυθαγόρου. (g) *Vita Pachomii* involves an extensive narrative about the succession from the founder of cenobitic monasticism which gives the Life a certain duality of form.

The greatest contrast between some of these cited formal analogies to Luke-Acts and the Lukan narrative is that they are parts of larger wholes which do not reflect the same duality of form that the parts do. For example, whereas the succession sections in the LXX, the succession section in Diodorus Siculus, and the six individual Lives in Diogenes Laertius themselves are formally similar to Luke-Acts, the larger wholes in which they are located do not reflect this duality. It is writings like Aristoxenos's Βίος Πυθαγόρου, Iamblichus's *De vita Pythagorica*, and *Vita Pachomii* that reflect a duality derived from the succession motif in the formal arrangement of the documents as wholes. It is worthy of note that the documents that are the closest analogies to Luke-Acts at the formal level are biographies, either of individual founders of communities or of a philosophical community itself.

3) The similarities of linguistic data, ritual acts associated with a succession, and evidences of a transfer are also present in the extant documents we have surveyed. (a) *Linguistic data*. The Lukan employment of διατίθημι (Luke 22:28–30) is paralleled by both Jewish and non-Jewish usage. The Lukan appropriation of καθίστημι (Acts 6:3) is likewise paralleled by Jewish and non-Jewish usage. The Lukan incorporation of χειροτονέω (Acts 14:23) is paralleled by both Jewish and non-Jewish usage. There is little in the Lukan use of linguistic markers that points in one direction or another among the literature of succession in antiquity.

(b) *Ritual acts.* In the first place, Luke-Acts' use of a speech by the foundation figure to his successors as a defining ritual act of transfer finds analogies in Josephus's account of the succession from Tiberius to Gaius in *Antiquitates judaicae* 18.6.9–10 §211–37, and in the Pseudo-Clementine *Homiliae* story of Peter's address to Clement as part of the succession. In the second place, Luke-Acts' employment of language about the Spirit's coming upon (ἐπί) the apostles echoes that of the LXX's use of such language for the Spirit's coming upon Elisha. That this occurs in the context of the foundation figure's ascent into heaven in both documents is significant. Only in the case of the succession from Jesus to the apostles and from Elijah to Elisha does the succession involve the predecessor's being in heaven after having left this earth. In the third place, Luke-Acts' use of the language of 'being clothed' (here, with the Spirit) is similar to that used in the story of Joshua's succession from Moses in *Liber antiquitatum biblicarum* 20:2–5 (Take Moses' garments and clothe yourself) and the LXX's narrative about the succession from Aaron to Eleazar in Num 20:23–28 (Moses takes Aaron's apparel off him and clothes his son, Eleazar). In this category, Luke-Acts' links are with both LXX and non-LXX sources, although the former predominate.

(c) *Signs of confirmation that the transfer has been made.* The remarkable correspondences between Jesus' career in Luke and that of the apostles in Acts is analogous to the LXX's practice of having the successor replicate in his career deeds associated with his predecessor (e.g., Joshua replicates a number of items from Moses' career, Elisha replicates several items from Elijah's life). To our knowledge, nowhere outside of the Deuteronomic history's section of the LXX is this technique found in so explicit a fashion in the period before or after Luke-Acts.

4) The succession from the apostles to the Seven in Acts 6 guarantees the continuation of a function (διακονία), just as the succession from Paul to the elders in Acts 14 and 20 ensures the continuation of a function (the care and nurture of the churches, including defending against grievous wolves among the flock). In both cases, the succession provides for the continuity in ministry that is needed. This is analogous not only to the LXX but also to the successions of emperors, jurists, and philosophers. The succession from Jesus to the Twelve involves the gift of both a status (eat at my table) and a role (judging) under the authority of the King (= the risen Christ). This legitimates the Twelve as the true judges who dispense righteous judgment, under their King,

in the restored Israel. Again, this is analogous not only to the LXX but also to the philosophical schools and the rabbinic tradition of authenticated teachers.

The impression created by this search for analogies in the areas of contents, form, details, and function is that Luke-Acts is in contents (i.e., use of multiple types of succession stories) most like the LXX; it is formally (i.e., duality of structure) most like the ancient Mediterranean writings whose surface structure is controlled by a succession principle (founder-successor[s]); in the category of details (i.e., linguistic markers, symbolic rites, confirming signs) is most like the LXX and certain other Jewish narratives that retell the biblical stories, and in function finds its analogies across a wide spectrum of Jewish and Greco-Roman sources. It is as though the author of Luke-Acts stands with one foot in the Greco-Roman culture of succession with its biographies of founders and their successors and the other foot in the biblical world of Ancient Judaism with its stories of successions, and from that dual stance creates a distinctive synthesis of the two that would nevertheless be recognizable to pagan, Jew, and early Christian alike as a succession narrative. In so doing, the author of Luke-Acts acts as modern genre critics suppose an author would do.

> In fact, the creation of a new type arises from old types. ... The new depends on a 'leap of the imagination' from the known to the unknown, to assimilate it and make it known, either through an amalgamation of two old types, or an extension of an existing type.[39]

Whatever name one gives to the genre of Luke-Acts, after this survey its affinities with a clearly defined body of analogous ancient writings are obvious.[40]

Given the formal similarities between Luke-Acts and analogous Greco-Roman writings,[41] the issue that remains unsettled for the two

---

[39] Burridge, 47. One of the changes Burridge mentions that is characteristic of flexible genres is "changes of scale." Another is "inclusion of one genre within another" (48).

[40] William G. Doty, 'The Concept of Genre in Literary Analysis,' *SBL Seminar Papers, 1972* (2 vols.; SBLSP 8; Chico, Calif.: Scholars Press, 1972), 2:439, says: "generic definitions are best understood as relational terms—they demonstrate how some literary works are similar." Burridge, 48, says: "If genre involves 'family resemblances,' then the key to correct generic understanding will be to relate literary works to other works to ascertain points of contact and divergence."

[41] Varro's *Antiquitates Rerum Divinarum* does not belong to the group of writings with which Luke-Acts has affinities (contra H. Cancik, *JBL* 116 [1997]: 684–85). Varro wrote forty-one books under the title *Antiquitates*. He divided his matter into two categories:

authors of this paper is: Is Luke-Acts more like biographies of individual founders that contain within them a succession list or narrative, or biographies of communities that employ a Life of their founder to define the Way and then follow that with a succession list or narrative? That is, is the concern of the document to describe Jesus' distinctiveness so that the inclusion of the successions provides part of his uniqueness, or is the aim to describe the distinctiveness of the Christian community so that the inclusion of a Life of the founder functions to define the basis of the uniqueness of the community? At this point, from our perspective, the decision is too close to call.

At the theological level, there are doubtless sectarian battles to be fought, with all sides likely finding that Luke-Acts offers both some comfort and some correction to all concerned. This, however, takes us beyond the prescribed aim of the article.

---

human and divine. He devoted twenty-five books to the former and sixteen to the latter. Under human things he dealt with persons, places, times, and actions. In general he followed a similar plan for divine things: i.e., sacred actions are performed by persons in certain places at definite times. Book One of *Rerum Divinarum* is an introduction. Books two through four deal with the persons who perform the rites (Bk. 2=pontiffs; Bk. 3=augurs; Bk. 4=sacred college of the Fifteen). Books five through seven deal with places (Bk. 5=shrines; Bk. 6=temples; Bk. 7=sacred places). Books eight through ten deal with the times (Bk. 8=festivals; Bk. 9=circus games; Bk. 10=theatrical performances). Books eleven through thirteen deal with the rites (Bk. 11=consecrations; Bk. 12=private worship; Bk. 13=public rites). Books fourteen through sixteen deal with the gods to whom the religious persons, places, times, and rites are directed (Bk. 14=the known gods; Bk. 15=unknown gods; Bk. 16=select major divinities). In fragment 12, Varro says the object of his research and writing is that people might reverence rather than despise these things. He works in the period of the Republic as it came to its end when Roman religion was more and more in decline. Varro's work on divine things is more like an encyclopedia than a history. Burkhart Cardauns, ed., *M. Terentius Varro Antiquitates Rerum Divinarum* (2 vols; Wiesbaden: Franz Steiner Verlag, 1976), gives a collection of the fragments (vol. 1) and a German translation and commentary (vol. 2). Augustine in *De civitate Dei*, Books 6–7, gives a summary of much of Varro's work. The Index of terms in volume 2 of Cardauns' work includes none belonging to the semantic field of succession.

CHAPTER THREE

READING AUNE'S READING OF TALBERT

David Aune has on two occasions made what others have called "telling criticisms"[1] of Talbert's arguments regarding gospel genre in general and the genre of Luke-Acts in particular.[2] Because of work on other projects, Talbert has thus far failed to make a sustained response to Aune, leading some to think that he has accepted Aune's critique as valid. This seems an appropriate place to indicate otherwise.

Gospel Perspectives II

Aune's critique in the article of 1981 was directed against Talbert's *What Is a Gospel?*, a volume usually credited with "the paradigm shift away from form-critical notions of the gospels' uniqueness."[3] In it there are seven criticisms to which we may direct attention.

The first consists of two parts. Argument 1a runs: "while Talbert has chosen to refute the critical consensus of NT scholarship as represented by Bultmann, the real Goliath is K. L. Schmidt."[4] "It is Schmidt, not Bultmann, who requires refutation."[5]

Argument 1b runs: Talbert assumes Bultmann's views retain validity after fifty years.[6]

Translation: 1a—Talbert did not do what I would have done. 1b— If I do not regard Bultmann's views as still valid, no one else does.

---

[1] Mikeal Parsons, 'Reading Talbert: New Perspectives on Luke and Acts,' in *Cadbury, Knox, and Talbert* (ed. M. C. Parsons and J. B. Tyson; SBLBSNA; Atlanta: Scholars Press, 1992), 162.
[2] D. E. Aune, 'The Problem of the Genre of the Gospels: A Critique of C. H. Talbert's *What Is a Gospel?*,' in *Gospel Perspectives* (ed. R. T. France and David Wenham; 6 vols.; Sheffield: JSOT Press, 1981), 2.9–60; idem, *The New Testament in Its Literary Environment* (Library of Early Christianity; Philadelphia: Westminster, 1987), 79.
[3] Richard A. Burridge, *What Are the Gospels? A Comparison with Graeco-Roman Biography* (SNTSMS 70; Cambridge: Cambridge University Press, 1992), 85; cf. Parsons, 'Reading Talbert,' 162.
[4] Aune, 'The Problem of the Genre of the Gospels,' 16.
[5] Ibid., 18.
[6] Ibid.

Response: Argument 1a—*What Is A Gospel?* "is essentially a negative argument: Bultmann's rejection of the biographical genre of the gospels is dismissed because other ancient βίοι were essentially mythic, cultic and world-denying. ... In the end, *What Is a Gospel?* ... destroys the arguments of earlier critics who thought it *is not* biography."[7] It did not attempt more. The different tasks were left to others. The question, then, should be: Has Talbert done what he set out to do? It should not be: Should Talbert have attempted more than he did? Argument 1b—That the entire form-critical affirmation of a gospel's literary uniqueness fell like a house of cards in spheres of scholarship influenced by Bultmann after *What Is a Gospel?* indicates that his views had in fact retained their validity for many even after fifty years. Conclusion: This argument is inappropriate and inaccurate.

The second argument also consists of two parts. Argument 2a runs: The focus on the myth of the immortals was the result of Talbert's preoccupation with Luke-Acts.[8]

Argument 2b runs: The terminology 'eternals ... immortals' is not that of the ancients.[9] Translation: Argument 2a—Talbert did not present all of the different ways it was believed men could become gods in antiquity. He dealt only with the one way, that which was closest to Luke-Acts (and the other synoptic gospels). I know more than he does which I show in my fifteen-page presentation of all the other models.[10] Argument 2b—The reality is contained in the terminology. If the terminology is not exactly that of the ancients, then the reality of two types of gods is null and void. Response: Argument 2a—This is a variation on the logic of argument 1a. Because Talbert does not do everything, especially what I would do, means that what he does do is inaccurate. However, if one's purpose is to show the mythical structure of the synoptics, what is the point of spending fifteen pages on models that are irrelevant? Why would one not rather spend the pages on the one model that is relevant for the synoptics, which, after all, are the focus of the debate? Argument 2b—This argument is analogous to that of some ancient Christians who opposed the Nicaean trinitarian formula because ὁμοούσιος is not used in scripture. It is akin to certain modern day fundamentalists who claim that unless the correct formula

---

[7] Burridge, *What Are the Gospels?*, 86.
[8] Aune, 'The Problem of the Genre of the Gospels,' 18.
[9] Ibid., 19.
[10] Ibid., 20–35.

is used, one is an outsider who has not appropriated Christian religious reality. Philo, for example, uses the categories 'gods and demigods' to describe the reality.[11] The reality about which he speaks, however, is exactly that conveyed, in context, by the categories 'eternals and immortals.' Conclusion: This argument in its two parts is specious, based on fallacious assumptions, and without relevant merit.

The third argument makes two claims. First, "To regard 'biography' as a monolithic literary form ... is a major methodological error of Talbert, ... to ignore the confluence of 'biography,' 'romance,' and even 'aretalogy' in the legendary lives of Alexander or the *Vita Apollonii* of Philostratus only compounds the error."[12] Second, to include under the rubric of biography all that Talbert does is to empty the comparison of all meaning.[13] Translation: I am calling for two disparate things at the same time. On the one hand, I claim Talbert regards biography as monolithic and on the other hand I complain that he includes under biography too diverse a list of writings. Response: First, such a contradictory critique in one paragraph implies that the author must have slept through the composition of this part of his argument. It makes no sense whatsoever.

Second, Talbert sees a great diversity in ancient biography: a difference between didactic and non-didactic biography; a difference between biographies with a mythical structure and those without it; a difference between those with one form of myth and those with another; a difference between biographies with functions A, B, C, D, and E, etc. In the chapter on the myth of the immortals, aretalogical elements of biographies are treated. The charge is without foundation in fact. Did he read the book? Third, Talbert does include under the biographical label a diverse group of writings. Why? It is because in the secondary literature, which is often uncited but not unknown, these documents were so included. Conclusion: This is the weakest argument so far. It is a contradictory claim that makes no sense.

The fourth argument runs: The gospels are not cult legends, so Talbert's attempt to show that some biographies are cultic is unnecessary.[14] Translation: Talbert does not argue the case the way I would have. Response: So what? Is not the result the same? Conclusion: Again, the

---

[11] Philo, *Legat.* 4.78; 13.93; 16.14; *Prob.* 105; *Contempl.* 6.
[12] Aune, 'The Problem of the Genre of the Gospels,' 36.
[13] Ibid.
[14] Ibid., 37–38.

same complaint: Talbert does not do what I would have done. The arguments seem to get weaker as we go along through the article.

Argument five, regarding Talbert's classification of didactic biographies in terms of five types, again has two parts. Argument 5a—"While Types D and E are dubious distinctions, it cannot be doubted that many ancient biographies functioned in the ways categorized in the first three types."[15] Argument 5b—"It is bold for Talbert to strike off on his own in proposing a new typology."[16] Do not change Leo's classification. Translation: 5a—Although I offer absolutely no evidence for a rejection of types D and E, I reject them because if I accept them I must accept also the cultic location of some biographies (which I have just rejected). 5b—I like Leo. I regard Leo's classifications as prescriptive. Why change? Response: Classifications of biographies, like genres of literature, are not prescriptive but descriptive. They shift as new questions are asked of the data. So a shift from a formalistic classification (Leo) to a classification in terms of functions (Talbert) results not from an overly bold act but from the natural tendency to ask new questions of the evidence as new circumstances arise. Judging from Classicists' responses to me over the years, the functional classification is often helpful. The evidence for types D and E is as abundant as for types A, B, and C. Conclusion: The critique is untenable, based on judgments pronounced with no evidence offered and on fallacious assumptions about the nature of classifications.

The sixth argument runs: In rejecting Bultmann's third pillar, Talbert is right but he fails to call attention to another strong argument.[17] Translation: Talbert is right but does not argue as I would have. Response: Thanks for the help. Conclusion: The argument is supportive in terms of its evidence and meaningless in terms of a critique.

The seventh argument comes after pages 44–48 sketch Aune's questions and proposals about gospel genre. At the end of his "constructive" work, he concludes: Talbert could have avoided his difficulties if he had "approached the ancient literature … with a different and more appropriate set of questions."[18] Translation: Here it is again. Talbert did not do it my way so it cannot be right. Response: I am growing weary of this broken record. Has Aune ever read Mortimer J. Adler and Charles

---

[15] Ibid., 39.
[16] Ibid.
[17] Ibid., 43.
[18] Ibid., 48.

van Doren, *How To Read A Book* (rev. ed.; New York: Simon & Schuster, 1972)? Conclusion: There is more heat than light in this review. Rhetoric, however, is no substitute for substance.

The New Testament in its Literary Environment

In this volume of 1987 David Aune leveled three criticisms against Talbert's claim that Luke-Acts reflects the a+b pattern of didactic biographies which presented first the life of a founder and then a list or narrative of his successors. (1) The usual pattern of life+successor+teachings which Talbert claimed was typical of Diogenes' *Vitae Philosophorum* is found in only six of the eighty-two lives. (2) Contrary to Talbert's view, Diogenes is concerned only with who succeeded whom, not with the legitimacy of their views. (3) To speak as Talbert does of a succession *narrative* in ancient biography is an "inappropriate description of brief *lists* of students or successors."[19] Let us take these objections one by one.

In the interests of accuracy, we should allow Aune to state his first critique in his own words.

> The only examples of this genre are Diogenes Laertius' *Lives of Philosophers*, a lengthy compendium of the lives and teachings of eighty-two ancient philosophers from Thales to Epicurus, written ca. A.D. 250 at the earliest. Talbert regards the similarities between Diogenes' *Lives* and Luke-Acts as remarkable, for both contain the life of the founder of a religious community, a list or narrative of successors, and a summary of the community's teaching.[20]

There are two pieces to this critique. In the first, Aune says that the only example of the genre of an a+b biography is Diogenes Laertius and that source is late. In *Literary Patterns*, I referred to a pre-Christian biography of Aristotle and to first century B.C. Herculaneum Papyri 1018, 1021, and possibly 1044, in addition to Laertius.[21] In *What Is a Gospel?*, I spoke of a pre-Christian Life of Aristotle and various collections of Successions of which Diogenes Laertius is the best preserved.[22] In 'Discipleship in Luke-Acts,' I mentioned *Vita Pachomii* and Hilary of Arles' *Sermo de vita Honorati*.[23] At no time did I ever say the sole

---

[19] Aune, *The New Testament in Its Literary Environment*, 79.
[20] Ibid., 79.
[21] Charles H. Talbert, *Literary Patterns, Theological Themes, and the Genre of Luke-Acts* (SBLMS 20; Missoula: Scholars Press, 1974), 130–31, 133.
[22] Charles H. Talbert, *What Is a Gospel?* (Philadelphia: Fortress, 1977).
[23] Charles H. Talbert, 'Discipleship in Luke-Acts,' in *Discipleship in the New Testament*

example of the a+b genre was Laertius or imply its only examples were late. The previous essay on 'Succession in Mediterranean Antiquity,' moreover, should put the lie as well to this part of Aune's argument.

The second part of Aune's first argument is his assertion that I claim Laertius' biographies "usually" exhibit an a+b pattern, whereas in fact only six lives out of eighty-two do so. In *Literary Patterns* I noted that the a+b pattern is characteristic of five lives of founders of philosophical schools in Laertius and listed them as Aristippus, Plato, Zeno, Pythagoras, and Epicurus.[24] My comment was: "The similarities between the lives of founders of philosophical schools presented by Laertius and Luke-Acts are remarkable."[25] In 'Discipleship in Luke-Acts,' it was specified that only certain lives in Laertius reflect the a+b pattern and six were specified: Socrates, Aristippus, Plato, Zeno, Pythagoras, and Epicurus.[26] From first to last I have contended that only five or six founders of philosophical schools mentioned by Laertius reflect the pattern, not Laertius as a whole.

Aune's second argument is that Diogenes is concerned only with who succeeded whom, not with the legitimacy of their views. If one grants that such a+b biographies are a phenomenon wider than Laertius, then other evidence can clarify the dispute. *Vita Pachomii* 119 says that Pachomius' successor Orsisius zealously emulated the life of the founder. Hilary of Arles' *Sermo de vita Honorati* 8 says Honoratus' successor's task was to do what the founder had done. These two Christian appropriations of the a+b biographical form used for founders explicitly say that the succession narrative was to demonstrate continuity between founder and successor. The succession list found in *m. Avot* certainly has as its aim to assert continuity between the rabbis of the time of writing and the oral law of Moses. The succession narrative of Laertius' *Vita Epicuri* shows continuity, not identity, between founder and successors. From the previous essay on 'Succession in Mediterranean Antiquity,' it has become clear that continuity between predecessor and successor in LXX stories is a guarantee that succession has taken place. The a+b form, then, is concerned to demonstrate continuity between founder and true successors and discontinuity between the founder and false followers.

(ed. Fernando Segovia; Philadelphia: Fortress, 1985), 62–75.
[24] Talbert, *Literary Patterns*, 127; 137, n. 16.
[25] Ibid., 129.
[26] Talbert, 'Discipleship in Luke-Acts,' 63; 74, n. 8.

Aune's third argument is that the a+b pattern of biography has only lists of a founder's successors, not a narrative as Luke-Acts does. In *Literary Patterns* I specified that the biographies of Zeno and Epicurus in Laertius have brief narratives of successors and that the pre-Christian biography of Aristotle ended with an anecdote about his choice of a successor.[27] In 'Discipleship in Luke-Acts,' I pointed out that *Vita Pachomii* had a long succession narrative. The previous essay on 'Succession in Mediterranean Antiquity' has, moreover, shown that the LXX employed detailed succession narratives in which the successor acted in various ways like his predecessor. Once it is recognized that the a+b pattern is wider than Laertius' five or six examples, succession lists are seen alongside succession narratives as part of the total scene.

Having looked at Aune's 'three telling criticisms' and more, what are we to conclude? Aune has not read carefully or reported accurately but opposes a straw man of his construction. His negative assertions do not apply to my thesis and, therefore, constitute no refutation of my thesis about the genre of Luke-Acts. Indeed, the more comprehensive data base on succession in antiquity presented in the previous essay should make my initial argument even more persuasive to any fair-minded reader.

At the end of this process one cannot help but wonder: why has Aune so repeatedly misread and so inaccurately reported the work he is allegedly evaluating? In this case he seems like a blind man in a dark room at midnight trying to make sense of a printed text. Having followed his literary career over the years, I must regrettably say that this is not the only occasion where this has occurred.

---

[27] Talbert, *Literary Patterns*, 137, n. 16; 130–31.

CHAPTER FOUR

PROPHECIES OF FUTURE GREATNESS: THE
CONTRIBUTIONS OF GRECO-ROMAN BIOGRAPHIES
TO AN UNDERSTANDING OF LUKE 1:5–4:1

What handle can the interpreter grasp to bring Luke 1:5–4:15 within the sphere of our understanding? Since the question of the sources of Luke 1–2 is well nigh impossible to answer[1] and that of Luke 3:1–4:15 has become increasingly difficult,[2] no argument can be framed with confidence on the basis of a comparison of the final form of the Gospel with its sources. An alternate route, the one chosen in this paper, is to attempt to indicate how a Greco-Roman reader/hearer of Luke-Acts would have understood Luke 1:5–4:15.[3]

Before taking this route, however, it is necessary to justify the focus on 1:5–4:15 as a coherent unit within the Third Gospel. A survey of the contents of the early chapters of Luke seems to support the focus. Before 1:5–4:15 we find the prologue (1:1–4); after it there is the frontispiece of the public ministry (4:16–30). Within 1:5–4:15 is a unit dealing with John the Baptist and Jesus in three episodes:[4] (1) 1:5–56, the annunciations of the births of John and Jesus; (2) 1:57–2:52, the births and early lives of the Baptist and Mary's son; and (3) 3:1–4:15, the adult ministry of John and the prelude to Jesus' public career. Each of these three episodes is built around a series of correspondences between the

---

[1] For a concise survey of the discussion, see Raymond E. Brown, *The Birth of the Messiah* (Garden City, N.Y.: Doubleday, 1977), 244–50; Charles H. Talbert, *Literary Patterns, Theological Themes and the Genre of Luke-Acts* (SBLMS 20; Missoula: Scholars Press, 1974), 45, 50.

[2] Cf. Joseph B. Tyson, 'Source Criticism of the Gospel of Luke,' in *Perspectives on Luke-Acts* (ed. Charles H. Talbert; ABPRSSS 5; Danville, Va.: Association of Baptist Professors of Religion, 1978), 24–39.

[3] This type of approach has proved effective at other points in the study of Luke-Acts: e.g., G. B. Miles and G. Trompf, 'Luke and Antiphon: The Theology of Acts 27–28 in the Light of Pagan Beliefs about Divine Retribution, Pollution, and Shipwreck,' *HTR* 69 (1976): 259–67; Fred Veltman, 'The Defense Speeches of Paul in Acts,' in *Perspectives on Luke-Acts*, 243–56; Vernon K. Robbins, 'By Land and By Sea: The We-Passages and Ancient Sea Voyages,' in *Perspectives on Luke-Acts*, 215–42.

[4] Talbert, *Literary Patterns*, 44–48.

material about John and that dealing with Jesus that reflects the Lukan artistry; each is concerned to portray Jesus' superiority over John the Baptist. In all three episodes John is depicted as a prophet (1:16–17; 1:76; 3:1–6), not the Messiah (3:15ff.), whereas Jesus is pictured in all three as the Davidic Messiah (1:32–33; 1:69; 2:4, 11; 3:23–38) and Son of God (1:35; 2:49; 3:22). This internal coherence argues for 1:5–4:15's being a single thought unit in the Lukan narrative.

The major objection to such a claim is the possibility that the Third Gospel once began with 3:1ff.[5] Three reasons have recently been advanced to support this contention. First, there are alleged historiographical parallels to 3:1ff. in other Greek writings which argue for this passage's having been the original opening of the Lukan Gospel. Second, Acts 1:1, 22 may be interpreted to mean that the Gospel once began with the baptism of Jesus. Third, the placing of the genealogy in the third chapter of Luke makes more sense if that had been done before an infancy narrative had been prefixed. This problem, I think, is more apparent than real. On the one hand, the reasons for thinking that the Third Gospel originally began with 3:1ff. are not compelling.[6] (1) The evidence of the first argument cuts both ways. Of the two examples cited by Raymond Brown, the first (Josephus, *B.J.*, 2.14.4 §284) comes in the middle of Josephus' narrative, not at the start of any main section. The second parallel (Thucydides, *Hist.* 2.2.1) may be the beginning of a section but is certainly not the start of the document as a whole. Given these facts, we may acknowledge that 3:1ff. is the beginning of the third episode of the unit 1:5–4:15. One should note, however, that 1:5 gives a similar, if not as elaborate, beginning for the first episode; and 1:26–27 and 2:1ff. give analogous beginnings in the first and second episodes for the material that relates to Jesus. The first argument is not persuasive. (2) The second argument depends on a given interpretation of Acts 1:1, 22. It seems just as plausible, however, to take Acts' reference to the baptism of John as a marker for the beginning of the adult career of Jesus as for the start of the Gospel. (3) Finally, the position of the genealogy is due to theological considerations. It is integral to the unit which begins with the baptism and ends with the

---

[5] Most recently, Raymond E. Brown, 'Luke's Method in the Annunciation Narrative of Chapter One,' in *No Famine in the Land* (ed. J. W. Flanagan and A. W. Robinson; Missoula: Scholars Press, 1975), 180; idem, *The Birth of the Messiah*, 240.

[6] Cf. Paul S. Minear, 'Luke's Use of the Birth Stories,' in *Studies in Luke-Acts*, ed. L. E. Keck and J. L. Martyn (Nashville: Abingdon, 1966), 111–30.

temptation narrative and which focuses on the Son of God.[7] There is no need to resort to the hypothesis of the Third Gospel's beginning at 3:1ff. to account for its presence in chapter 3 rather than in chapters 1–2. On the other hand, the issue before us ultimately has nothing to do with earlier stages in the Third Gospel's development but with the question whether or not *in the present form* of Luke, 1:5–4:15 is a coherent narrative unit. The answer to that, I think, is 'yes.' This paper will focus, then, on Luke 1:5–4:15 as a unit within the Lukan Gospel which treats the life of Jesus prior to his public career.

What is the thrust of the material about Jesus in Luke 1:5–4:15? Anticipations of Jesus' destiny predominate. These anticipations are given in various forms.

1) There are two angelophanies.[8] (a) In the first, Luke 1:26–38, the angel Gabriel comes to Mary not only to announce the miraculous conception (1:35a) but also to tell of the child's destiny.

> He will be great, and will be called the Son of the Most High; and the Lord God will give to him the throne of his father David, and he will reign over the house of Jacob forever; and of his kingdom there will be no end. (1:32–33, RSV) ... and the child to be born will be called holy, the Son of God. (1:35b)

(b) In the second, Luke 2:8–20, an angel of the Lord appears to the shepherds in the field announcing the birth of one who would be a Savior, Christ the Lord (2:11).

2) There are four prophecies. (a) Luke 1:67–79, the first, is a prophecy of Zechariah when he was filled with the Holy Spirit (v. 67). In the context of his predictions about John (vv. 76–79), there is praise to God for raising up a "horn of salvation" in the "house of his servant David" (v. 69, RSV). This, of course, refers in its Lukan context to Jesus. (b) Luke 2:25–35, the second, gives us the prophecy of Simeon, to whom it had been revealed that he should not taste death before he had seen the Lord's Christ (v. 26). In the Spirit, on seeing Jesus he blesses God.

---

[7] Talbert, *Literary Patterns*, 117–18.

[8] On the form of these two narratives see G. F. Wood, 'The Form and Composition of the Lucan Annunciation Narratives' (STD thes., Catholic University of America, 1962); Benjamin Hubbard, 'Commissioning Stories in Luke-Acts: A Study of Their Antecedents, Form and Content,' *Semeia* 8 (1977): 103–26.

> Lord, now lettest thou thy servant depart in peace, according to thy word;
> for mine eyes have seen thy salvation
> which thou hast prepared in the presence of all peoples,
> a light for revelation to the Gentiles,
> and for glory to thy people Israel. (2:29–32, RSV)

(c) In the third, Luke 2:36–38, we hear of the prophetess Anna who spoke of Jesus "to all who were looking for the redemption of Jerusalem" (v. 38, RSV). (d) Finally, Luke 3:16–17 gives John the Baptist's messianic preaching. He speaks of the mightier one who is coming who will baptize with the Holy Spirit and with fire, a prophecy the author of Luke-Acts apparently believed was fulfilled at Pentecost (Acts 2:3–4, 33).

3) Closely related to the series of four prophecies is Luke 1:41, 42–45, which consists of a portent followed by a prophetic interpretation. When the pregnant Elizabeth heard the greeting of Mary, the babe leaped in her womb. Filled with the Holy Spirit, Elizabeth then exclaimed: "Why is this granted to me, that the mother of my Lord should come to me? For behold, when the voice of your greeting came to my ears, the babe in my womb leaped for joy" (vv. 43–44, RSV).[9]

4) Luke 3:21–22 has similarities to 1:41–45. It too has an event that is prophetic in nature followed by a verbal interpretation. Though not usually read as such, Luke 3:21–22 is a prayer scene consisting of a vision followed by an audition which interprets it. The Third Evangelist has turned the narrative of Jesus' baptism into an episode of prayer in which there are an accompanying vision and audition. This is typically Lukan. (a) The Lukan emphasis on the prayer life of Jesus is well known (e.g., Luke 3:21; 5:16; 6:12; 9:18; 9:28–29; 11:1; 22:32; 22:39–46; 23:34; 23:46).[10] (b) It is also characteristic of the Evangelist to have prayer accompanied by visions and auditions.[11] For example, Luke 9:28–36 mentions that Jesus was praying, that a heavenly apparition occurred—Moses and Elijah appeared—and an interpretative audition followed—"this is my Son…" (RSV). Acts 10 offers another excellent example. In this chapter both Cornelius and Peter are involved in prayer; both

---

[9] Cf. Gen 25:22–23. John Drury, *Tradition and Design in Luke* (Atlanta: John Knox, 1976), 60, says: "In both instances the phenomenon is prophetic."

[10] Cf. Allison Trites, 'The Prayer Motif in Luke-Acts,' in *Perspectives on Luke-Acts*, 168–86.

[11] Cf. 2 Esd 9:26ff.; 2 Bar 21:1ff. for Jewish parallels.

have visions; both receive auditions which interpret what is seen. The same tendency may be found elsewhere in Acts 12:5ff.; 1:14 plus 2:1ff.; Luke 22:39–46; 1:10ff. In Luke 3:21–22 while Jesus is praying there is a heavenly apparition. The Holy Spirit descends in bodily form as a dove upon him.[12] The symbolism of the dove in Mediterranean antiquity (i.e., the beneficence of the deity in love)[13] is then interpreted by a *bath qol*: "You are my Son, my beloved, in you I am well pleased."[14] Here is another anticipation of Jesus' destiny, one that will become more striking when viewed in the context of the pagan practice of divination by means of the flight of birds. In Luke 1:5–4:15, therefore, angelophanies, prophecies in the Jewish sense of the word, a portent followed by an interpretation, and a vision plus an audition combine to give numerous verbal anticipations of Jesus' destiny.

Three other pericopes also deserve attention. There are two stories about the youth in which Jesus displays his wisdom and prowess (2:41–51; 4:1–13). In the episode of the twelve year old Jesus in the temple, the wisdom of the lad predominates.[15] In the test in the wilderness, the young Son of God demonstrates his spiritual power by means of his wise use of scripture and thereby defeats his adversary. Finally, there is the genealogy (3:23–38) which traces Jesus' lineage back through David to the father of the human race, Adam, and through him to God.[16] The impact of this material will be felt fully only after our foray into the Greco-Roman milieu of Luke-Acts.

How would such material—verbal anticipations of Jesus' destiny, stories of a young prodigy, and a genealogy—have been understood by

---

[12] Leander E. Keck, 'The Spirit and the Dove,' *NTS* 17 (1970–71): 63–67, argues that ὡς περιστεράν originally was adverbial, specifying the action of the Spirit. On Hellenistic soil there was a shift from adverbial to adjectival meaning, clearly evident in Luke. In the Third Gospel it is the dove-like form that is meant.

[13] E. R. Goodenough, *Jewish Symbols in the Greco-Roman Period* (13 vols.; New York: Pantheon Books, 1953–68) 8:40–41, after a survey of the uses of the dove in pagan, Jewish, and Christian tradition, concludes: "Beneath the variety of settings the dove itself shows a unity, and that unity, we may now see, lies essentially in the fact that the dove represents the beneficence of divinity in love, the loving character of divine life itself."

[14] Ultimately the textual question must be settled by determining the mind of the Evangelist. If Luke 1–2 is an integral part of the Gospel, then Luke 1:35 indicates Jesus was not begotten Son of God at his baptism. The Western reading is thereby excluded.

[15] Henk J. de Jonge, 'Sonship, Wisdom, Infancy: Luke 2:41–51a,' *NTS* 24 (1978): 317–54.

[16] Rodney T. Hood, 'The Genealogies of Jesus,' in *Early Christian Origins* (ed. A. P. Wikgren; Chicago: Quadrangle Books, 1961), 1–15, still seems to me to offer the best clue to Luke's genealogy.

a Greco-Roman reader? The question can be sharpened. Elsewhere I have argued that Luke-Acts belongs to a type of biography in antiquity which has the life of a philosopher who is a founder of a school followed by a narrative (or list) of his successors and selected other disciples.[17] The very form (a+b) would have been a clue to the readers/hearers about what to expect. In this light, how would a Greco-Roman listener hear a biography which had in its beginnings the components we have found in the Third Gospel in 1:5–4:15?

Suetonius's *Vitae XII Caesarum* is a good place to begin. In *Divus Augustus* there is one section (94), set aside for "an account of the omens which occurred before he was born, on the very day of his birth, and afterwards. ..." In this unit one finds at least fourteen omens which include: (a) portents interpreted by predictions (6 of the 14 items) which belong in the same general category as Luke 1:41–45; (b) dreams (3 of the 14 items)—e.g., a man dreamed of the savior of the Roman people, then on meeting Augustus for the first time, declared he was the boy about whom he had dreamed (cf. Luke 2:25–35); (c) prophecies (2 of 14 items), that is, verbal anticipations of the child's greatness and destiny (cf. the prophecies of Luke 1–3); (d) childhood prodigies (2 of 14 items), which tell us already that such childhood exploits were regarded as omens of the youth's destiny (cf. Luke 2:41–51; 4:1–13); (e) reference to a miraculous conception by Apollo (1 of 14 items), though the treatment of Augustus's family belongs to another section of the narrative about his pre-public life. In this section of omens from the beginning of Augustus's life we find all of the types of material that we noted in Luke 1:5–4:15 except a genealogy. It is interesting to note that here, as in Luke 1:5–4:15, the main thrust is on anticipations of the hero's destiny. *Divus Augustus* is, moreover, typical of Suetonius's efforts.

In *Tiberius* 14, Suetonius speaks of Tiberius's "strong and unwavering confidence in his destiny, which he had conceived from his early years because of omens and predictions." There follow seven such omens and predictions, all of which belong to the category of prophecies. There are no childhood prodigies, nor is there a miraculous conception. In 1–4 we hear of the stock from which Tiberius derived his origins.

Suetonius's *Divus Claudius* 1–2 treats the emperor's ancestry. In 7 there is one portent of a prophetic nature. When Claudius entered the Forum

---

[17] Talbert, 'Literary Patterns,' in *What Is a Gospel? The Genre of the Canonical Gospels* (Philadelphia: Fortress Press, 1977), ch. 8.

for the first time carrying the fasces, an eagle lighted upon his shoulder. This was regarded as prophetic because of the Roman use of the flight of birds of omen to discern the decrees of Fate.[18] A classic case, as described by Plutarch, is that of Numa who was chosen king after Romulus.[19] Numa said that before assuming the kingship his authority must first be ratified by Heaven. So the chief of the augurs turned the veiled head of Numa toward the south, while he, standing behind him with his right hand on his head, prayed aloud and turned his eyes in all directions to observe whatever birds or other omens might be sent from the gods. When the proper birds approached, then Numa put on his royal robes and went down where he was received as the "most beloved of the gods" (θεοφιλέστατον). In such a thought world, the Lukan baptismal narrative would have been viewed as an omen of Jesus' status as the beloved Son of God.

Three other Lives from Suetonius's work will suffice. In *Nero* 1–6, the emperor's family is treated. In 6 we are told that omens at his birth led to "direful predictions." Four examples follow, including one on the day of his purification (cf. Luke 2:22ff.). In *Vespasianus* 1–2, Suetonius treats the emperor's family line. At the beginning of 5 we hear that Vespasian began to hope for imperial dignity "because of the following portents." At least fifteen examples follow, including the prophecy of Josephus when he was captured during the first Jewish Revolt against Rome. Suetonius's *Divus Titus* includes both prophecies of his future rule (2 and 5:2) and a note about his youthful excellencies in body and mind (3). From Suetonius's *Vitae XII Caesarum* one can conclude that this biographer believed a Life should include something about a hero's family lineage, prophecies of his future greatness, and examples of childhood prodigies as part of his pre-public career. Sometimes there might be a reference to a miraculous conception. Is Suetonius to be considered typical of the Greco-Roman biographical tradition in this regard? The answer is 'yes.'

Portents, prophecies, and omens are widely used in biographical literature of Mediterranean antiquity for the period of a hero's life before he enters upon his public career. For example, Quintus Curtius,[20]

---

[18] Cf. Plutarch, *Rom.* 9 and Livy 1.7.1 for the use of such means to settle the quarrel between Romulus and Remus. Plutarch, in this context, speaks of the continuing Roman practice of taking auguries from the flight of birds.

[19] Plutarch, *Num.* 7.1–3.

[20] Quintus Curtius, *Hist. Alex.* 1 (a portent plus an interpretative prophecy).

Plutarch,[21] Philostratus,[22] Pseudo-Callisthenes,[23] the *Historiae Augustae*,[24] and the biographical section in Josephus's *Antiquitates judaicae* dealing with Moses[25] all contain this type of information in the pre-public lives of great men. A. D. Nock rightly said: "It was normally expected that a great man would be heralded by signs and prophecies."[26] The convention, being subject to perversion, could be ridiculed in satire, as in Lucian's *Alexander (Pseudomantis)*. Before Alexander and his partner Cocconas entered into their public routine, they went, says Lucian, to Chalcedon and buried bronze tablets, stating that very soon Asclepios and his father Apollo would come to Pontus and settle. When the tablets were found, the people voted to build a temple. Alexander then came proclaiming an oracle that he was the scion of Perseus. Next a Sibylline prediction of his activity was produced. This series of prophecies set the stage for the false prophet's public activity. Such prophecies are a convention in biographical literature.

Childhood prodigies are just as frequently a part of the Lives of great men in Mediterranean civilization. It was a commonplace of Hellenistic biography to relate tales of the precocious intelligence and of the unusual power and authority of the youths of destiny.[27] Quintus Curtius,[28] Plutarch,[29] Philostratus,[30] Pseudo-Callisthenes,[31] the *Historiae Augustae*,[32] Josephus,[33] and Philo[34] reflect the practice.

---

[21] Plutarch, *Rom.* 2.4; *Per.* 6.2–3; *Alex.* 3.1, 4–5; *Mar.* 3.3–4.1; *Lyc.* 5, etc.
[22] Philostratus, *Vit. Apoll.* 1.5.
[23] Pseudo-Callisthenes, *Hist. Alex. magn.*.
[24] *Hadr.* 2.4, 8, 9; *Sev.* 1.7–8; *Ant. Pius* 3.1–5.
[25] *A.J.* 2.9.2–3 §215–16. John Drury, *Tradition and Design in Luke's Gospel*, 47, says: "The resemblance of this to the prophetic canticles in Luke 1 and 2 needs no advertisement." Cf. also *1 En.* 106:13–19 (prophecy about Noah's destiny at his birth) and the *Genesis Aprocryphon* 2 which has a similar story about Noah.
[26] A. D. Nock, *Conversion: The Old and the New in Religion from Alexander the Great to Augustine of Hippo* (Oxford: Oxford University Press, 1933), 240.
[27] De Jonge, 'Sonship, Wisdom, Infancy: Luke 2:41–51a,' 341.
[28] Quintus Curtius, *Hist. Alex.* 1.
[29] Plutarch, *Rom.* 8 (overthrow of a tyrant); 6; *Alex.* 5.1 (wisdom); *Sol.* 2; *Them.* 2.1; *Cic.* 2.2; *Thes.* 6.4 (prowess and wisdom); *Dion* 4.2.
[30] Philostratus, *Vit. Apoll.* 1.7.11.
[31] Pseudo-Callisthenes, *Hist. Alex. magn.* (a number of childhood wonders, e.g., one of wisdom, one of strength, one of self-control, one of peacemaking, two of reliance on persuasion instead of war, one of respect for his father).
[32] *Sev.* 1.4.
[33] *A.J.* 2.9.6 §231; 2.9.7 §233; 2.10.1–2 §238ff. Cf. also *1 En.* 106:11 where Noah blesses God while still in the hands of the midwife.
[34] *Mos.* 1.5.20–24; 1.6.25–29. Cf. also *Jub.* 11–12 (childhood prodigies of Abraham).

References to miraculous conceptions are also an integral part of the biographical tradition, especially when the hero's Life is told in terms of the myth of the immortals.[35] Quintus Curtius,[36] Plutarch,[37] Philostratus,[38] and Pseudo-Callisthenes[39] give abundant examples of this tendency.

Finally, one expects to find material on the hero's family lineage which may eventuate in a genealogy. One may compare Plutarch,[40] Philostratus,[41] the *Historiae Augustae*,[42] and Josephus.[43]

The point is made. The biographical tradition of the Greco-Roman world would have conditioned a person in the Mediterranean region at the end of the first century A.D. to expect an account of the hero's career before he embarked on his public activity which included material on his family background, perhaps a reference to a miraculous conception, along with omens and other predictions of his future greatness, including childhood prodigies. When the reader confronted Luke 1:5–4:15, this narrative unit fulfilled these expectations in a remarkable way.

What was the purpose of such material in the narrative of a hero's life prior to his public career? For the sake of analysis, it will help if we divide the materials into two categories: omens, portents, and prophecies on the one hand, and birth, family, and childhood prodigies on the other.

1) Many Greco-Roman people believed that there existed a divine order of things which could be known by humans either through the initiative of the gods (i.e., revelation of when they were either angry or benevolent) or through the initiative of human beings skilled in unlocking such secrets (e.g., astrology). The prophecies of the biographies fit into

---

[35] Charles H. Talbert, 'The Concept of Immortals in Mediterranean Antiquity,' *JBL* 94 (1975): 419–36.
[36] Quintus Curtius, *Hist. Alex.* 1.
[37] Plutarch, *Thes.* 2; 6; 36.3 (begotten by Poseidon); *Rom.* 2.5; 4.2; *Alex.* 3.1–2.
[38] Philostratus, *Vit. Apoll.* 1.4.6.
[39] Pseudo-Callisthenes, *Hist. Alex. magn.*.
[40] Plutarch, *Thes.* 3; *Fab.* 1; *Brut.* 1–2; *Pyrrh.* 1; *Lyc.*1.4 (genealogy tracing his lineage back to Heracles).
[41] Philostratus, *Vit. Apoll.* 1.4.
[42] *Hadr.* 1.1–2; *Ant. Pius* 1.1–7.
[43] *A.J.* 2.9.6 §229 (genealogy tracing Moses back to Abraham); *Vita* 1 (the genealogy of Josephus).

this context. When Philostratus says of the portent at the birth of Apollonius, "No doubt the gods were giving a revelation—an omen of his brilliance, his exaltation above earthly things, his closeness to heaven,"[44] he was speaking of the belief that Tacitus alludes to with reference to Vespasian. Certain events, says Tacitus, revealed "the favour of heaven and a certain partiality of the gods toward him."[45] Through omens the gods revealed their preferences. Tacitus also tells how astrologers could, on their initiative, uncover fate. He says that Otho accepted the astrologer Ptolemy's "prophecies as if they were genuine warnings of fate disclosed by Ptolemy's skill. ..."[46] In a similar manner Suetonius can say that Domitian knew the very hour and manner of his death because "in his youth astrologers had predicted all this to him. ..."[47] Since either divine initiative or human skill could reveal one's destiny, Suetonius could write of Augustus:

> Having reached this point, it will not be out of place to add an account of the omens which occurred before he was born, on the very day of his birth, and afterwards, from which it was possible to anticipate and perceive his future greatness and uninterrupted good fortune.[48]

Sometimes, of course, such omens were not believed until after their fulfillment. Tacitus tells us that the secrets of Fate and the signs and omens which predestined (*destinatum*) Vespasian and his sons for power "we believed only after his success was secured."[49] And even a disregard of omens often pointed to acceptance of the assumption that there existed a higher order which was revealed through signs. So Tacitus tells us that Galba's disregard for omens was due to the fact that we "cannot avoid the fixed decrees of fate, by whatever signs revealed."[50] Given this way of thinking, it is to be expected that a biography of a great man would often contain one or more omens of the destiny allotted the individual and that they would be given during the period prior to his public career.

2) When we focus on the family lineage, birth, and childhood of the hero, we find sometimes an emphasis on the supernatural dimensions

---

[44] Philostratus, *Vit. Apoll.* 1.5 (LCL).
[45] Tacitus, *Hist.* 4.81.
[46] Tacitus, *Hist.* 1.22.
[47] Suetonius, *Dom.* 14.
[48] Suetonius, *Aug.* 94 (LCL).
[49] Tacitus, *Hist.* 1.10.
[50] Tacitus, *Hist.* 1.18.

of them, sometimes an emphasis on their natural character. On the one hand, sometimes a miraculous conception is joined with the theme of its manifestation in youthful prowess. For example, in Plutarch's *Romulus*, Numitor beholds Remus's superiority in stature and strength in body and notes that his acts correspond with his looks, when as yet the twins' identity was unknown. From this, Plutarch says, he grasped the truth of Remus's identity—that is, he was a divinely conceived child of a noble family.[51] Or in his *Theseus*, Plutarch remarks about the youthful triumphs of the hero who was offering "noble deeds and achievements as the manifesting mark of his noble birth."[52] On the other hand, sometimes the youth's behavior is understood as a natural phenomenon as in Plutarch's *Demetrius*. He gives a story of Demetrius's boyhood and says: "This ... is an illustration of the strong natural bent of Demetrius towards kindness and justice."[53] Whether the emphasis is on the supernatural or the natural, such stories of youthful behavior were taken as anticipations of the hero's future character. Plutarch says of Alcibiades: "His character, in later life, displayed ... many strong passions. ... This is clear from the stories recorded of his boyhood."[54] Again, the biographical tradition used a combination of birth, family, and boyhood stories to give anticipations about the future life of the hero. It would not be amiss to say that all of these components functioned also as prophecies of the character of the public career of the subject of the biography. If this was their purpose in the Greco-Roman biographies, then this is how a reader/hearer of Luke would most probably have taken the material of a similar nature in Luke 1:5–4:15.[55]

Virtually the totality of the material about Jesus in Luke 1:5–4:15 would have been regarded as an anticipation of his later public greatness. The angelophanies, the prophecies of a Jewish type, the portent plus its interpretation, the vision plus its audition, the two stories of childhood prodigies, and the genealogy (and miraculous conception) would combine to foretell/foreshadow the type of person Jesus would

---

[51] Plutarch, *Rom.* 7.3–4.
[52] Plutarch, *Thes.* 7.
[53] Plutarch, *Demetr.* 4.4.
[54] Plutarch, *Alc.* 2.1.
[55] John Drury, *Tradition and Design*, 131, says the order of the temptations in Luke places the Jerusalem temptation last because Jerusalem is the end and goal of Luke's gospel. "The temptations are thus made prophetic of Jesus' course."

be in his public ministry which began at Luke 4:16–30.[56] By writing in this way, the Evangelist was simply following the conventions of Greco-Roman biographical literature.

The Jewish cast to Luke's materials[57] is no obstacle to this thesis. Philo's *De vita Mosis*, the biographical section on the career of Moses in Josephus's *Antiquitates judaicae*, and Josephus's autobiography show that the Hellenistic biographical tradition made its impact on Judaism before and alongside of its impact on Christianity. Charles Perrot's collection of haggadic materials relating to the infancy/childhood of Noah, Abraham, Isaac, Samson, Samuel, Elijah, and Moses makes the same point.[58] The tendency in Mediterranean culture at large provoked a renewed interest in the early lives of heroes in Jewish circles which surfaced in the haggadah. To find material with a Jewish cast but presented in the mold of biographical convention is no impossibility, therefore. It is again rather what one would expect in an early Christian gospel.

Are we justified in speaking of a genre of an account of the pre-public careers of great men in Mediterranean antiquity? I think so. If so, then it would be a bit more inclusive than the recognized genre of infancy narratives of famous men.[59] In any case, the evidence assembled in this paper has enabled us to see that Luke made use of the conventional form of expression in his time and place for telling the story of the pre-public life of a hero.[60]

Mediterranean culture usually assumed that there was a divine order with some type of predetermined plan for human life. This order or plan was disclosed either through divine or human initiative in 'prophecy' of some sort. Prophecy, both oral and written, belonged to

---

[56] Raymond Brown, *The Birth of the Messiah*, 28, 481–82 (following Laurentin, *Jesus*, 147–58) recognizes this principle for Luke 2:41–51. This essay suggests the principle holds for the totality of Luke 1:5–4:15 as it relates to Jesus.

[57] E.g., echoes of Old Testament material that are often called midrashic and the use of an annunciation form characteristic of the Jewish scriptures.

[58] Charles Perrot, 'Les recits d'enfance dans la haggada,' *RdSR* 55 (1967): 481–518, esp. 507.

[59] Raymond Brown, *The Birth of the Messiah*, 561, says the first two chapters of the Third Gospel belong to the genre of "infancy narratives of famous men."

[60] As always, the question of genre is separable from the question of historicity. Cf. Charles H. Talbert, 'Oral and Independent or Literary and Interdependent? A Response to Albert B. Lord,' in *The Relationships among the Gospels: An Interdisciplinary Dialogue* (ed. W. O. Walker, Jr.; San Antonio: Trinity University Press, 1978), 99–100.

the propaganda strategies of Mediterranean religion generally.[61] It was not the preserve of Jewish and Christian traditions only. In using the argument from prophecy, then, Christians were merely working within the framework of common cultural assumptions. The particulars varied but the underlying structural assumptions were similar.

---

[61] A. D. Nock, *Conversion*, 250.

CHAPTER FIVE

JESUS' BIRTH IN LUKE AND
THE NATURE OF RELIGIOUS LANGUAGE

At no point is the *theological* difference between the two post-World War II generations more clearly seen than in their dominant understandings of the nature of religious language. The first post-World War II generation assumed a view of religious language typified by Rudolf Bultmann: it is the unfolding of believing self-understanding.[1] The preaching of the kerygma evokes faith. Faith has cognitive dimensions: implicit is a certain understanding of the self's relation to God, to others, the created order and to itself. Religious language is an explication of this believing self-understanding. This stance, of course, had roots in the liberal view that theology is the result of reflection on religious experience. In liberal theology, however, the religious experience on which reflection is done is secondary religious experience; that which is common to humans as humans (so Schleiermacher). In the Bultmannian system however, reflection is on primary religious experience, of a variety that is peculiar to Christians as Christians (i.e., to adherents of a particular religion).

The current generation assumes a view of religious language as political/projectionist. Its roots are in the thought of Feuerbach, Marx and Durkheim. (a) For Feuerbach, theology is but a mystified form of anthropology. God is the projection of universal humanity in a cosmic image.[2] (b) For Marx, social existence determines consciousness. Religious language is mere ideology, the idea system of the dominant class, reflecting the socio-economic interests of that class, and functioning to enforce the status and self-interest of that class. A changed social existence, however, will result in a new consciousness and eventually in the abolition of both religion and religious language.[3] (c) For Durkheim, religion is something eminently social. Religious language is a collective

---

[1] Rudolf Bultmann, *Theology of the New Testament* (2 vols.; New York: Scribner, 1951–1955), 2:237–41.
[2] Ludwig Feuerbach, *The Essence of Christianity* (New York: Harper, 1957).
[3] Karl Marx and Friedrich Engels, *On Religion* (New York: Schocken, 1964).

representation of collective realities. Religion was established to support and preserve group goals. It functions to give such goals sanctity and authority.[4]

Taken together, Feuerbach, Marx and Durkheim have bequeathed to our generation a distinctive view of religious language: (1) it is a projection/reflection of the existing social order; (2) it functions to maintain existing social arrangements; and (3) if the social system is changed, it will result in a corresponding alteration in religious language. It is this view of religious language as political/projectionist that is assumed by the current generation.[5]

At no point is the *methodological* difference between the two post World War II generations more clearly seen than in the shift from a historical to a literary paradigm for reading the Bible. The historical reading of the Bible is a diachronic method interested in tradition history and 'what really happened.' Its quest for sources atomizes the text and detracts from its canonical form and context.[6] The literary reading of the Bible is a synchronic method interested in the textures and interrelationships of the final form of the text and in its effect on the text's readers. It suspends judgement, for the most part, on questions of sources and historicity.[7] Although the first post-World War II generation's historical method did not entirely exclude literary considerations, and although the current generation's literary reading does not completely eliminate the diachronic concerns of the historical method, each generation is characterized by its own dominant methodological approach.

What I propose to do in this essay is twofold. First and foremost, I aim to employ a modified type of reader-based interpretation of the Lukan birth narratives (second-generation methodology) in order to show how such a literary-critical reading supports a view of religious language that is closer to that typified by Bultmann than to that represented by Durkheim (first-generation theology).[8] By reader-based criti-

---

[4] Emile Durkheim, *The Elementary Forms of Religious Life* (New York: Free Press, 1965).

[5] In New Testament studies, for example, it is this view of religious language that underlies Wayne A. Meeks's widely cited article, 'The Man from Heaven in Johannine Sectarianism,' *JBL* 91 (1972): 44–72.

[6] Edgar Krentz, *The Historical-Critical Method* (Philadelphia: Fortress, 1975).

[7] Norman Peterson, *Literary Criticism for New Testament Critics* (Philadelphia: Fortress, 1978).

[8] I have no wish to endorse the Bultmannian theological programme which, I believe, is seriously flawed. I wish only to contend that religious language like that found in the Bible is better understood in theological than in political terms and that

cism I mean an approach to the text that asks first of all about what the auditors in Mediterranean antiquity would have heard when the text was read aloud in their presence.[9] It is my belief that an answer to this question then permits an inference about the author's general intent. Second, in the light of such a reading, I intend to comment briefly on an alternative interpretation of Luke 1–2 which illustrates how biblical study should *not* be done.

A Modified Reader-Based Interpretation of Luke 1–2

The text under consideration in this essay is Luke 1–2. These two chapters are part of the larger thought unit, 1:5–4:15, in the overall arrangement of the Third Gospel. Luke 1:5–4:15 belongs to the genre of accounts of the pre-public life of a hero often found in ancient biographies. The biographical tradition of the Greco-Roman world would have conditioned a person in the Mediterranean region at the end of the first century A.D. to expect an account of a hero's career before he embarked on his public activity which included material on his family background, perhaps a reference to a miraculous conception, along with omens and other predictions of his future greatness, including childhood prodigies. In Mediterranean antiquity stories of a hero's pre-public life were told as a way of explaining the hero's later life. Suetonius, *Divus Augustus* 94, puts it this way:

> Having reached this point, it will not be out of place to add an account of the omens which occurred before he was born, on the very day of his birth, and afterwards, from which it was possible to anticipate and perceive his future greatness and uninterrupted good fortune.

It was a working out of the principle: the adult is foreshadowed in the child.[10] Given this tendency, the Evangelist's audience would hear the birth narratives (Luke 1–2) as the Third Gospel's answer to the question: How is such a life (that recorded in Luke 4:16–25:52) possible?[11]

---

this was characteristic of Bultmann (as well as of others of his generation).

[9] This, of course, is different from modern reader-response criticism which focuses exclusively on the modern readers. Cf. Jane Tompkins, *Reader-Response Criticism: From Formalism to Post-Structuralism* (Baltimore: Johns Hopkins University Press, 1980).

[10] See chapter 4, 'Prophecies of Future Greatness: The Contribution of Greco-Roman Biographies to an Understanding of Luke 1:5–4:15.'

[11] This is an entirely appropriate question for a biography. The biographical character of the Gospels has been settled. Cf. Richard A. Burridge, *What Are the Gospels?* (Cambridge: Cambridge University Press, 1992).

The distinctive way Jesus' birth is told would determine the auditor's perception of Luke's answer.

In order to clarify the Lukan answer, it will be necessary to deal with two related questions: (1) what options were available in Mediterranean culture for speaking about an individual's origins? and (2) what would ancient Mediterranean auditors have understood the various options to mean?[12]

What options existed in ancient Mediterranean culture for talking about an individual's origins? At least five different schemes come immediately to mind.

1) One way of speaking was to say that a person had a human father and a human mother. For example, Matt 1:6b says: "And David was the father of Solomon by the wife of Uriah" (RSV). The Third Evangelist employed this option in Luke 1:5–7, 13, 18, 24, 57, where he tells the reader that John the Baptist was the son of Zechariah and Elizabeth. John, like Solomon, had a human father and a human mother. This, of course, was the normal way of talking about an individual's origins.

Implicit within such a description of human origins were certain religious or philosophical underpinnings. (a) *Theological corollary*—The normal way of speaking about human origins assumes at least a semi-autonomous world system within which at least semi-autonomous human acts of creativity take place. For example, given the sexual order of the natural world, a man and a woman can normally produce an offspring by means of their semi-autonomous sexual acts. If the system works properly, God is not overtly a direct or an immediate part of the equation. Of course, if the system is flawed in some way, it may take some adjustment by God to get it to work properly (e.g., as in the case of John the Baptist). Even in such a case, however, the child is the result of a father's and a mother's creative activity within the world system. (b) *Christological corollary*—In such a scheme, the one who is born is purely human, nothing more. So Solomon may be wise and may be king but he is not divine, and John the Baptist may be inspired but he remains a creature. (c) *Soteriological corollary*—The one whose origins are explained

---

[12] This essay assumes that the various options were 'in the air' in the Mediterranean world of antiquity so that even an early Christian would have been cognizant of them. Note in the discussion of each option indications of Christian knowledge.

by reference to a human father and a human mother is the product of what is humanly possible, even if on occasion God must make what is humanly possible possible.

An ancient Mediterranean author of a narrative about origins told in terms of one's having a human father and a human mother would have heard it as having such associations. That the Third Evangelist did not tell the story of Jesus' origins in this the normal way is indicative that such a scheme did not adequately say what he wanted his auditors to hear.

2) On at least one occasion in the New Testament it is said that an individual was 'without father or mother.' So Heb 7:3 characterized Melchizedek. In Mediterranean antiquity this is the way true gods are usually described.[13] Lactantius, *Epitome divinarum institutionum* 1.7.1 says:

> Mercury, that thrice greatest ... not only speaks of God as 'without a mother,'... , but also as 'without a father,' because He has no origin from any other source but Himself.

The *Apocalypse of Abraham* 17:8–11, moreover, provides the following acclamation of God:

> Eternal One, Mighty One, Holy El, God autocrat
> self-originate,[14] incorruptible, immaculate,
> unbegotten, spotless, immortal;
> self-perfected, self-devised,
> without mother, without father, ungenerated.

Likewise in the *Acts of Peter* 23, Simon Magus says to Peter that the Romans are not fools, and turning to them he says: "Ye men of Rome, is God born?"[15] In 24, a prophet is cited: "Born not of a woman but from a heavenly place came he down." On occasion in antiquity, one could hear that such and such a one was without father or mother.

Implicit within such a claim would also be certain religious or philosophical corollaries. (a) *Theological corollary*—In this scheme divine intervention is deemed necessary. The individual's presence in the world is not the product of autonomous or semi-autonomous human creativ-

---

[13] Jerome H. Neyrey, "Without Beginning of Days or End of Life' (Hebrews 7:3): Topos for a True Deity,' *CBQ* 53 (1991): 439–55.

[14] Cf. *Sib. Or.* 3.10; 8.429; frg. 1, line 17.

[15] The background for Simon's remark is the Mediterranean distinction between deities who were 'eternal' and those who were 'immortal.' Cf. C. H. Talbert, 'The Concept of the Immortals in Mediterranean Antiquity,' *JBL* 94 (1975): 419–36.

ity. It is not the result of human creativity at all. It rather results from an inbreaking divine activity. So Simon, in the *Acts of Peter*, says a god comes down, and Marcion (Tertullian, *Marc*. 4:7–8) speaks of Christ appearing in Galilee as a full-grown man. (b) *Christological corollary*—The one whose presence is the result of divine intervention is himself divine, not human. Without father and mother means to be self-generated. This is a trait of a true god, not a human. (c) *Soteriological corollary*—Such a life is due to the transcendent deity's intervention in the world, devoid of human involvement. In this scheme one encounters a system of human passivity. All the activity is God's.

An ancient Mediterranean auditor would have understood a narrative that portrayed an individual's origins as 'without father or mother' in terms of these corollaries. That Luke did not tell the story of Jesus' origins in this particular fashion indicates that he did not regard such a scheme as adequately conveying to his auditors what he wanted them to hear.

3) In other circumstances, it could be said that one had a divine father and a divine mother. Horus, the son of Isis and Osiris, comes immediately to mind. The Egyptian god Osiris and his consort, the goddess Isis, produced an offspring, Horus. Horus was the son of two deities: Isis, wife and mother, and Osiris, husband and father (e.g., Aristides, *Apol.* 12).

Such a scheme also had certain religious or philosophical corollaries associated with it. (a) *Theological corollary*—In this system of origins deity is understood as both male and female. God does not transcend sexuality; God is, rather, sexual. Deity is not merely male or merely female; deity is both; God/ess. (b) *Christological corollary*—The one produced by such a divine union is himself divine. Horus is a god, not a human. (c) *Soteriological corollary*—Such a life is due to the sexual involvement of male and female deities. Divine creativity is by means of sexual activity.

This is doubtless the way a Mediterranean auditor would have heard a narrative that spoke of origins in terms of two divine parents. That the Lukan Evangelist did not tell of Jesus' origins in these terms indicates that such a scheme did not adequately communicate to his auditors what he wanted them to hear.

4) At other times it could be said that one had a human father and a divine mother. For example, it was believed that Persephone was the daughter of the goddess Demeter and the mortal Iasion who made

love in a ploughed field (*Od.* 5.125–28); that Achilles was the son of Thetis, a goddess, and a mortal, king Peleus (Arnobius, *Disp. adv. nat.* 4.27; Chariton, *Chaer.*),[16] and that Aeneas was the son of Venus and a mortal (Ovid, *Metam.* 14.125–28; Arnobius, 4.27).

Again, such a scheme of origins contained within it certain religious or philosophical corollaries. (a) *Theological corollary*—God is understood as the world, either the earth (Gaia) or the ocean (Thetis), viewed as animate and divine and understood as the mother of all that is. Some feminist scholars contend that Hera, Athene, Aprodite, Isis, Demeter, Cybele are but individualized manifestations of the one feminine divine principle, the primordial mother goddess.[17] In so far as this is the case, it is a pantheistic understanding of deity and world. (b) *Christological corollary*—The one so produced partakes of the natures of both parents and so participates in both the human and the divine spheres. Exactly how the two spheres are related in the one person varies, depending upon the context. (c) *Soteriological corollary*—In this system such a life is the result of the divine possibilities inherent in the world which have been brought to fruition by the intervention or involvement of a human catalyst.

A Mediterranean auditor of a narrative that spoke of origins in terms of a human father and a divine mother would have heard these things implied. That Luke did not utilize this scheme in his depiction of Jesus' origins implies that he did not think such a system adequately conveyed to his auditors what he wanted them to hear.

5) On still other occasions, it could be said that an individual had a divine father and a human mother. For example, it was believed that Dionysius was the son of Zeus and Semele, daughter of Cadmus, founder of Thebes (Diodorus Siculus, 4.2.1–4; Ovid, *Metam.* 3.259–318); that Hercules was the son of Zeus and Alcmene, a daughter of Perseus (Diodorus Siculus, 4.9.1); that Asclepios was the son of Apollo and the mortal Coronis (Diodorus Siculus, 4.71.1); that Romulus and Remus

---

[16] B. P Reardon, ed., *Collected Ancient Greek Novels* (Berkeley: University of California Press, 1989), 54.

[17] E.g., Miriam Robbins Dexter, *Whence the Goddess?* (New York: Pergamon Press, 1990), pp. 186–87; and Christine Downing, 'The Mother Goddess among the Greeks,' in *The Book of the Goddess: Past and Present* (ed. Carl Olson; New York: Crossroad, 1983), 49–59. This assertion by feminist scholars runs counter to Hesiod's *Theogony* which attempts to integrate popular piety into a scheme which is essentially alien to its primitive roots.

were the offspring of the god Mars and the woman Ilia (Dionysius of Halicarnassus, *Ant. rom.* 1.77.2–1.78.4); that Osiris, a king of Egypt, was the son of Zeus and a human daughter (Diodorus Siculus, 1.23); that Alexander the Great was the son of either Jupiter (Quintus Curtius, *Hist. Alex.* 1) or the god Ammon of Egypt (Pseudo-Callisthenes, *Hist. Alex. magn.*) and the mortal Olympias; that Augustus was the offspring of Apollo and the mortal Atia (Suetonius, *Aug.* 94:4). This position did not, of necessity, involve sexual relations between the deity and the human mother (Plutarch, *Num.* 4) but could be spoken of as occurring by means of *spirit/pneuma* (Plutarch, *Is. Os.* 36).

This scheme of speaking about an individual's origins also involved a system of allied assumptions of a religious or philosophical nature. (a) *Theological corollary*—In this system, God is regarded as other than the world. The world is the arena of His activity. This, of course, is a theistic system. (b) *Christological corollary*—The one so produced shares in both the divine and the human spheres. (c) *Soteriological corollary*—Such a life is the result of human submission to the divine will. Human activity is involved, but it is in response to the divine initiative. An ancient Mediterranean auditor would have associated a narrative that spoke about origins in terms of a divine father and a human mother with these religious or philosophical connections.

In Mediterranean antiquity there were, then, at least these five options for speaking about an individual's origins. Each of these options, moreover, had certain philosophical or religious corollaries that would have been recognized, consciously or unconsciously, by auditors. That the Third Evangelist chose the fifth option as the vehicle for his telling of the story of Jesus' origins must surely indicate that implicit within such a scheme were the religious or philosophical points that he wanted his auditors to pick up.

When the five options are laid out and the religious or philosophical corollaries of each position are exposed to view and it is possible to recognize how each would have been heard by ancient auditors, it is not difficult to see which Luke regarded as the most appropriate vehicle for his Christian convictions. Given those convictions, it is not difficult to see why he eschewed the other four options.

1) The option that speaks of origins in terms of a human father and a human mother is problematic on all three counts. Theologically, Luke wanted his auditors to hear that Jesus' life was the result of the deity's direct intervention, not the result of autonomous human creativ-

ity. Christologically, he wanted them to hear that Jesus participated in both human and divine spheres, not the human only. Soteriologically, he wanted them to hear that such a life is not the product of what is humanly possible, but the result only of God's direct creative intervention. If auditors would have heard Option One in terms of problematic associations, it was inappropriate.

2) The option that speaks of one as without father and mother would be problematic on two counts. Theologically, this position is consonant with Christian convictions. God's direct intervention is necessary. Christologically, however, it is deficient in that it eliminates the humanity of the one so described. Moreover, soteriologically it is problematic in that it eliminates all human involvement. If ancient readers would have associated Option Two with questionable corollaries, it was not suitable.

3) The option that speaks of origins in terms of a divine father and a divine mother is problematic on all three counts. Theologically, it is inappropriate for Luke because it understands deity in terms of sexuality: God is sexual, male and female. Christologically, it eliminates the humanity of the one so produced. Soteriologically, God's creative activity is viewed in sexual terms whereas Luke wanted his auditors to hear that God transcends sexuality. If Mediterranean auditors would have connected Option Three with such baggage, it was to be avoided.

4) The option that views origins in terms of a divine mother and a human father is problematic for Luke on two counts. Theologically, this stance is unacceptable to him because it regards God as the world, the mother of all that is. This pantheistic system is alien to Luke's Jewish roots. Christologically, however, its corollary is consonant with what he wants to affirm. The one so produced shares, in some way, in both divine and human spheres. Soteriologically, however, it is problematic because it regards salvation as possible whenever a human catalyst develops the divine possibilities inherent in the world. If potential readers would hear a narrative told in terms of Option Four in this way, it was not suitable.

5) The option that regards origins in terms of a divine father and a human mother apparently fits Luke's expectations on all counts. After all, this is the option he chose. Theologically, God is other than

the world but acts directly in the world. Christologically, the one so produced shares in both divine and human spheres. Soteriologically, such a life is due to human submission to the divine will. Of the options available for speaking about Jesus' origins in order to explain how such a life was possible, Option Five functions best as a vehicle for Luke's Christian convictions. It is, then, no surprise that the Third Gospel tells the story of Jesus' birth in just the way that it does. The God who is other than the world intervenes in the world to create one who is both divine and human and whose birth models the means of salvation for all people: submission to the divine will. In only one area does the Lukan infancy narrative deviate from some of the Greco-Roman traditions that speak of an individual's being the offspring of a divine father and a human mother. Under no circumstances would Luke think of the conception of Jesus as occurring by means of sexual contact between God and the woman. Like Plutarch, Luke speaks in a way that has the conception take place by means of Spirit (Plutarch, *Is. Os.* 36). Mary asks; "How shall this be, since I have no husband?" The angel says: "The Holy Spirit will come upon you, And the power of the Most High will overshadow you" (Luke 1:34–35, RSV). The God who in Jewish tradition was transsexual remains so in the Christian story of Jesus' origins in the Lukan Gospel. A narrative told in terms of Option Five with the safeguards built in to avoid any inference about sexual contact between deity and woman would be heard by ancient auditors in a way that was consonant with the expectations of the Third Evangelist.

Read in terms of a modified form of reader-based criticism, Luke 1–2 is best seen as the explication of Christian believing self-understanding by means of the Evangelist's use of the literary genre of the pre-public life of a hero figure such as is found in ancient Mediterranean biographies. Such a second-generation post-World War II methodology justifies a first-generation view of religious language.[18]

---

[18] The second post-World War II generation's view of religion and religious language was already successfully critiqued in the first generation by Reinhold Neibuhr. A generation that no longer reads Neibuhr can find a reasonably sympathetic summary of his positions on this issue in Roger A. Johnson, *et al.*, *Critical Issues in Modern Religion* (Englewood Cliffs, N.J.: Prentice-Hall, 1973), 175–208.

Evaluation of an Alternative Reading of Luke 1–2

The reading offered above of the narratives of Jesus' birth in Luke runs counter to that offered by Richard A. Horsley's *The Liberation of Christmas*.[19] Horsley's book is a variation on the same theme as that pursued by Klaus Wengst three years earlier.[20] It could have been appropriately subtitled: 'A Marxist Reading of Jesus' Birth.' Horsley extracts from the birth narratives three themes: (1) the rulers (= the oppressors); (2) the people (= the oppressed); and (3) the songs of liberation (= celebration of the political overthrow of the oppressors by the oppressed). He then moves to a modern analogy: (1) the United States (= the oppressor); (2) the Nicaraguan revolutionaries (= the oppressed); and (3) the infancy narratives (= consciousness-raising stories reinforcing the overthrow of the oppressor by the oppressed). For Horsley, Jesus' birth, interpreted in terms of a second post-World War II generation's political view of religious language, is a story about people's political liberation from political exploitation and domination. If, as Horsley argues, the Christmas story in North America has become subservient to capitalist economic ends and so functions to legitimate the festival of retailing and consumption of goods, in *The Liberation of Christmas* it has become subservient to Marxist goals and functions to legitimate class warfare. If an ancient text has any meaning other than what a modern reader imposes on it from her own perspective, Horsley's reading of the stories of Jesus' birth misses the whole point of the narratives.[21] Theological texts (= texts that view life in terms of a transcendent deity) cannot be legitimately demythologized into political tracts (= texts that view life solely in terms of a struggle between the 'haves' and the 'have-nots' in the areas of class, race and gender). Such reductionism violates their very nature.

Horsley's book proves, to me at least, that it is impossible to read a religious text properly (= in a way that does not violate the religious

---

[19] Richard A. Horsley, *The Liberation of Christmas: The Infancy Narratives in Social Context* (New York: Crossroad, 1989).

[20] Klaus Wengst, *Pax Romana: Anspruch and Wirklichkeit* (München: Chr. Kaiser Verlag, 1986).

[21] Equally off-target is Geoffrey Parrinder, *Son of Joseph: The Parentage of Jesus* (Edinburgh: T. & T. Clark, 1992), who contends that the Virgin Birth tradition was due to ascetical trends in the early church which led to a depreciation of sex and family life. Whereas this might have been true for later popular religion as reflected in the apocryphal Gospels (e.g., the *Protevangelium Jacobi*), it was certainly not true for Luke, given this essay.

nature of the text) if one's view of religious language is skewed. The foundation documents of Christianity cannot, I think, be read with integrity (= without reductionism) if the interpreter assumes, either consciously or unconsciously, a view of religious language as political/projectionist.

CHAPTER SIX

THE WAY OF THE LUKAN JESUS: DIMENSIONS OF LUKAN SPIRITUALITY

The purpose of this paper is to use one facet of Lukan Christology to cast light on the current struggle to find an acceptable form of spirituality for our time. It will begin with historical description and then move to a use of this description as a basis for an evaluation of the current scene.[1]

The Lukan picture of Jesus, viewed as a whole, corresponds to the pattern that has been called exaltation Christology.[2] Conceived by the Holy Spirit, born of the virgin Mary, the earthly Jesus lives and dies as a benefactor,[3] is then taken up to live an immortal, exalted existence as heavenly Lord who from time to time intervenes on behalf of his cause and his devotees.[4] In this christological pattern, Jesus' continuing reign from heaven has as its basis his resurrection from the dead, his ascension, and his exaltation. His remarkable life as benefactor has as its basis his miraculous conception. The miraculous conception says that Jesus' earthly life is due to God's act. Like Adam, Jesus is one whose existence resulted from the direct, creative intervention of God. Within this frame of reference, two questions related to this christology must be asked and answered: (1) What kind of life does God's creative, redemptive act produce? and (2) What is the relevance of such a life for Jesus' disciples?

---

[1] The literature on New Testament spirituality is limited and what is available is oftentimes of little use either for accurate description or for assistance in the current theological enterprise. Perhaps the best available is Louis Bouyer, *The Spirituality of the New Testament and the Fathers* (vol. 1 of *A History of Christian Spirituality*; New York: Seabury, 1963).

[2] R. H. Fuller, *The Foundations of New Testament Christology* (New York: Scribner's, 1965).

[3] F. W. Danker, 'The Endangered Benefactor in Luke-Acts,' in *SBL Seminar Papers, 1981* (SBLSP 20; Chico, Calif.: Scholars Press, 1981), 39–48.

[4] Charles H. Talbert, 'The Concept of Immortals in Mediterranean Antiquity,' *JBL* 94 (1975): 419–36.

What Kind of Life Does God's Intervention Produce?

A correct understanding of the Lukan Jesus' earthly life is possible only if one recognizes that the Evangelist depicts it in developmental terms. Three observations prove this to be the case. The first is found in Luke 2:41–51, the story of the twelve year old Jesus in the temple. Enclosed in a frame, verses 40 and 52,[5] it focuses on the youth's growth and development. Verse 52, "And Jesus increased in wisdom and stature, and in favor with God and man," uses the term προκόπτειν (to increase).[6] In the Greek world this term was used in philosophical circles to depict an individual's process of moral and spiritual development between beginning and perfection. Epictetus, for example, speaks of "one who is making progress" (ὁ προκόπτων) because he has learned from the philosopher (*Diatr.* 1.4.1). He says: "Whatsoever the goal toward which perfection in anything definitely leads, progress (προκοπή) is an approach thereto" (1.4.4). He asks:

> Where, then, is progress? If any man among you, withdrawing from external things, has turned his attention to the question of his own moral purpose, cultivating and perfecting it so as to make it finally harmonious with nature, elevated, free, unhindered, untrammelled, faithful, and honorable ...—this is the man who in all truth is making progress (ὁ προκόπτων). (1.4.18–21, LCL)

Philo uses it the same way. He speaks of three grades of people: ὁ ἀρχόμενος, the man who is just beginning his training; ὁ προκόπτων, the one who is making progress; and ὁ τέλειος, the perfect or mature person (*Leg.* 3.159). In *Quod deterius potiori insidari soleat* 51 he uses προκοπή to speak of moral progress in life. In *De posteritate Caini* 132 he contrasts προκόπταις (those making progress) with τελειότητι (those attaining perfection). In *De somniis* 2.234–35 he describes the perfect man (τέλειον) as neither God nor man, but as on the border-line between the uncreated and the perishing form of being. The man who is on the path of progress (προκόπτοντα) is placed between the living and the dead, between those who have wisdom for their life-mate and those who rejoice in folly. Philo, of course, regards the source of one's progress not as nature but as God. Later, Greek-speaking Christians made use of this terminology and assumed a similar conceptual world. In *Vita Pachomii* 2 we hear that the monastic father made progress (πρόκοψας);

---

[5] Henk J. de Jonge, 'Sonship, Wisdom, Infancy: Luke 2:41–51a,' *NTS* 24 (1978): 317–54.

[6] For the data in the following paragraph, see G. Stählin, *TDNT* 6:703–19.

that he took joy in those who made progress (τῶν προκόπτων) in virtue and increased in faith (28). We also hear that some of the brothers had not attained perfection (τελειότητα, 43). Among monks as well as moral philosophers life's journey was described as making progress toward perfection. In the New Testament's nine uses of προκοπή and προκόπτειν two are very close to the widespread use in popular philosophy in speaking of the personal moral and spiritual progress of individuals (1 Tim 4:15—Timothy; Luke 2:52—Jesus). In Luke 2:52 the emphasis is on the spiritual progress of the youth, Jesus. Although this facet of the development of the Lukan Jesus has been recognized by research, it is usually treated in isolation from the rest of the Lukan narrative.[7] It needs to be seen, however, in the context of the unfolding of the divine plan in Luke-Acts.

The second observation is that the Third Evangelist traces an unfolding history of salvation in his two-volume work.[8] The author signals new stages in what God is doing by reference to significant divine inbreaks (sometimes accompanying human prayer). For example, in Acts the movement to the Gentiles is a major new development in salvation history. Its actualization is accomplished only by the direct intervention of God. In Acts 10 the prayers of Cornelius and Peter are accompanied by visions and auditions which direct the course of events. The intent of God to open a new front in the expansion of the gospel is signaled by an unexpected outpouring of the Holy Spirit while Peter is still speaking. In Acts 9 the person to be used as an instrument for the mission to the Gentiles is overpowered by the Lord in an event which includes a vision (the light—v. 3) and an audition (the voice—vv. 5–6). In Acts 13:1–3 the beginning of the missionary outreach of Barnabas and Paul results from a prophetic word spoken in the midst of the church's worship. In the Third Gospel there are also significant new stages in the unfolding of God's plan in the life of the Lukan Jesus which are marked by divine intervention. For instance, in Luke 3:21–22, in the midst of prayer, the Lukan Jesus experiences a vision (v. 22a) and an audition (v. 22b). This, he says later (4:16–21), is the basis for his ministry of power in Galilee (4:16–9:50). That the Evangelist intends the reader to see the event as a development within the Lukan Jesus is

---

[7] Stählin's failure to distinguish adequately between the level of the historical Jesus (for whom it is impossible to trace any development) and the level of the Lukan Jesus kept him from pursuing the obvious development in the Third Gospel.

[8] To acknowledge this fact does not commit one to the thesis of Conzelmann.

evident both from the second person form of address in 3:22b ("Thou art my beloved Son" RSV) and from the first person speech in 4:18–19 ("The Spirit of the Lord is upon me, because he has anointed me" RSV). Furthermore in Luke 9:18ff. and 9:28ff., the confession of Peter and the transfiguration are portrayed as prayer scenes in which there is a recognition on the part of the Lukan Jesus of a new departure in the unfolding of God's plan for his way—rejection, suffering, death. That the Evangelist thought in terms of Jesus' own understanding is confirmed by 9:51 which speaks of the Lukan Jesus' intentionality.

The third observation is found in Luke 13:31–35, a Lukan paragraph composed of a number of independent traditions which portrays the Lukan Jesus as looking toward Jerusalem and his death. In the course of the unfolding of the thought unit, Jesus says: "Behold, I cast out demons and perform cures today and tomorrow, and on the third (day) I am being perfected" (τελειοῦμαι—first person singular, present indicative passive).[9] That this completion refers to his death is evident from what follows: "it cannot be that a prophet should perish away from Jerusalem" (RSV). In any case, here the Third Evangelist depicts the Lukan Jesus as saying that he will be perfected or brought to completion in his death. This is much the same thing that is said in Heb 2:10 and 5:8–9 where Jesus' being made perfect (τελειῶσαι and τελειωθείς) refer to his having learned obedience through suffering. The significant thing to note at this point is that the Evangelist regards the life of Jesus in developmental terms and leads his readers to believe that the Lukan Jesus was aware of and consciously participated in this development.

To sum up, the Third Evangelist portrays an ever unfolding plan of God in the history of salvation, both in the career of the Lukan Jesus and in the life of the church of the apostolic age. In the Gospel of Luke, the Evangelist's choice of terminology at one point shows that he interprets the significance of this unfolding in the life of Jesus in terms of the Hellenistic concept of the progress of the individual in spiritual growth between beginning and perfection.

Once this is grasped, it is possible to look at the Lukan Jesus' life in terms of five stages; (a) his dedication to God by his parents as an infant (Luke 2:22–24); (b) his personal agreement with their parental decision as a youth (Luke 2:40–52); (c) his empowering by the Holy

---

[9] G. Delling, *TDNT* 8:84, incorrectly interprets it to mean Jesus' *work* will be brought to conclusion by God.

Spirit (Luke 3:21–22); (d) his acceptance of rejection, suffering, and death as part of his way (Luke 9:19, 22; 9:28–31; 9:44; 9:51; 18:31–33, etc.); and (e) his resurrection, ascension, and exaltation (Luke 24; Acts). In the paragraphs that follow there will be a brief examination of each of these five stages, with a focus on the third and fourth.

(a) *Dedication to God.* Luke 2:22–24 falls into an AB:B'A' pattern: verses 22a and 24 (cf. Lev 12:8) which deal with the purification of the mother after childbirth being A and A'; verses 22b and 23 which deal with the redemption of the first-born being B and B'. The prescription of Exod 13:2 concerning the first-born is here literally fulfilled in the case of Jesus. Jesus, the first born (Luke 2:7), is not ransomed (Exod 13:13). No such ransom is paid by Jesus' parents (Num 3:47; 18:16). Contrary to normal custom, Jesus is dedicated to God and remains his property.[10] That Luke's auditors would have heard the text in these terms is likely given the references to the redemption of the first-born in both the iconographic and the literary traditions of later Christianity.[11] Gentile readers would, indeed, have been aware of the ritual.

(b) *Youthful Agreement with Parental Decisions.* Luke 2:41–51 gives the story of the youthful Jesus' trip to Jerusalem at Passover time. Verse 42 says that his trip at age twelve was according to custom. This is probably in preparation for his entrance into religious responsibility which, according to *m. Avot* 5:21, came at age thirteen. When his parents returned and finally found him in the temple, his mother reproached him: "Son, why have you treated us so? Behold your father and I have been looking for you anxiously"(v. 48, RSV). The Lukan Jesus' response, "How is it that you sought me? Did you not know that I must be in my Father's house?" (v. 49, RSV), can only be understood if seen in the context of his childhood dedication. The closest parallel to the Lukan emphasis in 2:22–24 is found in 1 Sam 1-2. There Hannah gives Samuel, at his birth, to the Lord for as long as the child lives. Consequently Samuel lives in the presence of Eli at the tent of meeting. If the Lukan

---

[10] Bo Reicke, 'Jesus, Simeon, and Anna (Luke 2:21–40),' in *Saved By Hope* (ed. J. I. Cook; Grand Rapids: Eerdmans, 1978), 96–108, esp. 100.

[11] For the iconographic tradition, see Dorothy Shorr, 'The Iconographic Development of the Presentation in the Temple,' *Art Bulletin* 28 (1946): 30; for the literary tradition, see Ps-Bonoventura, *Meditations on the Life of Christ* (ed. and trans. I. Ragusa and R. B. Greene; Princeton: Princeton University Press, 1961), 61. For the combination, see Heidi Hornik and Mikeal Parsons, 'Ambrogio Lorenzetti's *Presentation in the Temple*: A 'Visual Exegesis' of Luke 2:22–38,' *PRSt* 28 (2001): 31–46.

Jesus, in a similar manner, was dedicated to God and not redeemed, then he belonged to God permanently. This would explain why, in the Lukan narrative, Jesus would not understand why his parents did not know where to find him in Jerusalem. Since he was God's, he could be expected to be in his Father's house, as in the case of Samuel. At the level of the plot of the Lukan narrative, the boy Jesus had made a personal identification with the decisions his parents had made about him at his birth.

(c) *Empowering for Service*. The Third Evangelist has turned Luke 3:21–22, the so-called narrative of Jesus' baptism, into an episode of prayer. After his baptism and while Jesus is praying, there is a heavenly apparition. The Holy Spirit descends in *bodily form* as a dove upon him. To Greco-Roman hearers of Luke's narrative this would evoke echoes of the Roman use of the flight of birds of omen to discover the decrees of fate.[12] For example, Plutarch in describing how Numa was chosen king after Romulus tells how Numa insisted that before he assumed the kingship his authority would first have to be ratified by heaven. So the chief of the augurs turned the veiled head of Numa toward the south, while he, standing behind him with his right hand on his head, prayed aloud and turned his eyes in all directions to observe whatever birds or other omens might be sent from the gods. When the proper birds approached, Numa then put on his royal robes and went down where he was received as the "most beloved of the gods." In such a thought world the Lukan narrative would be viewed as an omen of Jesus' status. Exactly what that status was can be discerned from the bird involved, a dove, and the interpreting voice from heaven.

In Mediterranean antiquity the dove was symbolic of "the beneficence of divinity in love, the loving character of divine life itself."[13] For the Holy Spirit to come on the Lukan Jesus in the form of a dove's descent would say to Mediterranean hearers that Jesus was beloved of God. That this is Luke's intent can be seen from the interpretation offered of the event by the voice from heaven; "You are my Son, my beloved, in you I am well pleased."

This post-baptismal gift of the Holy Spirit is interpreted by Luke as Jesus' anointing for ministry as God's servant, an equipping of him

---

[12] See chapter 4, 'Prophecies of Future Greatness: The Contribution of Greco-Roman Biographies to an Understanding of Luke 1:5–4:15.'

[13] E. R. Goodenough, *Jewish Symbols in the Greco-Roman Period* (13 vols.; New York: Pantheon Books, 1953–1968), 8:40–41.

for his task. Luke 4:16–21, the formal opening of Jesus' ministry in the Third Gospel, has Jesus read from Isaiah: "The Spirit of the Lord is upon me, because he has anointed me to preach good news to the poor" (RSV). Then, after returning the scroll, Jesus sat down and said: "Today this scripture has been fulfilled in your hearing" (RSV). The reference is, of course, back to the baptism-prayer scene with its descent of the Holy Spirit on Jesus (cf. Acts 4:27; 10:38).

It is noteworthy that in the plot of the Third Gospel Jesus found it necessary to receive an empowering for ministry before he embarked on his public career. He had been conceived by the Holy Spirit; he had been dedicated to God by his parents as a babe; he had personally identified with his parents' decisions about him and consciously assumed the yoke of the kingdom of heaven. Yet none of these could substitute for the necessary anointing-empowering given him when he prayed after his baptism. What is needed for adequate ministry in the Lukan understanding is a prior empowering by God's Spirit. It was this that the Lukan Jesus received in 3:21–22 and of which he was conscious in 4:16–21. It was out of this empowering that he entered into his Galilean ministry (4:16–9:50). The keynote there is power.

(d) *Acceptance of Rejection, Suffering, and Death.* Luke 9:7–50 marks a crucial turning point in the plot of the Third Gospel. It functions to conclude the Galilean ministry which began with 4:16; it also sets in motion a new departure in the unfolding of God's plan in the narrative of Luke-Acts. Two questions about Jesus' identity give focus to the passage as a whole. Herod asks, "Who is this?" (9:9, RSV) Jesus himself reiterates the query. "Who do you say that I am?" (9:20, RSV) Luke 9's answer is that Jesus is the one who, through prayer, moves into a new stage of the spiritual process, a stage that involves rejection, suffering, and death.

On the one hand, it is a Lukan concern to show that prayer is the instrument by which God directs the development of the history of salvation.[14] It is no surprise, therefore, to find the Evangelist in Luke 9 signaling a new development in the Lukan Jesus' career by two paragraphs that show Jesus at prayer (9:18ff.; 9:28ff.). Both references to prayer in Luke 9:18 and 9:28–29 are distinctively Lukan. Both link Jesus' prayer with his coming suffering. In 9:22 the Lukan Jesus' word about his suffering, rejection, and death is the response to Peter's con-

---

[14] A. A. Trites, 'The Prayer Motif in Luke-Acts,' in *Perspectives on Luke-Acts* (ed. C. H. Talbert; Danville, Va.: ABPR, 1978), 169.

fession that arises out of his session of prayer. In 9:28–31 Jesus' prayer transports him to the heavenly world where a conversation with two heavenly residents ensues about his exodus (his departure from this world which includes his death, as well as his resurrection and ascension). The Lukan Jesus' grasp of his future suffering is once again tied to his prayer.

On the other hand, if prayer was the medium through which the Third Evangelist believes Jesus came to an awareness of God's will for a new departure in his life, the content of that will involved not immediate exaltation but rather rejection, suffering, and death. The one who had been anointed with the Spirit would be rejected and killed.

How can it be that the Spirit-empowered Jesus must suffer? The answer lies in the eschatology of main line Christianity in the first century. This eschatology combined a 'now' and a 'not yet' (cf. Paul in 1 Cor 4, 15; Phil 3). The New Age had broken in with the resurrection of Jesus, but the Old Age continues until the Parousia. Believers live where the ages overlap. How to hold on to these two realities (now—not yet) has always been among the most difficult tasks for Christian life and thought. There is perennially the temptation to allow one to swallow the other. Either the emphasis is so focused on the powers of the New Age at work in believers that an eschatological reservation is lost, or the focus is so directed to believers' involvement in the structures and limitations of this life that the power of the Holy Spirit in the midst of weakness is overlooked.

The Third Evangelist, having presented Jesus in his Galilean ministry as a Spirit-empowered conqueror of evil, now is concerned to show that even such a Spirit-empowered figure is subject to the limitations of this age. He is not immediately and automatically triumphant because of the Spirit unleashed in his life in healing, exorcism, and powerful teaching. He will be rejected and killed. Only the other side of this subjection to the limitations of this age will he enter into his final glory. Theologically, it is necessary to juxtapose 'anointed with the Spirit' and 'destined to die' because to say less would be to break the delicate balance between the 'now' and the 'not yet' of Christian existence.[15]

---

[15] "Sufferings ... point the sufferer ... toward the future, and thus stamp 'not yet' upon the consummation of salvation. To this extent they have an antifanatical function. ..." (E. S. Gerstenberger and W. Schrage, *Suffering* [trans. J. E. Steely; Nashville:

What purpose could such suffering serve for the Lukan Jesus? In order to answer this question, two items of background information are necessary, one from Luke and the other from the New Testament at large.

On the one hand, the Third Evangelist frames Jesus' earthly career within two temptation sequences (Luke 4:1–13; 23:35, 36–37, 39). The first, Luke 4:1–13, must be read against the background of Jesus as both the culmination of all that God had been doing in the history of Israel and the second Adam. The genealogy of Luke 3:23–38 portrays Jesus both as the culmination of Israel's history and as second Adam. The order of the temptations in Luke 4:1–13 echoes not only the threefold temptation of Adam and Eve in Gen 3:6 (cf. 1 John 2:16) but also the temptation of Israel in the wilderness as given by Ps 106 (cf. 1 Cor 10:6–9). The temptations of the Lukan Jesus in 4:1–13 thereby become antitypical of the experience of Israel in the wilderness and of the original pair in the garden. Whereas those who came before were disobedient, Jesus as second Adam and as the true culmination of Israel's heritage is obedient. He has reversed Adam's fall and Israel's sin. This temptation narrative thus understood has the effect of setting all that follows in Jesus' earthly career under the sign of 'Jesus' obedience.' Remember: in the Lukan plot, Jesus is the unredeemed first-born who belongs wholly to God. The second temptation sequence comes in Luke 23:35, 36–37, 39. It is also a threefold temptation, this time of the crucified Jesus. The Lukan Jesus has spoken earlier of the divine necessity of his death (9:22, 44; 18:31–33).[16] In the garden he has surrendered to the divine will even if it means death (22:39–46). Now he faces the temptation to use divine power for self-preservation (a power he still has—22:51). Three times he is confronted with the demand: "save yourself" (23:35, 37, 39). That he does not is his obedience unto death, the perfection of his obedience to the Father (remember 13:32). The Lukan frame around the public ministry of Jesus defines the Lukan Jesus' career as the way of obedience, even unto death.

Abingdon, 1980], 213). That Luke was concerned about such a problem is argued by C. H. Talbert, 'The Redaction Critical Quest for Luke the Theologian,' in *Jesus and Man's Hope* (ed. D. Y. Hadidian; 2 vols; Pittsburgh: Pittsburgh Theological Seminary, 1970), 1:171–222.

[16] Should one think of the divine necessity in terms of the law of the unredeemed first-born?

On the other hand, in the New Testament one stream of early Christian thought saw Jesus' death not only as an atonement for sin and as a defeat of the powers of evil but also as Jesus' ultimate act of obedience or faithfulness to God (e.g., Phil 2:8; Rom 5:18–19).[17] Jesus died rather than sin. In this context, Jesus' suffering and death were regarded as the arena in which his obedience to God was perfected. Heb 2:10 says: God made "the pioneer of their salvation perfect through suffering" (RSV). Heb 5:8–9 says: "Although he was a Son, he learned obedience through what he suffered; and being made perfect he became the source of eternal salvation to all who obey him" (RSV).[18] 1 Pet 4:1–2 says:

> Since therefore Christ suffered in the flesh, arm yourselves with the same thought, for whoever has suffered in the flesh has ceased from sin, so as to live for the rest of the time in the flesh no longer by human passions but by the will of God. (RSV)

Paul, Hebrews, and 1 Peter speak of a suffering endured by Christ which is the arena in which obedience to God is perfected.[19] Luke's view of Jesus' suffering belongs to this facet of New Testament thought.

It is in the context of a view of suffering that is integral to the process of spiritual growth that Luke 9 should be understood. The Lukan Jesus, through prayer, has come to see that he is about to enter a new

---

[17] The entire discussion of 'the faithfulness of Jesus' in Pauline thought is relevant here. Most recently, see Luke T. Johnson, 'Romans 3:21–26 and the Faith of Jesus,' *CBQ* 44 (1982): 77–90, and the bibliography listed there.

[18] Eduard Schweizer, *Lordship and Discipleship* (Naperville: Allenson, 1960), 72, says that Hebrews here regards Jesus' death as the final, finishing stage of his obedient suffering. There are roots both in the Jewish and in the Greek worlds. The Hellenistic background is that which regarded suffering as an education (παιδεία) which leads to progress and in the end perfection. The Old Testament has as one interpretation of suffering that pain can be a means of discipline employed by God (e.g., Jer 15:18–19, where Jeremiah's own sufferings have the purpose of bringing him closer to God). Such suffering is to be cherished (e.g., Ps 94:12; 119:71). This view is found also in post-biblical Judaism (e.g., *2 Bar.* 13:3–10, where one is chastened in order to be sanctified). In Hellenistic Judaism the perfection that was suffering's goal was understood as complete and exclusive devotion to God. Progress toward it was a lifelong process but could be completed in death (cf. 4 Macc 7:15). On the Jewish background, see Jim Alvin Sanders, *Suffering as Divine Discipline in the Old Testament and Post-Biblical Judaism* (Rochester, N.Y.: Colgate Rochester Divinity School, 1955) and E. S. Gerstenberger and W. Schrage, *Suffering*, Part One (OT).

[19] Wolfgang Schrage (*Suffering* [Nashville: Abingdon, 1980], 217) argues that 1 Pet 1:7 does not intend to say that suffering liberates from all the dross of the world and sin and turns one's gaze from peripheral matters to the center; rather in the fire of suffering it is revealed what is faith and what is not. Two responses are necessary. First, in revealing what is not faith suffering strips away the dross. Second, 1 Pet 4:1–2 most definitely asserts a purifying function for suffering whether or not 1 Pet 1:7 does.

phase of God's plan for him. He is moving beyond the initial stage of empowering into a dimension of life which, though still empowered, is characterized by rejection (9:22). In this phase he will learn obedience through what he suffers. His obedience to God in the face of rejection, persecution, suffering, and finally death will signal his victory over sin as one who belongs totally to God.

The importance of rejection, persecution, suffering, and the threat of death in the process of spiritual growth is that each of these holds up the possibility of the loss of something which the self either holds dear or is tempted to hold on to. One is threatened with the loss of economic security, of status, of reputation, or of life itself. Circumstances remove the possibility of one's holding on to any of these finite treasures as security. The suffering of rejection detaches one from these real or potential false gods. One learns obedience to God alone through what is suffered. Rejection or suffering shatters real or potential idols and allows God to draw one to himself alone. This redemptive dimension of suffering would not be possible without the prior stage of empowering. From the Third Evangelist's perspective, only as God lives within is there the potential for suffering to be experienced as the perfection of one's obedience. The way of the Lukan Jesus, then, was from empowering through suffering to glory.

(e) *Resurrection, Ascension, Exaltation*. The Lukan view of Jesus' glorification can only be grasped if seen in the context of the early Christian understanding of Jesus' resurrection. In earliest Christianity the resurrection of Jesus encompassed three different realities: (1) Jesus' victory over death; (2) Jesus' removal from human time and space into another dimension (that of God); and (3) Jesus' new function as cosmic Lord. In Luke-Acts the unity of these three realities is broken and they become three separate events on a chronological time-line: (1) the resurrection of Jesus is reduced to the reality of his victory over death; (2) the ascension becomes in Luke-Acts Jesus' removal to heaven; and (3) the exaltation designates the moment of Jesus' new status as Lord and Christ. By taking the different pieces of a whole individually, the Evangelist can focus on the meaning of each without distraction. Taken together, they represent the Lukan Jesus' entry into glory (cf. Luke 24:26).

To sum up, Luke gives us a developmental picture of Jesus in which his individual progress spiritually is depicted as the gradual unfolding of the divine plan in Jesus' way.

What Relevance Does Jesus' Development Have?

This second question, that of relevance, is construed both as descriptive and as constructive. It asks both how the Third Evangelist saw the relevance of the way Jesus and how this Lukan perspective may feed into current constructs for spiritual formation.

There are several strands of evidence that make clear how the author of Luke-Acts viewed the relevance of Jesus' way for that of his disciples. The first strand of evidence is that of the basic architectonic principle that governs the arrangement of the entire two-volume work, namely, the remarkable correspondences both in content and sequence between the events and persons found in Luke and those in Acts. What happens in the career of Jesus in the Third Gospel has its parallel occurrence in the history of the church in the Acts of the Apostles.[20] This is one way to say that the life of Jesus is the norm for the lives of his followers.

A second strand of evidence consists of a cluster of closely related concepts. (a) Christianity is described in Acts as "the Way" (cf. Acts 9:2; 19:9, 23; 22:4; 24:14, 22; also see 16:17; 18:25–26).[21] (b) As in the Heb 2:10 and 12:2, Jesus is described in Acts as the ἀρχηγός (3:15; 5:31; cf. Luke 19:28). (c) A disciple in Luke's understanding is one who follows behind Jesus (cf. Luke 23:26 where Simon of Cyrene carries the cross "behind Jesus," a distinctively Lukan note). Taken together, these components describe a Way opened up by Jesus, the pioneer, for his disciples to follow behind him.

The third strand is found in so many specifics of the Lukan story of Jesus where the Lord is depicted as a model for Christians to emulate (e.g., the temptation narrative in 4:1–13; the prayer in the garden in 22:39–46).[22] Among the items in which the Lukan Jesus is held up as a model for his followers is his suffering-death. This is made very clear

---

[20] C. H. Talbert, *Literary Patterns, Theological Themes and the Genre of Luke-Acts* (Missoula: Scholars Press, 1974), 15–18.

[21] S. Lyonnet, "La voie' dans les Actes des Apotres,' *RechSR* 69 (1981): 149–64; J. Pathrapankal, 'Christianity as a 'Way' according to the Acts of the Apostles,' in *Les Actes des Apotres* (ed. J. Kremer; Gembloux: J. Duculot, 1979), 533–39. E. Repo, *Der 'Weg' als Selbstbezeichnung des Urchristentums* (Helsinki: Suomalainen Tiedeakatemia, 1964). For the history of scholarship concerning the absolute use of the term 'Way' in Acts, see F. Bovon, *Luke the Theologian* (Allison Park, Pa.: Pickwick, 1987), 321–23.

[22] M. Bouttier, 'L'humanite de Jesus selon Saint Luc,' *RechSR* 69 (1981): 33–43.

by the correspondences between the martyr death of Jesus in the Third Gospel and the martyrdom of Stephen in Acts 6–7 (cf. also Luke 22:28–30; Acts 14:22).[23]

All three strands of evidence mentioned here point to the same conclusion. Jesus' way is normative for his followers. As a pioneer, the Lukan Jesus has opened a way for life to be lived from cradle to the grave and beyond. It is a developing way but with certain set components. Those who belong to him walk the way he has opened,[24] energized by the same power-Spirit that led him.

Over and beyond how the Third Evangelist described the relevance of Jesus' way for disciples, there is the question of how the Lukan perspective fits into the larger picture of the history of Christian spirituality. The history of Christian mysticism lights up the process by which human spiritual consciousness generally unfolds. Evelyn Underhill contends that just as human embryos pass through the same stages of physical growth, so too with spiritual man. The normal individual, no less than the mystic, moves through certain stages of spiritual growth:

> If he moves at all, he will move through a series of stages which are, in their own small way, analogous to those experienced by the greatest contemplative on his journey towards union with God.[25]

Underhill also argues that "Christians may well remark that the psychology of Christ, as presented to us in the Gospels, is of a piece with that of the mystics."[26] I would qualify her remark by saying that at least in Luke this seems to be the case. Underhill speaks of five stages of spiritual development: awakening, purification, illumination, purgation or the dark night of the soul, and the unitive life. Of these, two are relevant parallels to what one finds in the Lukan depiction of Jesus: illumination and purgation or the dark night.[27] In *illumination* there is the initial experience of the presence of God in power which may be accompa-

---

[23] C. H. Talbert, *Luke and the Gnostics* (Nashville: Abingdon, 1966), 76.

[24] Luke's view corresponds to what James M. Gustafson, 'The Relation of the Gospels to the Moral Life,' in *Jesus and Man's Hope* (Pittsburgh: Pittsburgh Theological Seminary, 1970–1971), 2:110–16, means when he says the Jesus of the gospels functions as a 'paradigm.'

[25] Evelyn Underhill, *Mysticism* (New York: Meridian Books, 1974), 445.

[26] Ibid., 448.

[27] It would be an arguable position to say that the Lukan Jesus reflects all five of Underhill's stages: (1) awakening (Luke 2:41–52); (2) purification (Luke 3:21—Jesus' baptism by John the Baptist being the culmination); (3) illumination (Luke 3:21–22); (4) the dark night (Luke 9–23); and (5) union (Luke 24 and Acts).

nied by auditions, visions, and other manifestations. This would seem to correspond loosely to the Lukan Jesus' experience of empowering after baptism and to his disciples' baptism in the Holy Spirit. In the *dark night* the pleasure of the former stage is often replaced by pain of one kind or another. The purpose of the suffering is the healing of the self at levels that cannot otherwise be touched. This seems to correspond to the phase of the Lukan Jesus' career that begins in Luke 9 and continues through his passion and to which his disciples are called to participate in Luke 9:23. What is important to see in all of this is that the Lukan portrayal of the Christian Way as seen in the development of the Lukan Jesus' career is very close to what a modern scholar has been able to discern as typical for the spiritual giants of later Christian faith.

For those of us who teach religion in an academic context, the Bible and church history have often been used to correct erroneous ways of thinking among our students. What we now need to hear is their call to us, as well as to our students, to expand our models of religious experience. Luke has presented us with the Way of Jesus in five stages: dedication to God as an infant; confirmation of parental decisions as a responsible youth; empowering for service; rejection and suffering as the perfection of obedience; and glorification. Contemporary reductions abound. Myriads of Christians live out of a model that is composed of dedication, confirmation and glorification. Some live out of a paradigm that includes dedication, confirmation, rejection and suffering, and glorification. Others attempt to live with a schema that embraces dedication, confirmation, empowering for service and glorification. Only rarely do we ever meet a Christian whose model of the Christian Way is inclusive enough to embrace all five of the Lukan components. For those of us with attenuated models of religious experience and development, the Lukan Jesus both shatters our expectations of what to anticipate in ourselves as we walk the Way of the Lord who calls us to follow 'behind him.'

CHAPTER SEVEN

MARTYRDOM IN LUKE-ACTS AND THE LUKAN SOCIAL ETHIC

In Luke-Acts the deaths of Jesus and Stephen are portrayed as martyrdoms.[1] When we focus on the Lukan Jesus' death, two things need to be said. On the one hand, in contrast to other New Testament witnesses like Paul (e.g., 1 Cor 15:3; 2 Cor 5:21; Rom 3:25) and Matthew (e.g., 26:28), Luke avoids any connection between Jesus' death and the forgiveness of sins.[2] In the speeches of Acts, both Peter (Acts 2:38; 3:19; 5:31; 10:43) and Paul (Acts 13:38; 17:30; 26:18) preach the forgiveness of sins as the risen Christ directed (Luke 24:47). Yet neither combines the forgiveness of sins with the death of Jesus on the cross. In contrast to Mark 10:45 ("For the Son of man also came ... to give his life as a ransom for many," RSV), Luke 22:27b ("I am among you as one who serves," RSV) avoids any mention of an atoning death. In Luke 22:37 (Isa 53:12) and Acts 8:32–33 (Isa 53:7–8), although Isa 53 is quoted, there is no mention of the sacrificial death of the servant. In Luke-Acts, neither baptism (Acts 2:38, 41; 8:12, 13, 16; 8:37–39; 9:18; 10:47–48; 16:15; 19:5; 22:16) nor the Lord's Supper (Luke 22:16–20; 24:30ff.; 24:41ff.; Acts 2:42–46; 20:7, 11; 27:35) is connected with Jesus' death (contrast Rom 6:3ff. and 1 Cor 11:23ff.). In Luke-Acts forgiveness of sins flows from the earthly Jesus, especially at mealtime (Luke 5:29–32; 15:1ff.; 19:7ff.), and after the resurrection from the exalted Lord (Acts 2:38; 4:11; 5:31—"God exalted him at his right hand as leader and savior, to give repentance to Israel and forgiveness of sins," RSV).[3]

On the other hand, Luke portrays the death of Jesus as a martyrdom, the unjust murder of an innocent man by the established powers due to the pressure of the Jewish leaders. Jesus is innocent of the charges

---

[1] C. H. Talbert, *Luke and the Gnostics* (Nashville: Abingdon, 1966), ch. 5; Gerhard Schneider, *Die Passion Jesu nach den Drei Älteren Evangelien* (Munich: Kösel, 1973), 167.

[2] Luke 22:19–20 and Acts 20:28 are often cited as exceptions to this claim. Neither actually is. Both speak about the death of Jesus as the seal of the new covenant.

[3] Richard Zehnle, 'The Salvific Character of Jesus' Death in Lucan Soteriology,' *TS* 30 (1969): 420–44; I. H. Marshall, *Luke: Historian and Theologian* (Grand Rapids, Mich.: Zondervan, 1970), 169.

against him (Luke 23:4, 14, 15, 22, 41, 47). He is delivered up by the Jewish chief priests and scribes (Luke 22:66 and 23:1–2; 23:13 and 18, 21, 23, 24; cf. Acts 5:27, 30; 13:27) and executed by Gentiles (Luke 23:24; Acts 4:27). His death is parallel to the sufferings of the prophets of old at the hands of the Jews (Luke 13:33; Acts 7:52—"which of the prophets did not your fathers persecute? And they killed those who announced beforehand the coming of the Righteous One, whom you have now betrayed and murdered," RSV). So Jesus stands at the end of a long line of martyrs. Like the martyrs in 2 Macc 7:2, 11 and 4 Macc 6:1 and 10:23, Jesus is silent before his accusers (Luke 23:9). As in the martyrdom of Isaiah, Jesus' martyrdom is due to the Devil (Luke 23:3, 53). As in the case of the martyrs slain by Herod (Josephus, *Ant.*, 17.6.2–4 §149–67), there is an eclipse at Jesus' death (Luke 23:45). His demeanor in martyrdom leads to the conversion of one of the thieves crucified with him (Luke 23:40–43). Jesus' death as a martyr is a fulfillment of Old Testament prophecies (Luke 24:25–27, 46; Acts 13:27–29), a part of God's plan (Acts 2:23).

When we focus on the Lukan picture of Stephen's demise, we find that the story of Stephen parallels that of Jesus. Both are tried before the Council (Luke 22:66ff.; Acts 6:12ff.). Both die a martyr's death. Acts 7:59, "Lord Jesus, receive my spirit" (RSV), echoes Luke 23:46, "Father, into thy hands I commit my spirit" (RSV). Acts 7:60, "Lord, do not hold this sin against them" (RSV), echoes Luke 23:34, "Father, forgive them; for they do not know what they are doing."[4] Both stories contain a Son of man saying: Luke 22:69 and Acts 7:56. This is remarkable since Acts 7:56 is the only occurrence of the title Son of man outside the Gospels and on any lips except those of Jesus. Both men's deaths issue in evangelistic results (Luke 23:39–43; Acts 8:1ff.; 11:19ff.). Moreover, the story of Stephen's martyrdom fulfills Jesus' words: Luke 21:12–19, especially verse 16 ("some of you they will put to death," RSV;

---

[4] This verse is textually questionable. It is omitted by such witnesses as P^{75} and B. It is included by such witnesses as ℵ*. The language and thought are Lukan (Father—Luke 10:21; 11:2; 22:42; 23:46; forgive because of ignorance—Acts 3:17; 13:27; intercede for executioners—Acts 7:60). Sayings of Jesus are found, moreover, in each of the main sections of the crucifixion narrative (23:28–31, 43, 46). If one is missing here the pattern would be disturbed. It could have been omitted either because it was believed to have conflicted with vv. 28–31 or because the events of A.D. 66–70 were thought to show that it was not answered. The probabilities are that it is an integral part of the Third Gospel.

cf. also Luke 12:1–12). The deaths of both Jesus and Stephen are portrayed as martyrdoms in Luke-Acts. Having noted this fact, it is now necessary to focus on two facets of the Lukan theology of martyrdom.

Martyrdom as Rejection

These martyrdoms are understood by the Evangelist in the first instance as the *rejection of God's spokesmen* which results in the rejection of the rejectors by God. This aspect of the Lukan mind can be grasped if we look at those martyrdoms in the context of the Evangelist's understanding of Israel. This understanding may be set forth in five summary statements.

1) Before Israel's refusal of the gospel, Luke regards her as a reality existing on two levels: first, as an historical people defined by race and nationality, the Jewish nation (e.g., Luke 7:5; 23:2; Acts 10:22; 24:10, 17; 26:4; 28:19); and second, as the people of God (e.g., Luke 1:68; 2:32; 7:16; Acts 7:34; 13:17).[5] Recognition of this fact is crucial to further discussion.

2) The third Evangelist makes a great deal of the Jewish rejection of Jesus and the Christian message (e.g., Luke 2:34; 4:28–29; 13:34; 19:14; 19:39; 19:44; 20:13–16; 23:1–2; 24:20; Acts 4:1–2, 17–18; 5:17–18, 40; 7:58; 13:45; 14:19; 17:5–9; 17:13; 18:5–6, 12–17; 19:8–9; 20:3; 21:27–30, etc.). At the same time, he makes clear the fact that the earliest believers were Jewish (Acts 1:13–14, 21) and that there were many Jewish converts to Christianity (Acts 2:41, 47; 4:4; 5:14; 6:7; 13:43; 17:4; 21:20, etc.) both in Jerusalem and elsewhere. Hence the Lukan narrative shows how the Christian movement divided Israel into two groups: the repentant and the unrepentant. Israel did not reject the gospel but became divided over the issue.

3) In the Lukan perspective the repentant portion of the Jewish nation is Israel, the people of God. It is to them and for them that the promises have been fulfilled. This restored Israel is the presupposition of all the missionary work that follows to the Gentiles (Acts 15:15–18). God first rebuilds and restores Israel and then as a result the Gentiles seek the

---

[5] A. George, *Etudes sur Poeuvre de Luc* (Paris: Gabalda, 1978): 87–125.

Lord. The unrepentant portion of the nation, however, has forfeited its membership in the people of God (Acts 3:23). A formal statement of the rejection of the unrepentant portion of the Jewish nation is delivered three times, once in each main area of missionary activity. Acts 13:46 has Paul and Barnabas say to the unbelieving Jews in Antioch of Pisidia: "It was necessary that the word of God should be spoken first to you. Since you thrust it from you, and judge yourselves unworthy of eternal life, behold, we turn to the Gentiles" (RSV). In Acts 18:6 the scene is Corinth. Here, when the unbelieving Jews opposed him, Paul said: "Your blood be upon your heads! I am innocent. From now on I will go to the Gentiles." Finally, in Acts 28:25–28 Paul says to the unbelieving Jews in Rome: "Let it be known to you then that this salvation of God has been sent to the Gentiles; they will listen" (RSV).

4) It is incorrect to say *only* that for Luke it is when the Jews have rejected the gospel that the way is open to the Gentiles.[6] It is equally incorrect to say only that when Israel has accepted the gospel that the way to the Gentiles is opened.[7] Both, indeed, are parts of the total view of Luke.[8] That is, both Acts 15:15–18 on the one hand and Acts 13:46; 18:6; and 28:25–28 on the other are parts of the total perspective of the third Evangelist. In the first place, the Jewish Christian community in Jerusalem, as the restored Israel, is the means through which salvation comes to the Gentiles (Acts 15:15–18). The Gentiles are incorporated into believing Israel. They are, however, incorporated without circumcision and the law, that is, without first becoming proselytes (Acts 15). In the second place, the explanation why the Lukan church feels no obligation to evangelize the national-racial entity of Israel is that these unrepentant ones have excluded themselves from Israel, the people of God (Acts 13:46; 18:6; 28:25–28). Hence, in Luke's view, by the end of Acts the people of God are no longer a race or a nation but those who believe (Luke 20:9–18). The unbelieving Jews remain an historical people who experience the fall of Jerusalem and the destruction of the temple (Luke 13:35a; 19:41–44; 21:20–24; 23:27–31), but they do not belong to Israel, the people of God. The destruction of the temple and

---

[6] Hans Conzelmann, *Die Apostelgeschichte* (Tübingen: J.C.B. Mohr, 1963), 78; Ernst Haenchen, *The Acts of the Apostles, A Commentary* (trans. B. Noble; Philadelphia: Westminster, 1971), 100ff.

[7] Jacob Jervell, *Luke and the People of God* (Minneapolis: Augsburg, 1972), 41–74.

[8] S. G. Wilson, *The Gentiles and the Gentile Mission in Luke-Acts* (Cambridge: Cambridge University Press, 1973), 231–33.

of the holy city, moreover, are understood as the consequences of the rejection of Jesus by the racial-national Israel.⁹

5) The question whether Luke, like Paul in Rom 9–11, envisioned a final conversion of the entire Jewish people prior to the parousia, prompted by the inclusion of the Gentiles in the people of God, is debatable. Most scholars think that the Lukan Paul of Acts 28:25–28, unlike the historical Paul of Rom 11, seems resigned to a Gentile church.¹⁰ A few Lukan scholars think that Luke, like Paul in Rom 11:20, looked forward to a time when the Jews as a people would be reinstated.¹¹ Acts 1:6; Luke 21:24, 28; and Luke 22:28–30 are about the only supports for this stance that are not simply too far-fetched. There is enough question about even these texts, however, to make it improbable that the Gentile Christian community from which Luke-Acts came expected any final conversion of the nation as a whole before the parousia. The Evangelist would not have ruled out the conversion of any individual Jew, but as far as the direction of the church's mission was concerned, it was to Gentiles. In this Luke is akin to Justin Martyr, who believed that a remnant of Jews was still being saved by conversion to Christianity in his own day (*Dial.* 32; 55; 64). Justin, furthermore, allowed these Jewish Christians who lived within the church to practice the law (*Dial.* 47:2).

In the Lukan narrative we note that those responsible for the deaths of Jesus and Stephen are the chief priests and their associates, not the Pharisees. On the one side, in the Third Gospel the Pharisees vanish as soon as Jesus enters Jerusalem in 19:45 (the last we hear of Pharisees is in 19:39 on the outskirts of the city.). The opponents in the passion narrative are the chief priests, rulers, Sadducees, and the Council (Luke 19:47; 20:1, 19, 27; 22:4, 50, 52, 54, 66; 23:1, 10, 13; cf. 24:20—"how our chief priests and rulers delivered him up to be condemned to death, and crucified him," RSV). On the other side, in Acts 1–5 the enemies of the church are all associated with the temple (Acts 4:1, 5–6, 8, 15, 23; 5:17, 21, 22, 24, 26, 27, 34, 41). Likewise, Stephen in Acts 6:12 is brought before the Council, where he is interrogated by the high priest (7:1).

---

⁹ This became standard Christian argument. Cf. Eusebius, *Hist. eccl.* 3.5.3–6.
¹⁰ E.g., Marshall, *Luke: Historian and Theologian*, 186–87.
¹¹ A. W. Wainwright, 'Luke and the Restoration of the Kingdom of Israel,' *ExpTim* 89 (1977): 76–79; Robert Karris, 'Missionary Communities: A New Paradigm for the Study of Luke-Acts,' *CBQ* 41 (1979): 80–97.

If the clear sense of language is followed in Acts 7:54ff., then the Council members must have participated in the death of Stephen. In the Lukan perspective, therefore, it is the rulers of the nation and the administrators of the temple, that symbol of Jewish national identity, who are portrayed as the instruments behind Jesus' martyrdom and as agents involved in Stephen's death. This is the Evangelist's way of saying that it is the racial-national entity that has rejected God's messengers, not once but twice. What could be attributed to ignorance the first time (Acts 3:17) is clearly deliberate the second time. If the martyrdom of Jesus symbolized the first rejection of God's messenger, the martyrdom of Stephen symbolized the second. The racial-national Israel twice rejected God's messenger. The result is spelled out clearly by Luke. Luke 20:9–18 and Acts 3:23 make it plain. Those who have rejected Jesus have been rejected by God. The first dimension of the Lukan understanding of martyrdom, therefore, is that such a death represents the *rejection of God's messenger* by those supposed to be God's people.

Martyrdom as Legitimation

A second dimension of the Lukan understanding of martyrdom is that *such deaths serve to legitimate* Jesus and the Christian cause and to function as *catalysts for evangelistic outreach*. This aspect of the Lukan mind can be grasped if we look at these martyrdoms in the context of the understanding of martyrdom in Greco-Roman, Jewish, and early Christian thinking.[12]

Greco-Roman Views of Martyrdom

We may begin with a look at the Greco-Roman view of martyrdom. On the one hand, martyrdom was regarded positively in many circles in antiquity. It was a commonplace that true philosophers lived their doctrine as well as expounding it. The philosopher's word alone, unaccompanied by the act, was regarded as invalid (e.g., Seneca, *Ep.* 52.8–9; Dio Chrysostom, *De philosophia* 70.6). Some very harsh things were said about philosophers' sincerity—or lack of it—in antiquity. Josephus (*C. Ap.* 1.8) exaggerated when he said that no Greek philosopher would

---

[12] On the general topic of martyrdom, cf. W. H. C. Frend, *Martyrdom and Persecution in the Early Church* (Oxford: Blackwell, 1965); Norbert Brox, *Zeuge und Märtyrer* (Munich: Kösel, 1961); H. A. Fishel, 'Martyr and Prophet,' *JQR* 37 (1947): 265–80, 363–86.

ever die for his philosophy. The same sentiments are found, however, in Lucian (*Pisc.* 31): "in their life and actions ... they contradicted their outward appearance and reversed (philosophy's) practice." Epictetus (*Diatr.* 1.29.56) says: "What, then, is the thing lacking now? The man ... to bear witness to the arguments by his acts." Seneca (*Ep.* 24.15) joins the chorus: "There is a very disgraceful charge often brought against our school—that we deal with the words, and not the deeds, of philosophy." In view of this cynicism about philosophers' sincerity, sometimes only the willingness to die or actual death could validate a philosopher's profession.

Several examples of philosophers sealing their profession with either their deaths or their willingness to die illustrate this fact. Tertullian (*Apol.* 50) tells us that Zeno the Eleatic, when asked by Dionysius what good philosophy did, said it gave contempt of death. When he was called on to prove it, given over to the tyrant's scourge, he was unquailing as he sealed his opinion even to death. In *Vita Secundi*, Secundus, because of an incident that had caused his mother's suicide, put a ban on himself, resolving not to say anything for the rest of his life—having chosen the Pythagorean way of life. The Emperor Hadrian arrived in Athens and sent for Secundus to test him. When Secundus refused to speak, Hadrian sent him off with the executioner with instructions that if he did speak his head should be cut off. If he did not speak, he should be returned to the Emperor. When he was returned to Hadrian after having been willing to die for his vow of silence, Secundus was allowed to write answers to the twenty questions asked by the Emperor—which answers were put in the sacred library. His willingness to die had validated Secundus's philosophy. Origen (*Cels.* 8.66) commends Celsus when the pagan says:

> If you happen to be a worshipper of God and someone commands you either to act blasphemously or to say some other disgraceful thing, you ought not to put any trust in him at all. Rather than this you must remain firm in face of all tortures and endure death rather than say or even think anything profane about God.

The sealing of one's profession in death as a martyr sometimes issued in furthering the cause of the philosopher. Plato's *Apologia* tells the story of Socrates' death. In chapter 39 Socrates says:

> I fain would prophesy to you; for I am about to die, and that is the hour in which men are gifted with prophetic power. And I prophesy to you who are my murderers, that immediately after my death punishment far heavier than you have inflicted on me will surely await you.

What is meant in this context is that there will be more accusers than there are now. His position vindicated by death, Socrates' disciples will attack the Athenians as never before.

On the other hand, however, Greco-Roman teachers gave two serious cautions about martyrdom. Martyrdom is not to be sought. Seneca (*Ep.* 24.25) says: "Above all, he should avoid the weakness which has taken possession of many—the lust for death." Martyrdom does not provide certain results. That is, it does not guarantee the furtherance of one's cause. It may win some but not necessarily others (Lucian, *Peregr.* 13; Marcus Aurelius 11.3.2).

Jewish Tradition Regarding Martyrdom

The view of martyrdom in ancient Judaism has similarities to this Greco-Roman stance but there are also differences. On the one side, there was a positive attitude toward martyrdom. Two streams of thought ran alongside one another. One stream spoke of the prophets dying as martyrs at the hands of God's people (e.g., Jer 2:20; Neh 9:26; 1 Kgs 10:10, 14; 2 Chr 24:20–22; *Jub.* 1:12; *Liv. Pro.*; *Mart. Isa.*; cf. also Matt 23:31–39; Heb 11:36ff.; 1 Thess 2:15; Mark 12:1–12). Here the emphasis is on the sinfulness of God's people (cf. Luke 13:33–34; Acts 7:52). The other stream spoke of the faithful among God's people dying as martyrs at the hands of the Gentiles. Here, as in Greco-Roman paganism, it was believed that the true prophet sealed the truth of his testimony with death. In 4 Macc 7 the aged scribe Eleazar refused to eat swine's flesh as demanded by the Syrians or even to pretend to eat it (cf. 2 Macc 6:18ff.). Instead he endured willingly the scourge, the rack, and the flame (2 Macc 7:4). In 4 Macc 7:15 the author cried out: "O life faithful to the Law and perfected by the seal of death." It was also believed that such martyrs gained thereby the resurrection from the dead (2 Macc 7:9, 14, 23, 28–29—the seven brothers and their aged mother; Josephus, *B.J.* 1.33.3 §651ff.—those who tore down the golden eagle Herod the Great had erected over the gate of the Temple; 4 Macc 9:18; 16:25; *b. Berakhot* 61b—Akiba). Such martyrs' deaths moreover were believed to benefit the nation (2 Macc 7:37–38; 4 Macc 6:27–29; 17:22), effecting a new relationship between God and the people. Sometimes the martyrs' actions made converts to Judaism. For example, *b. Avodah Zarah* 18a, tells of R. Hanina b. Teradion who in the time of Hadrian was arrested for teaching Torah to groups. He was burned to death. After watching, the executioner then threw himself into the fire. Whereupon a *bath qol* (voice from heaven) exclaimed: R. Hanina and the executioner have been assigned to the world to come.

On the other side, we find the same two cautions among Jewish teachers that we found in the pagan world. Overeagerness for martyrdom is denounced as self-annihilation (e.g., *Genesis Rabbah* 82).[13] Martyrdom is no guarantee of another's conversion (e.g., 2 Macc. 6:29).

Martyrdom in Early Christianity

Ancient Christianity was deeply indebted to the pagan and Jewish views about martyrdom in defining its own stance. On the one hand, there was a positive attitude toward martyrdom. Like pagans and Jews, most Christians believed that the truth of their profession must be sealed in blood if it came to that (e.g., Revelation; Justin, *2 Apol.* 12). It is, of course, true that some Gnostics refused to undergo martyrdom (cf. Irenaeus, *Haer.* 1.24.3–6—Basilides; Tertullian, *Praescr.* 1—Basilides; *Scorp.* 1—Valentians and other Gnostics). Christians also believed, like the Jews, that martyrdom benefited the martyr (Revelation; 2 Tim 4:6–8; Matt 10:32–33; cf. the *Martyrium Apollonii*, where Apollonius says: "Proconsul Perenius, I thank my God for this sentence of yours which will bring me salvation."). Christians also believed, like the Jews, that martyrdom benefited the community of Christians (e.g., *Mart. Pol.* 1.1; Eusebius, *Hist. eccl.* 4.15.3, who says Polycarp put an end to the persecution by his martyrdom.). Christians, even more than pagans and Jews, believed that martyrdoms had 'evangelistic' benefits. They helped spread the gospel. For example, Justin, *Dialogus cum Tryphone* 110, says: "The more we are persecuted, the more do others in ever-increasing numbers embrace the faith." Tertullian, *Apologeticus* 50, says: "We conquer in dying. ... The oftener we are mown down by you, the more in number we grow; the blood of Christians is seed." *Epistula ad Diognetum* 6.9 says: "Christians when they are punished increase the more in number every day." In 7.7–8, it says: "Can you not see them thrown to wild beasts, to make them deny their Lord, and yet not overcome? Do you not see that the more of them are punished, the more numer-

---

[13] Stanley Hauerwas in a private conversation suggested that Jews and Christians would have reservations about an overeagerness for martyrdom because they believed that life belonged to God. Therefore, one is not free to dispose of it at will. For the Jewish casuistry developed to help Jews avoid martyrdom, see David Daube, *Collaboration with Tyranny in Rabbinic Law* (New York: Oxford University Press, 1966).

ous the others become?" Compare also the *Martyrium Apollonii* and the *Martyrium Potamiaenae et Basilidis*. Lactantius (d. A.D. 325), *Divinarum institutionum libri VII* 5.19, says: "It is right reason, then, to defend religion by patience or death in which faith is preserved and is pleasing to God himself, and it adds authority to religion."

On the other hand, Christians shared the pagan and Jewish reservations about martyrdom. An overeagerness for martyrdom is denounced (e.g., *Mart. Pol.* 4: "We do not approve those who give themselves up, for the gospel does not teach us to do so"; *Act. Cypr.* says: "Since our discipline forbids anyone to surrender voluntarily."). Martyrdom was not regarded as a certain proof.[14]

Summary of Luke's Attitude toward Martyrdom

When we compare Luke-Acts with its environment we find many points of contact. Like pagans and Jews, as well as later Christians, Luke-Acts assumed that martyrdom legitimated a philosopher's/prophet's profession, and that such a death might very well issue in the conversion of others to the innocent one's cause, though Christian emphasis is more often here than in pagan or Jewish circles (cf. Luke 23:42–43; Acts 8:1b, 4ff.; 11:19ff.). In Luke-Acts, the two Jewish streams of martyrology flow together in the picture of Jesus' death. Jesus is a prophet rejected and killed by God's people (cf. Luke 13:33 ff.; Acts 7:52); he is also a devout Jew executed unjustly by the Gentiles (Acts 4:25–28). Stephen's death reflects only the first of three streams—prophetic martyrdom at the hands of God's people. Further, Luke-Acts agrees with Jewish thought in the belief that by martyrdom the man of faith gains eternal life (so Jesus and Stephen—cf.. Luke 21:19), and the belief that the martyrdom of a righteous man benefits the community (so Luke 22:19–20 says that Jesus' blood sealed the new covenant).

Luke shares with the milieu generally the two main reservations about martyrdom. On the one hand, martyrdom is not to be sought (cf. Luke 22:42—"Father, if thou art willing, remove this cup from me; nevertheless not my will, but thine, be done," RSV). Jesus did not have a lust for death but sought to avoid it, if God would permit it. On the other hand, martyrdom is not proof of the truth of one's cause and does

---

[14] H. Musurillo, *The Acts of the Christian Martyrs* (Oxford: Clarendon, 1972), passim.

not lead to the conversion of everyone (cf. Luke 23:39–43, where only one of the two thieves crucified with him is converted; the other rails at Jesus).

How then would Luke's first readers/hearers have perceived his account of the martyrdoms of Jesus and Stephen? Three things would likely have stood out. First, neither man died because of a lust for death. Both were healthy selves. Second, both legitimated their profession as they sealed it with their blood. Both were sincere in their stands. Third, this legitimation is evidenced in the conversion of others as a result of their deaths. Martyrdom has an evangelistic function. In the ancient world this Lukan motif would have served as part of the confirmation of the Christian message. Its persuasiveness was that of a selfless commitment on the part of stable persons.

The Social Implications of Luke's View

What are the *implications* of this view of martyrdom for our understanding of the Lukan social ethic? What kind of political and social stance does Luke attribute to Jesus? This question is prompted by *Jesus, Politics, and Society*, by Richard Cassidy.[15] Cassidy argues that the Lukan Jesus is portrayed as a Gandhi-like figure advocating nonviolent resistance. Is this position tenable in light of our previous discussion? I think not.

Cassidy works with three possible stances:[16] (a) nonresistance (where people refrain not only from physical violence but also from directly confronting those responsible for existing ills; they identify with those suffering from such evils; they offer no defense if they themselves are subjected to violence by those who have power; their hope is that their example will eventuate in changes in the attitudes and actions of others); (b) nonviolent resistance (where people avoid violence to persons but confront in a nonviolent way those responsible for existing social ills; their hope is that the challenge will serve to create a dialogue that may eventually result in a favorable change of behavior); and (c) violent resistance.

These or similar stances had their representatives among Jewish people at the time of Christian origins. The Zealots were the advocates of

---

[15] Richard Cassidy, *Jesus, Politics, and Society: A Study of Luke's Gospel* (Maryknoll, New York: Orbis Books, 1978).
[16] Ibid., 40–41.

armed revolution against Rome. Josephus gives us at least two examples of nonviolent resistance in Jesus' time. The first is found in *Antiquitates judaicae* 18.3.1 §261–309 and *Bellum judaicum* 2.9.3 §184–203. This is an account of a five-day sit-in to protest Pilate's introduction of images into Jerusalem. When threatened with death if they did not end their protest, the Jews cast themselves on the ground and bared their throats, declaring that they gladly welcomed death rather than violate their law. The protest caused Pilate to remove the offensive images from the city. A second is found in *Antiquitates judaicae* 18.8 §244–272 and *Bellum judaicum* 2.10 §184–198. This tells of a general strike by Jews that left fields untilled in the sowing season for more than a month. The protest prevented Caligula's statue from going up in the temple.

Although during the Hasmonean rule at least some of the Pharisees functioned as a political party, from the rise of Herod the Great until the end of the first Jewish revolt against Rome, the Pharisees seem to have moved away from direct political involvement and to have adopted an attitude of indifference regarding rulers and the forms under which they ruled. It seems likely that the Pharisees did not oppose Roman rule in Judea.[17] Their concern in this period was with the proper ordering of the life of God's people according to the law.

The Lukan Jesus' stance is more complex than Cassidy's description allows. Two components must be recognized in Luke's picture of Jesus' social and political stance. First, although the Lukan Jesus shows no deference toward political rulers (e.g., Luke 13:31–33), this does not mean that he is involved, Gandhi-style, in a nonviolent resistance to them. Like the Pharisees, the Lukan Jesus manifests an *indifference* to the political rulers. For someone who believed that all power and authority resided with God and all history unfolded according to his purpose, human rulers were of little consequence. Since the rulers shared no common assumptions that would facilitate dialogue with him, the Lukan Jesus opted for silence in their presence. Second, toward the Jewish structures (the church), however, the Lukan Jesus showed no indifference. Here he was involved in *nonviolent resistance*. Confrontation between the Lukan Jesus and the Jewish leaders was frequent (e.g., Luke 5:12–6:11; 11:37–54; 13:10–17; 14:1–24; 16:14–15; 19:47–20:47). Only at Luke 19:45 is there any hint of possible violence. The Evangelist has so shaped the cleansing story, however, that

---

[17] Ibid., 122–23.

it becomes merely Jesus' entry into the site of his subsequent teaching (Luke 19:47–21:38). Moreover, Luke 22:49–51 has Jesus explicitly reject violence against Jewish authority. Nonviolent confrontation aimed at dialogue and hoping for a change of behavior seems the best description of the Lukan Jesus' stance toward the Jewish structures. This was doubtless due to the fact that Jesus and the Jews shared common assumptions about God and values. With such a people dialogue could be profitable.

The Lukan view of martyrdom offers specific support to this correction of Cassidy's thesis. Were the deaths of the Lukan Jesus and Stephen designed by either to influence the political structures of the times (that is, Roman political structures)? Were their deaths the result of Rome's resistance to their political agitation? The answer to both questions must be in the negative. In Luke-Acts these deaths were the outcome of a struggle within the people of God, which at that time was also a racial-national entity. The deaths, moreover, had their positive influence on those within the people of God: the thief converted on the cross was almost certainly a Jew, and the spread of the gospel in Acts 8 and 11 was by Christians (cf. Phil 1:12–14, where Paul's imprisonment and threatened martyrdom caused most of the Christians to be bold in preaching). The Lukan Jesus and his followers, like the Pharisees of Jesus' time, had as their concern the proper ordering of the life of God's people.[18] If the Lukan Jesus adopted an attitude of indifference regarding rulers and the forms under which they ruled, the Christians in Acts basically looked with favor on the Roman structures because, when they worked at their best, they protected the preachers of the gospel from attack (e.g., Acts 17:1–9; 18:12–17; 19:23–41; 21:30–32; 23:12–35), and, even when they were flawed (e.g., Acts 24–28), they facilitated the preaching of the gospel.

The Lukan Jesus' primary vehicle for social change—if such language is even legitimate in describing Lukan thought—was the structure of life in the community of his disciples. Among his followers the Lukan Jesus sought a revolution in social attitudes. His disciples were to live in the present in light of God's reversal of all human values in the Eschaton. Such a stance, of course, was regarded by some as "turning the world upside down" (Acts 17:6), even if that was not a primary or even a conscious intention of the Christians. By embodying structures

---

[18] H. C. Kee, *Christian Origins in Sociological Perspective* (Philadelphia: Westminster, 1980), 42.

of social relationships that reflected the new life in the Spirit under the Lordship of Jesus, the Christian community functioned in the larger society as an agent of social change.

It would be improper, I think, to close without at least raising the question of the relevance of the Lukan perspective for modern life. Two contemporary Christian ethicists reflect the stance we have found in Luke-Acts: John Howard Yoder[19] and Stanley Hauerwas.[20] Yoder's thesis is that the first duty of the church for society is to be the church. That means to be a society which through the way its members deal with one another demonstrates to the world what love means in social relations. In this way the church fulfills its social responsibility by being an example, a witness, a creative minority formed by obedience to nonresistant love. From this point of view, the church does not attack the social structure of society directly, as one power group among others, but indirectly by embodying in its life a transcendent reality. Hauerwas acknowledges both his debt to Yoder and to the Gospel of Luke. The Lukan Jesus, he argues, did not go to the top (to Caesar or to Pilate) to get something done. Nor did he go to the Left (the Zealots). He went instead to the poor and the sinners. He established a community to embody God's grace. By insisting on being nothing less than the community of love, moreover, the church forces the world to face the truth of its own nature. "The most vital form of Christian social ethics must actually be a concern about the kind of community that Christians form among themselves."[21]

To conclude: The Lukan Jesus is no more a social activist of the Gandhi variety than of the Zealot type. Like the Pharisees of the historical Jesus' time, he is preoccupied with the ordering of the life of the people of God. It is through the leaven of the life of the community of the Lukan Jesus' disciples that the world is turned upside down. This

---

[19] Yoder is known to a wide reading audience by his *The Politics of Jesus* (Grand Rapids: Eerdmans, 1972). There he argues that "a social style characterized by the creation of a new community and the rejection of violence of any kind is the theme of New Testament proclamation from beginning to end" (p. 250). He has strong support from Jacques Ellul, *Violence* (New York: Seabury, 1969), who shows the fallacy of the logic of the assumption that violence, while wrong in the oppressor, becomes right when used by Christians for desirable social change. The best summary of Yoder's position is found in Stanley Hauerwas, *Vision and Virtue* (Notre Dame, Ind.: Fides, 1974), in a chapter entitled, 'The Nonresistant Church: The Theological Ethics of John Howard Yoder,' 197–221.

[20] Stanley Hauerwas, 'The Politics of Charity,' *Int* 31 (1977): 251–62.

[21] Hauerwas, *Vision and Virtue*, 216.

Lukan perspective on social ethics, moreover, is now incorporated in at least one stream of contemporary Christian theological ethics. The advisability of basing contemporary Christian ethical thought on Lukan perspectives is a matter for Christian ethicists to decide after debate. What the Lukan point of view is with regard to social ethics, however, seems to me beyond debate.

CHAPTER EIGHT

THE PLACE OF THE RESURRECTION IN THE THEOLOGY OF LUKE

According to Luke, the resurrection takes place according to divine plan and functions variously: to signal God's reversal of Jesus' rejection; to attest to Jesus' victory over death; to confirm Jesus as the mediator of salvation; to establish the Eucharist as the extension of table fellowship with Jesus; and to make mission possible.

The apocryphal *Gospel of Peter* (35–42) purports to give an account of Jesus' resurrection.

> Now in the night whereon the Lord's day dawned, as the soldiers were keeping guard two by two in every watch, there came a great sound in the heaven, and they saw the heavens opened and two men descend thence, shining with a great light, and drawing near unto the sepulchre. And that stone which had been set on the door rolled away of itself and went back to the side, and the sepulchre was opened and both of the young men entered in. When therefore the soldiers saw that, they waked up the centurion and the elders (for they also were there keeping watch); and while they were yet telling them the things which they had seen, they saw again three men come out of the sepulchre, and two of them sustaining the other, and a cross following after them. And of the two they saw that their heads reached unto heaven, but of him that was led by them that it overpassed the heavens. And they heard a voice out of the heavens saying: "Hast thou preached unto them that sleep?" And an answer was heard from the cross, saying: "Yea."[1]

None of the canonical Gospels, Luke included, recounts the resurrection itself. They rather focus on the aftereffects, like the empty tomb and the appearances of the one who was raised. Luke's Gospel speaks about the resurrection of Jesus by using three types of tradition: (1) passion predictions and references to such (9:22 [cf. 24:6–7]; 18:33); (2) stories of and references to an empty tomb (24:1–11 [cf. 24:22–23]; 24:12 [cf. 24:24]); and (3) stories about (24:13–32, 35; 24:36–49) and references

---

[1] M. R. James, *The Apocryphal New Testament* (Oxford: Clarendon, 1955), 92–93.

to (24:34) appearances of the risen Christ. The task of this article is not to do an exegesis of these texts but rather to explore the role of Jesus' resurrection in Lukan theology. This will be done by examining in order the theological, christological, soteriological, ecclesiological, and missiological ramifications of the resurrection in Luke (and Acts).

Theological Ramifications

Theologically, what is the role of Jesus' resurrection in Luke? For the third evangelist, God raised Jesus as part of the divine plan. In Luke 9:22, Jesus predicts: "The Son of Man must [δεῖ] suffer many things, and be rejected by the elders and chief priests and scribes, and be killed, and on the third day be raised [ἐγερθῆναι, aorist passive]" (RSV).

1) The passive "be raised" is a divine passive. Jesus will be raised by God. This is explicitly stated in Acts 2:24 ("God raised him up"); 2:32 ("Jesus God raised up"); 3:15 ("God raised from the dead"); 4:10 ("God raised from the dead"); 5:30 ("God raised Jesus"); 10:40 ("God raised him on the third day"); 13:32 ("God raising Jesus"); 17:31 ("God raising him from the dead"). This was also common early-Christian confession (e.g., pre-Pauline—1 Cor 15:4; Rom 4:24; Pauline—1 Cor 15:15; Deutero-Pauline—Eph 1:20; Petrine—1 Pet 1:21; Ignatian—*Trall.* 9.2).

2) Jesus' being raised, moreover, is a part of the divine plan. In Luke-Acts there is a divine purpose that stands behind the events of history.[2] It is spoken of as "the purpose of God" (βουλὴ τοῦ θεοῦ) in Luke 7:30; Acts 2:23; 4:28; 5:38–39;13:36; 20:27; as God's "will" (θέλεμα) in Luke 22:42; Acts 21:14; 22:14; as God's "authority" (ἐξουσία) in Acts 1:7. Sometimes the divine plan is described by the term "must" (δεῖ) or "it was necessary" (ἔδει), as in Luke 2:49; 4:43;13:33;17:25; 21:9; 22:37; 24:7, 26, 44; Acts 1:16, 21; 3:21; 4:12; 9:16; 17:3; 23:11; 27:24; and here in Luke 9:22. Mark 8:31 and Matt 16:21 reflect the same use of "must" relative to Jesus' resurrection. The realization of the divine plan is often spoken of in terms of fulfillment. Luke 1:20; 4:21; 21:24; Acts 1:16; 3:18; 13:27, all use πληροῦν ("fulfill"). Luke 9:51 uses συμπληροῦσθαι (literally, "when the days were fulfilled"; "drew near," RSV).

---

[2] John T. Squires, 'The Plan of God in Luke-Acts,' (Ph.D. diss., Yale University, 1987).

Luke 18:31 and 22:37 employ τελεῖν ("accomplish," RSV). Luke 18:31 reads: "Behold, we are going up to Jerusalem, and everything written of the Son of Man by the prophets will be fulfilled." This includes Jesus' resurrection ("and on the third day he will rise"). Luke 24:44–46 continues the same thread. The risen Jesus says:

> "Everything written about me in the law of Moses and the prophets and the psalms must be fulfilled." Then he opened their minds to understand the scriptures, and said to them, "Thus it is written, that the Christ should suffer and on the third day rise from the dead." (RSV)

The divine plan can be known by humans. Prophecy of various sorts makes it known, including the prophecy of the pre-Easter Jesus. So, in Luke 24:6–8, the angels say to the women who have found the tomb empty:

> "Remember how he told you, while he was still in Galilee, that the Son of Man must be delivered into the hands of sinful men, and be crucified, and on the third day rise" [Luke 9:22]. And they remembered his words. (RSV)

The divine plan is made known by Jesus' prophetic words. In Luke, Jesus' resurrection is God's doing and is a part of his overall plan.

Christological Ramifications

Christologically, the resurrection functions both as part of Luke's attempt to maintain the identity of the pre- and the post-Easter Jesus and as God's reversal of the human no to Jesus. First, the resurrection serves as part of a larger motif emphasizing 'this same Jesus.' There is a pattern in Luke-Acts that seeks to guarantee that the one who dies, is buried, is raised, and ascends in Jerusalem and its environs is the same Jesus who worked in Galilee. (1) Luke 23:49 says: "And all his acquaintances and the women who had followed him from Galilee stood at a distance and saw these things" (RSV). The echoes of 6:12–16 (the choice of the twelve apostles) and 8:1–3 (a notice that the twelve were with him and also some women) are unmistakable. The continuity of the witnesses ensures that the Jesus who died is the same as the one who worked in Galilee. (2) Luke 23:55 reads: "The women who had come with him from Galilee followed, and saw the tomb, and how his body was laid" (RSV). Again, an echo of 8:1–3 is heard. Again, the effect is to guarantee that it is the same Jesus who was buried. (3) Luke 24:6–7 has the two angels remind the women who find the tomb empty of something Jesus said "while he was still in Galilee" (i.e., the passion prediction of 9:22), "and they remembered his words" (24:8). The words of the one who had predicted his resurrection while in Galilee are fulfilled, as the empty tomb evidences. The prophecy-fulfillment schema underwrites the identity of the Galilean prophet and the risen one. (4) Acts 1:11 has two angels address the witnesses of Jesus' ascension: "Men of Galilee [remember Luke 6:12–16], why do you stand looking into heaven? This Jesus, who was taken up from you into heaven, will come in the same way as you saw him go into heaven" (RSV). That the witnesses of the ascension are Galileans serves to underscore that it is the same Jesus who ascends. From the Lukan perspective, credentials for a witness to the resurrection of Jesus include that such a one has "accompanied us during all the time that the Lord Jesus went in and out among us, beginning from the baptism of John until the day when he was taken up from us" (Acts 1:21–22, RSV). Why? Only such a person could verify that it was the same Jesus from Galilee to ascension. Lukan christology is one with that of the Johannine community in its preoccupation with guaranteeing the identity of Jesus through the events of passion, resurrection, and ascension (e.g., the role of the beloved disciple—John 13:23; 18:15?; 19:26–27; 19:35; 21:7, 20–24).

Christologically, Jesus' resurrection in Luke-Acts also functions as God's reversal of the human no to Jesus.[3] This motif is most explicit in Acts. In Acts 2:23–24 Peter says: "This Jesus ... you crucified and killed by the hands of lawless men. But God raised him up" (RSV). In Acts 3:14–15 Peter again says: "But you denied the Holy and Righteous One, and asked for a murderer to be granted to you, and killed the Author of life, whom God raised from the dead" (RSV). In Acts 5:30–31 Peter and the apostles say: "The God of our fathers raised Jesus whom you killed by hanging him on a tree. God exalted him at his right hand as Leader and Savior, to give repentance to Israel and forgiveness of sins" (RSV). In Acts 10:39b-40 Peter says: "They put him to death by hanging him on a tree; but God raised him on the third day and made him manifest" (RSV). In Acts 13:28–30 Paul says: "Though they could charge him with nothing deserving death, yet they asked Pilate to have him killed. ... But God raised him from the dead" (RSV). If Jesus' death is the result of human rejection of God's

---

[3] I. H. Marshall, *Luke: Historian and Theologian* (Grand Rapids: Zondervan, 1970), 175.

messenger, his resurrection is God's vindication of him. This view of Jesus' resurrection is implicit in his words in Luke 22:69: "But from now on the Son of Man shall be seated at the right hand of the power of God" (RSV). Like a prophetic perfect in Hebrew, the future tense ('will be'), joined to the expression 'from the now,' speaks of events as if already realized, so certain is the speaker of their fulfillment by God (in this case, God's vindication of Jesus). The evangelist's words in Luke 16:31, at the end of the parable of the Rich Man and Lazarus, reflect the realism of post-resurrection experience: "If they do not hear Moses and the prophets, neither will they be convinced if some one should rise from the dead" (RSV).

Soteriological Ramifications

Soteriologically, the resurrection functions both to provide the means by which salvation may flow from Jesus and to define the nature of the ultimate victory over death.

1) In Luke-Acts salvation flows from the living Jesus.[4] This is true for the periods both before and after Easter. Thus, this is so before Easter (e.g., Luke 5:29–32; 7:36–50; 15:1–2, 3–32; 19:1–10). Even the promise to the thief on the cross was a promise made by the living Jesus (Luke 23:42–43). In the period after Easter, this is still true. Luke 24:46–47 links the proclamation of repentance and forgiveness of sins in Jesus' name to his resurrection from the dead. The emphasis is continued in Acts. In 2:33–36, 38 the call to "Repent, and be baptized everyone of you in the name of Jesus Christ for the forgiveness of your sins" (RSV) is predicated on Jesus' resurrection and exaltation (so also in 4:10, 12; 10:40–43; 13:30–39). In 5:31 the same point is explicit: "God exalted him at his right hand as Leader and Savior, to give repentance to Israel and forgiveness of sins" (RSV). In 26:23 one hears it yet again: "Christ ... by being the first to rise from the dead ... would proclaim light both to the people and to the Gentiles" (RSV). It is by virtue of his resurrection that salvation flows from Jesus in the period after his death. Luke shares this emphasis with other early Christians (pre-Pauline—Rom 4:25; 8:34b; Phil 2:9–11; Deutero-Pauline—1 Tim 3:16; Heb 4:14; 7:25; 8:12).

---

[4] Ibid., 169.

2) Jesus' resurrection serves in the Third Gospel to describe the nature of the ultimate victory over death.[5] For Luke, the resurrection of Christ is not the resuscitation of a corpse, as in the case of the widow's son at Nain (Luke 7:11–17; described in 7:22 as "the dead are raised up") and of Jairus's daughter (Luke 8:40–42, 49–56).[6] When a corpse is resuscitated, it will eventually die again of something else. Whenever one has experienced the ultimate victory over death, however, that one will never die again (cf. Rom 6:9, "For we know that Christ being raised from the dead will never die again; death no longer has dominion over him," RSV). Neither can the resurrection of Jesus in Luke be understood as a disembodied existence in the intermediate state, as such a state is assumed in the parable of Luke 16:22–26 and the words of Jesus to the repentant thief in Luke 23:42–43. Resurrection implies an embodied existence (cf. 1 Cor 15:42–50). Nor does Luke regard Jesus' resurrection as identical with his "departure" (ἔξοδος, 9:31; cf. his "coming" [εἴσοδος], Acts 13:24). Like the fourth evangelist, the third evangelist sees Jesus' departure as encompassing his death-resurrection-ascension-exaltation. Jesus' death is part of the Way to the climactic "being received up" (ἀναλήμψεωσ, 9:51; cf. Acts 1:2, 11), or "entering into his glory" (εἰσελθεῖν εἰς τὴν δόξαν αὐτοῦ, 24:26). Thus, Jesus' resurrection in Luke is one facet of his departure.

In earliest Palestinian Jewish Christianity the one event, the resurrection of Jesus, encompassed three different realities: his victory over death, his removal from human time and space into another dimension (that of God), and his new function as cosmic Lord (cf. 1 Cor 15:3–5; Rom 1:3–4). In Luke-Acts the temporal unity of these three realities is broken apart, and they are treated narratively as three separate events on a time line. The resurrection of Jesus is used to refer to the reality of his victory over death (Luke 24:1–11, 12, 13–35, 36–49). The ascension becomes Jesus' removal to heaven (Luke 24:51; Acts 1:9–11). The exaltation designates the moment of Jesus' new status as Lord and Christ (Luke 22:69; Acts 2:33–36; 5:31). Other early Christians near the same time as Luke-Acts make the same theological separation between resurrection (Eph 1:20; Col 3:1; 1 Tim 3:16; 1 Pet 1:3, 21; 3:21; Heb 13:20), ascension (Eph 1:20; 4:10; Col 3:1; 1 Tim 3:16; 1 Pet 3:22; Heb 4:14), and exaltation (Eph 1:20; Col 3:1; 1 Tim 3:16; 1 Pet 3:22; 1:21; Heb 1:3;

---

[5] Charles H. Talbert, *Reading Luke* (New York: Crossroad, 1984), 226–29.

[6] J. A. Fitzmyer, *The Gospel According to Luke X–XXIV* (Garden City, N.Y.: Doubleday, 1985), 1538.

8:1; 10:12). Luke's use of narrative as his theological vehicle necessitated his taking the three religious components of resurrection as understood by the earliest Palestinian Jewish Christians separately 'for the sake of analysis.' In so doing, however, Jesus' resurrection comes to refer only to his ultimate victory over death.

This ultimate victory over death is understood in corporeal terms. Both the first empty-tomb tradition (Luke 24:1–11) and the second appearance story (Luke 24:36–49) witness to the corporeality of the risen Christ. Luke 24:1–11 (and par.) has some distinctive traits. Luke contrasts what the women did find (the stone rolled away) with what they did not find (Jesus' body). The absence of the body echoes Luke 23:55, where the women observe the body of Jesus laid in the tomb, and is echoed later in the Emmaus account (24:23, "did not find his body"). The two angels' words interpret this empirical data: "Why do you seek the living among the dead? He is not here but has risen" (24:5, RSV, following the long text). Whatever the nature of Jesus' victory over death was, it involved the absence of his body from the tomb.

Assuming the long text,[7] a second empty-tomb tradition (Luke 24:12) is attached to the first in order to eliminate two erroneous explanations of the missing body of Jesus. First, the report was not due to the hysteria of some women. The second empty-tomb story in Luke furnishes a second witness that is needed for a valid testimony under Jewish law (cf. Num 35:30; Deut 17:6–7; 19:15). Second, it eliminates the possible explanation of the empty tomb as due to the theft of Jesus' body (cf. Matt 28:11–15 and John 20:1–18 for concern with the same issue). Just as in John 20:6–7, Peter's seeing the linen cloths lying by themselves argues against theft. A thief would have taken not only the body but also the expensive cloths. The tomb was in fact empty, says Luke. We do not have a case of hysterical women getting it wrong. Moreover, it was empty not because of the theft of Jesus' body but, as the angels said (Luke 24:5) and Jesus predicted in Galilee (Luke 24:6–7; cf. 9:22), because he has been raised from the dead in a corporeal fashion.

Luke 24:36–43 tells of an appearance of the risen Jesus to the eleven and some others in Jerusalem. This story also functions to establish the corporeality of the risen Christ (cf. 1 John 1:1–2; John 20:24–29; for a similar concern cf. Ign., *Smyrn.* 3.1–2; *Ep. Apos.* 11–12). When Jesus

---

[7] J. E. Alsup (*The Post-Resurrection Appearance Stories of the Gospel Tradition* [Stuttgart: Calver Verlag, 1975], 103) indicates the trend of recent research is to accept v. 12 as an integral part of the Third Gospel.

appeared, the disciples supposed they saw a spirit. The story rectifies the disciples' belief with two proofs. First, Jesus says: "See my hands and feet, that it is I myself, handle me, and see; for a spirit has not flesh and bones as you see that I have" (24:39, RSV). The pagan Lucretius (*Rer. Nat.* 1.304) enables one to sense the significance of this for Luke's readers. He says: "For nothing can touch or be touched except a bodily substance." This kind of saying was also known to an early Christian like Tertullian (*An.* 5; *Marc.* 4:8), who used it to argue for the corporeality of Jesus. In contrast to this, consider the gnosticizing *Coptic Gospel of Thomas*, "Jesus said: I will give you what eye has not seen and ear has not heard and hand has not touched and which has not come into the heart of man" (17).

Second, when Jesus says, "Have you anything here to eat?" the disciples give him a piece of broiled fish and "he took it and ate before them" (24:41–43, RSV; cf. Acts 1:4; 10:41). The significance of this act for Jewish sensitivities is clear: Angels do not eat (e.g., Tob 12:19; Josephus, *A.J.* 1.9.2 §197; Philo, *Abr.* 118); human beings do eat. For Luke, the risen Lord, no less than the pre-Easter Jesus, is flesh and bones, corporeal, truly human. Not only does the risen Jesus eat, but he also can be seen (even the wounds in his hands and feet) and touched.

The two stories (Luke 24:1–11 and 36–43) say the same thing about the nature of Jesus' victory over death. It is not to be understood as an escape from this perishable frame (the Greek immortality of the soul) but as a transformation of it. It is to be understood neither as a transformation into a purely spiritual, angelic being nor as the mere survival of his shade (cf. 1 Sam 28:8–14). Jesus remains flesh and bones, though immortal. His existence, although bodily, is nevertheless not limited by the normal human constraints (e.g., 24:31, "He vanished out of their sight," RSV; 24:36, "As they were saying this, Jesus himself stood among them," RSV). Again, the similarities with the Fourth Gospel are striking (John 20:19, "the doors being shut ... Jesus came and stood among them," RSV; 20:26, "the doors were shut, but Jesus came and stood among them," RSV).

In Luke-Acts Jesus is understood, in part at least, as the prototype of Christian existence. He is the pioneer (ἀρχηγός, Acts 3:15 ["Author," RSV]; 5:31 ["Leader," RSV]; cf. Heb 2:10; 12:2) who goes before, opening the Way for his disciples to follow. His existence is, then, a model for his followers (cf. Luke 4:1–13 and 22:39–46, where Jesus' dealing with temptation is an example for Christians facing the same difficulties). Given this mindset, if Luke speaks about the nature of

Jesus' victory over death, he is also making a comment about the nature of the victory over death for which Christians hope (cf. Phil 3:20–21; 1 John 3:2). Luke's answer, therefore, is very much the same answer as Paul's (1 Cor 15). Still, Luke does not make his confession in an analytical or systematic manner but rather offers his confession in the form of a narrative of the risen Christ who is understood as the prototype of Christian existence. In the nature of Jesus' victory over death, one sees the victory for which his disciples hope as well. It is a bodily existence in which marks that allow for the recognition of individuality remain, but it is not subject either to death or to the normal constraints of bodily existence as known this side of the transformation from mortal to immortal.

Ecclesiological Ramifications

Ecclesiologically, the resurrection of Jesus functions in Luke to clarify the nature of the Eucharist as mealtime with Jesus.[8] The Lukan Jesus is frequently involved in meals: (a) with sinners (5:29–32; 15:1–2; 19:5–7); (b) with Pharisees (7:36–50; 11:37–41; 14:1–6); (c) with disciples (22:19–20; 24:30; 24:41–43; Acts 1:4—the term is literally "to take salt with someone," but the Latin, Syriac, and Coptic translations read "to eat together"—cf. RSV, "while staying with them," 10:41); (d) with the multitudes and disciples (9:11–17). Three of the meals in which the earthly and risen Jesus is involved mention the breaking of bread (9:11–17; 22:19–20; 24:30).

1) Luke 9:11–17 portrays Jesus as one who satisfies the hungry, feeding them through his disciples (cf. Luke 1:53, "He has filled the hungry with good things"; 6:21, "Blessed are you that hunger now, for you shall be filled"). In Luke the feeding is in the neighborhood of Bethsaida ('House of fishing'). Although the crowd could not be satisfied by their natural circumstances, Jesus can meet their need. He takes the five loaves and two fishes, blesses and breaks them, and gives them to his disciples to set before the crowd. "And all ate and were satisfied" (v. 17, RSV).

---

[8] Talbert, *Reading Luke*, 229–31; Robert F. O'Toole, *The Unity of Luke's Theology* (Wilmington, Del.: Michael Glazier, 1984), 46–47.

2) Luke 22:14–38 is a farewell speech of Jesus that contains within it the Third Gospel's account of the Last Supper.[9] In ancient Jewish and Christian farewell speeches there are certain constants. A hero figure knows he is about to die (cf. 2 Pet 1:15, where the apostle describes his death as an exodus). He gathers his primary community about him and gives a farewell speech with two standard components: first, a prediction of what is to take place after he is gone; and second, an exhortation of how his community should behave after he has departed. (a) Luke 22:14 indicates Jesus has gathered his community about him. (b) Verses 15–18 function as Jesus' prediction of his impending death (e.g., "I shall not eat it again until it is fulfilled in the kingdom of God," v. 16, RSV; "I shall not drink of the fruit of the vine until the kingdom of God comes," v. 18, RSV). (c) Verses 19–38 give the predictions and exhortations. Within this section of predictions and exhortations come the Eucharistic words. Assuming the long text, verses 19–20 read:

> And he took bread, and when he had given thanks he broke it and gave it to them, saying "This is my body which is given for you. Do this in remembrance of me" (v. 19, RSV).

> And likewise the cup after supper, saying, "This cup which is poured out for you is the new covenant in my blood" (v. 20, RSV).

Here Jesus (a) asks his disciples to repeat the meal in his personal memory (v. 19, i.e., exhortation) and (b) says his death is the seal of the new covenant (v. 20, i.e., prediction or promise).

In Jewish thought, a covenant was sometimes sealed by a sacrifice (e.g., Gen 15; Exod 24:3–8, "Behold the blood of the covenant which the Lord has made with you," RSV). Matt 26:28a ("this is my blood of the covenant," RSV), Mark 14:24 ("This is my blood of the covenant," RSV), and 1 Cor 11:25 ("This cup is the new covenant in my blood," RSV) join Luke in this emphasis. This was not a sacrifice to deal with sins but one that sealed the pact.

In the Greco-Roman world, memorial meals for founders of semi-religious groups were sometimes held at the founder's request (e.g., the Epicurean school's remembrance of Epicurus and Metrodorus at their annual celebration provided for in Epicurus's will, so Diogenes

---

[9] Talbert, *Reading Luke*, 206–11; for a survey of the literature, see François Bovon, *Luke the Theologian* (trans. Ken McKinney; Allison Park, Pa.: Pickwick, 1987), 379–83.

Laertius, *Vit. phil.* 10.16–22). In an analogous manner, the Lukan Jesus exhorts his followers to repeat the meal as a personal remembrance of him.

3) In Luke 24:30 the risen Jesus "took bread and blessed, and broke it, and gave it to them" (RSV). This action echoes the previous meals of 9:16 and 22:19. At this point, although the disciples have previously been kept from recognizing Jesus (v. 16), now their eyes are opened and they do recognize him (v. 31a). The table fellowship that was interrupted by Jesus' death is here resumed at the risen Christ's initiative. Hereafter, the disciples will go on doing this in remembrance of him (22:19), and they will mediate to the multitudes the nourishment Jesus provides (9:16). Then, too, this incident is but one of several occasions on which the risen Jesus ate with his followers (Luke 24:41–43; Acts 1:4; 10:41). It serves as a bridge between the meals the earthly Jesus had with his disciples and the later church's Eucharist.[10]

In Acts we hear of the church's being involved in breaking bread (Acts 2:42, 46; 20:7; 27:33–36—all but the last text in the setting of Christian worship). Since 'breaking bread' is Eucharistic language in the Third Gospel and since elsewhere in early Christianity there is evidence of cultic meals with only bread and no mention of wine (e.g., *Acts John* 106–110; *Acts Thom.* 27, 49–50, 133; Pseudo-Clementine *Rec.* 4 and *Hom.* 14:7), this seems the appropriate way to construe the expression 'breaking bread' in Acts.

All of this yields the distinctive Lukan understanding of the Eucharist. If Paul understands the Lord's Supper as the moment when Christians remember Jesus' death[11] and the Fourth Gospel views the Eucharist as the cultic extension of the incarnation, Luke-Acts regards it as the extension of mealtime with Jesus. Such Eucharistic breaking bread with Jesus looks back to mealtime with Jesus during his earthly career and his request that it be continued (Luke 9:11–17; 22:19–20); it is now grounded in Jesus' resurrection appearances to his disciples in connection with the breaking of bread (Luke 24:30; Acts 1:4; 10:41); and it anticipates the coming Messianic banquet in the Kingdom of God

---

[10] Robert C. Tannehill, *The Narrative Unity of Luke Acts* (2 vols.; Philadelphia: Fortress, 1986), 1:290.

[11] For various ways this could be understood, see C. H. Talbert, *Reading Corinthians* (New York: Crossroad, 1989), 76–78.

(Luke 13:28–29; 14:15). In Luke-Acts, the resurrection of Jesus supplies the ground for the ongoing Eucharistic breaking of bread in the community of his disciples.

Missiological Ramifications

Luke-Acts sees the church in terms of mission. This mission is grounded in the resurrection of Jesus in at least three ways.[12] First, mission is based on the authoritative word of the risen Christ. Resurrection-appearance narratives are of two types. Some function merely to prove that Jesus is alive; others serve not only this purpose but also to allow the risen Christ to give further instructions to his disciples. Luke 24:36–49 falls into the latter category. After establishing that Jesus is alive and what the nature of his victory over death is (vv. 36–43), the story shifts focus so that verses 44–49 serve the needs of the disciples for further teaching, in particular, about the christological meaning of scripture.

> Thus it is written, that the Christ should suffer and on the third day rise from the dead, and that repentance and forgiveness of sins should be preached in his name to all nations, beginning from Jerusalem. (RSV; cf. Acts 1:8b)

The one who speaks this word of command is the one whose prophecies during his earthly career have now been fulfilled (v. 44; cf. 24:6–8). In the ancient world, fulfilled prophecy legitimated the one who made the prediction (cf. Deut 18:21–22). If Jesus' words have been fulfilled, he is a true prophet who speaks with authority. It is this authoritative prophet, now risen from the dead, who gives the command to mission.

Second, mission is enabled by the risen Christ's gift of the Spirit. Luke 24:49 reads: "And behold, I send the promise of my Father upon you; but stay in the city, until you are clothed with power from on high" (RSV; cf. Acts 1:4–5, 8a). One reason the risen Christ commands the disciples to remain in Jerusalem until the Spirit is given concerns the Lukan belief that a valid testimony to Christ requires two witnesses, in accordance with Deut 19:15, namely, the witness of the apostles and the witness of the Holy Spirit (cf. Acts 5:32, "we are witnesses to these things, and so is the Holy Spirit whom God has given to those who obey him," RSV; cf. 4:29–30, "grant to thy servants to speak thy word with all boldness, while thou stretchest out thy hand to heal,

---

[12] Talbert, *Reading Luke*, 231–33.

and signs and wonders are performed through the name of thy holy servant Jesus," RSV). Another reason the disciples are to remain in Jerusalem until they receive the gift of the Spirit has to do with the Lukan conviction that God has the initiative in salvation history, so that what human beings do must be done in response to divine leading and empowering (cf. Luke 5:1–11, where successful fishing is done only after and in obedience to the directions of Jesus). A third reason the disciples are not to depart Jerusalem before receiving the Spirit is quite simply that until this gift is bestowed on them, they will have no personal desire to bear witness. Acts 1:8 is not a command; it is a promise. "You shall receive power when the Holy Spirit has come upon you; and you shall be my witnesses" (RSV). If disciples have been empowered by the Spirit, they will bear witness. This is the promise the risen Jesus makes.

In Lukan missiology, the principle is clear cut: There is no mission without a prior empowering! This empowering was promised by the pre-Easter Jesus (Luke 11:13) and the resurrected Christ (Luke 24:49a; Acts 1:5, 8a), but it was made possible because of Jesus' resurrection-exaltation. Acts 2:32–33 puts it plainly:

> This Jesus God raised up, and of that we all are witnesses. Being therefore exalted at the right hand of God, and having received from the Father the promise of the Holy Spirit, he has poured out this which you see and hear. (RSV)

Third, those who will be involved in mission are placed under the protection of the risen Lord. Luke 24:50 says that prior to his ascension, the risen Jesus "led them out as far as Bethany, and lifting up his hands he blessed them" (assured them of God's favor and support; RSV).[13] Blessings were often part of final-departure scenes in Jewish literature (e.g., Gen 27:4; 48:15–16). This act of blessing is like that of the high priest, Simon, in Sir 50:19–20. With a priestly act, the risen Christ puts his disciples who are to be involved in mission under the protection of God before he leaves them (cf. Matt 28:20, "and lo, I am with you to the end of the Age," RSV; John 17:11, 15, "Holy Father, keep them in thy name. ... I do not pray that thou shouldst take them out of the world, but that thou shouldst keep them from the evil one," RSV, for similar concerns). After blessing the disciples, Jesus ascends heavenward. For their part, the disciples obediently return to Jerusalem, there to await the gift of the Spirit and the beginning of their mission to the nations.

---

[13] Frederick W. Danker, *Jesus and the New Age* (Philadelphia: Fortress, 1988), 400.

CHAPTER NINE

CONVERSION IN THE ACTS OF THE APOSTLES: ANCIENT AUDITORS' PERCEPTIONS

Conversion is a central focus of Acts, maybe *the* central focus.[1] There are at least ten conversion narratives in Acts[2] plus numerous statements by the narrator about such phenomena. In 1979, Paulist Press published *The Salvation of the Gentiles* by Jacques Dupont, which contained an essay on 'Conversion in the Acts of the Apostles.'[3] Dupont contended the following concerning conversion in Acts: (1) that it belonged to the moral category of conversion which was concerned with sin and forgiveness, (2) that it involved a 'turning from' as well as a 'turning to,' (3) that its catalysts were miracles and preaching, (4) that its roots were in divine grace, and (5) that it resulted in a continuing change of life. Looking back on Dupont's study, one may conclude that the only point that needs modification is the first one. In Acts, instances are identifiable of both the moral and the cognitive types of conversion (e.g., the account that includes Simon in Acts 8 is an example of cognitive conversion because his worldview, even after his baptism, includes magic; 13:4–12; 14:8–18; 17:22–31).[4] With this one adjustment,

---

[1] Thomas M. Finn, *From Death to Rebirth: Ritual and Conversion in Antiquity* (New York: Paulist, 1997), 27, says conversion is the major theme of Acts.

[2] Finn, *From Death to Rebirth*, 27, says there are twenty-one. In the summer of 1995, my student, Craig Joseph, and I attempted to build a database of ancient conversion accounts and, on the basis of an examination of that collection to determine whether or not there was a set form for a conversion story. We concluded that it is possible to isolate five stable components in these ancient conversion narratives: (1) the context, (2) the catalysts leading to conversion, (3) the counter-forces which pose an obstacle or opposition, (4) the conversion itself, and (5) the confirmation of the genuineness of the conversion by postconversion evidence. These results essentially confirmed an earlier attempt by Robert Allen Black, 'The Conversion Stories in the Acts of the Apostles' (Ph.D. diss., Emory University, 1985). A reading of Acts then showed ten narratives which contained these five components: (1) 2:1–47, (2) 3:1–4:37, (3) 8:4–25, (4) 8:26–40, (5) 9:1–22, (6) 10:1–48, (7) 13:6–12, (8) 13:13–52, (9) 16:11–15, and (10) 16:25–34.

[3] Jacques Dupont, *The Salvation of the Gentiles* (New York: Paulist, 1979) 61–84. Cf. further R. Michiels, 'La conception lucanienne de la conversion,' *ETL* 41 (1965): 42–78; and Augustin George, *Études sur l'oeuvre de Luc* (Sources bibliques; Paris: Editions Gabalda, 1978), 351–68.

[4] Nancy Shumate, *Crisis and Conversion in Apuleius' Metamorphoses* (Ann Arbor: Univer-

I want to employ Dupont's description of conversion in this study of Acts and ask a further question: How would ancient auditors have heard Acts' description of Christian conversion?[5] An answer to this question will be attempted, mostly but not exclusively, on the basis of a comparison of Acts with selected conversion narratives from antiquity.[6] We will take up in order the five parts of our modified version of Dupont's description of conversion in Acts.

Moral and Cognitive Conversions

First, if we grant the modification of Dupont's proposals as stated above, Acts describes some conversions as primarily moral, which involve issues of sin and forgiveness (e.g., 2:38; 3:19; 5:30–31; 10:43; 13:38; 26:17–18), and others as essentially cognitive, which involve a shift of basic paradigms about the world, that is, a movement from idolatry to the worship of the living God (e.g., 13:4–12; 14:8–18; 17:22–31). How would people outside of messianic Judaism have heard this depiction?

On the one hand, a moral type of conversion was known to both Jewish and pagan[7] persons alike.

---

sity of Michigan Press, 1996) works out the contrast between a moral type of conversion in which the stress is ethical, a movement from vice to virtue in which the convert recognizes his/her shortcomings in light of a heightened awareness of morality, and a cognitive type of conversion in which there is a collapse of an entire system of premises and assumptions about how the world works and its replacement by one radically different, a change of worldviews. In Acts, Jews and God-fearers are offered forgiveness for sins through Jesus (a moral type of conversion) while pagans are called upon to experience a shift from polytheism to monotheism (a cognitive type of conversion).

[5] The audience-oriented approach taken here is like that of Peter J. Rabinowitz, 'Whirl Without End: Audience-Oriented Criticism,' in *Contemporary Literary Theory* (ed. G. Douglas Atkins and Laura Morrow; Amherst: University of Massachusetts Press, 1989), 81–100; idem, 'Truth in Fiction: A Reexamination of Audiences,' *Crln* 4 (1977): 121–42; and idem, *Before Reading. Narrative Conventions and the Politics of Interpretation* (Ithaca, N.Y.: Cornell University Press, 1987), 15–46. Rabinowitz defines the 'authorial audience' as the readers that the author has in mind in creating the text. These readers possess the sociocultural knowledge and interpretive skills necessary to actualize the text's meaning. Unlike some contemporary uses of the expression 'implied reader,' the term 'authorial audience' locates the interaction of text and reader in a particular sociohistorical context.

[6] The database of conversion narratives from antiquity may be found in my *Reading Acts* (New York: Crossroad, 1997) in the section on Acts 9:1–31. Some scholars would also include Dio Chrysostom's *De exilio* and Aelius Aristides' Ἱερῶν λόγοι. I have reservations about both and so have omitted them.

[7] See Finn, *From Death to Rebirth*, 45–46, for a discussion of the term.

1) *Jewish*. One example will suffice. Although the material is not in the form of a conversion narrative, the synoptic traditions about John the Baptist (Matt 3:1-12; Mark 1:2-8; Luke 3:1-14) relate John's call for a repentance/conversion that involved the forgiveness of sins and a change of behavior in an ethical direction. Such a view of conversion was far from unique in ancient Judaism.

2) *Pagan*. Conversion to philosophy belongs to the moral type, although the categories employed are those of vice and virtue rather than sin and forgiveness. Two examples will suffice.[8] The first example is the case of Polemo. In *Bis accusatus* (ca. A.D. 165), Lucian presents the judicial case, Drink versus the Academy, in which Drink accuses the Academy of luring away her faithful servant, Polemo. In section 17, the Academy responds.

> One day he reached my door. He found it open: I was discoursing to a company of my disciples, as is my want, upon virtue and temperance. He stood there, with a flute-girl at his side and the garlands on his head, and sought at first to drown our conversation with his noisy outcry. But we paid no heed to him, and little by little our words produced a sobering effect, for Drink had not the entire possession of him: he bade the flute-girl cease, tore off his garlands, and looked with shame at his luxurious dress. Like one waking from sleep, he saw himself as he was, and repented his past life; the flush of drunkenness faded and vanished from his cheek, and was succeeded by a blush of shame; at last, not (as plaintiff would have you believe) in response to any invitation of mine, nor under any compulsion, but of his own free will, and in the conviction of my superiority, he renounced his former mistress there and then, and entered my service.[9]

This is a conversion from vice to virtue.

A second example of philosophical conversion of the moral variety is Lucian's *Nigrinus* (mid-second century A.D.). Lucian presents a dialogue between two friends, one (Lucian?) who has been converted by exposure to Nigrinus and the other who is befuddled by his friend's new behavior (1-5). The friend sets the tone with his comment about the other's behavior since he came back. "You don't deign to notice us anymore, you don't associate with us, and you don't join in our conversations; you have changed all of a sudden. ... [W]hat is the cause

---

[8] One could also refer to the conversion of the brother of Apollonius of Tyana in Philostratus, *Vit. Apoll.* 1.13.

[9] Translation from F G. Fowler and H. G. Fowler, *The Works of Lucian of Samosata* (4 vols.; Oxford: Clarendon, 1949), 3:155-56.

of all this?" The other answers: "I have come back to you transformed ... into a happy and blissful man—in the language of the stage, 'thrice blessed.'" The friend replies: "In so short a time?" The other responds: "Yes. Don't you think it wonderful, in the name of Zeus, that once a slave, I am now free; once poor, now rich indeed; once witless and befogged, now saner?" The friend replies: "I don't clearly understand what you mean." The other then tells of his experience. He was going to Rome to see an oculist about eye trouble. While there he went early one morning to pay his respects to Nigrinus the Platonic philosopher, something he had not done for some time. Nigrinus began to speak to him. He praised philosophy and the freedom it gives; he ridiculed the things that are commonly counted blessings like wealth and reputation, dominion and honor, purple and gold. As a result, the other says: "I couldn't imagine what had come over me." The other now regarded all these things as paltry and ridiculous and was, in his words, "glad to be looking up, as it were, out of the murky atmosphere of my past life to a clear sky and a great light." He forgot his eye ailment as he became sharpersighted in his soul. "There you have it! I am going about enraptured and drunk with the wine of his discourse" (LCL). This dialogue, then, is also indicative of a conversion from vice to virtue.

In both examples of conversion to philosophy given above, the conversion is moral. There is a renunciation of a lifestyle (drunkenness, luxury) that is now replaced with a higher virtue (sobriety, simplicity). At the same time, the philosophic convert remains within the pagan, polytheistic worldview. His conversion is moral not cognitive.[10]

On the other hand, a cognitive type of conversion was also known to both Jewish and pagan persons in antiquity.

---

[10] Wayne A. Meeks, *The Origins of Christian Morality: The First Two Centuries* (New Haven: Yale University Press, 1993), 28, agrees with A. D. Nock that "being or becoming religious in the Greco-Roman world did not entail ... moral transformation." His position is critiqued by Thomas M. Finn, review of Wayne A. Meeks, *The Origins of Christian Morality: The First Two Centuries*, CBQ 57 (1995): 602. There are texts that cast doubt on the long held stereotype about Greek religion: (1) Euripides, *Bacchae*, lines 72–77 ("O blessed he who in happiness knowing the rituals of the gods makes holy his way of life and mingles his spirit with the sacred band."); (2) Theophrastus, *Pietate*, extant in fragments attested by Porphyry (*Abst.*), discusses the relationship between ethics and sacrifice (e.g., "One must go to the sacrifices having a soul pure from evils."); (3) Porphyry, *De abstentia*, quotes an inscription at the entrance to the sanctuary at Epidauros: "Pure must one be when entering the temple. ... But purity is thinking holy things." Among pagans, it was not just in philosophy that conversion meant a changed lifestyle. This is not to deny that in some pagan religion ethics were irrelevant; it is to say that not all pagan cultic religion was devoid of ethical concern.

1) *Jewish*. The five major conversion narratives from ancient Judaism about which I know[11] have one thing in common: they all understand conversion as the movement from a worship of idols to the worship of the living God. This commonality is found in the following accounts: the conversion of Achior, an officer in the Ammonite army (Jdt 14; second century B.C.); the conversion of Aseneth (*Jos. Asen.*; 100 B.C.-A.D. 100);[12] the case for Izates as recounted by Josephus (*A.J.* 20.2.3-4, 34-48); Job (*T. Job* 2-5; 100 B.C.-A.D. 100); and Abraham (*Apoc. Ab.* 1-7; A.D. 100-200). The conversion of these Gentiles to Judaism was understood as a cognitive shift from a polytheistic frame of reference to a monotheistic worldview.

2) *Pagan*. Nancy Shumate's *Crisis and Conversion in Apuleius' Metamorphoses* offers a reading of the novel as a narrative of religious experience and specifically as a narrative of conversion. Throughout this work, Shumate contends that Lucius's conversion is not moral but cognitive. She asserts: "The axis upon which the conversion of Lucius turns is one of epistemological rupture rather than moral reform."[13] Conversion of this type involves a comprehensive and radical shift from one paradigm of interpreting and constructing reality to another. In spite of having a secondary moral component, this model is primarily a cognitive one.[14] It is a mistake to see Lucius's transformation as punishment for his moral sins (lust and striving after forbidden knowledge) and to see Isis as an agent of moral purification.[15] Rather, Lucius's conversion is a move from one plausibility structure to another, from one worldview to another. It is a process of changing a sense of root reality, the ground of being that orients and orders experience.[16] Shumate concludes:

> Lucius begins with his worldview bounded by conventional structures of meaning and is thrown off-balance when these structures collapse. For

---

[11] I am not counting the conversion of Naaman in 2 Kgs 5. This seems closer to adhesion than conversion.

[12] Randall D. Chesnutt, *From Death to Life: Conversion in Joseph and Aseneth* (JSPSup 16; Sheffield: Sheffield Academic Press, 1995), 150: "Conversion in Joseph and Aseneth is ... conceived as a transition from death and destruction which characterize the predicament of the godless to the life and immortality enjoyed by those who worship the true God, and creation imagery is the descriptive language used most often."

[13] Shumate, *Crisis and Conversion*, 34.
[14] Ibid., 139.
[15] Ibid., 147.
[16] Ibid., 173-74, 184.

this reason it is in the end the structuring function of Isis ... to which he is especially attracted.[17]

Both Jewish and pagan persons, therefore, knew of cognitive type conversions.

When Mediterranean auditors heard Acts read and encountered both its moral and cognitive types of conversion, they would have been sensitized already to both types of life transformation in their ancient milieu. In respect to the possibility of moral and cognitive conversions, Acts would have posed little formal discontinuity between Christian conversion and that of non-messianic Jews and Greco-Roman pagans.

'Turning From' and 'Turning To'

Second, Dupont argues further that conversion in Acts involves both a 'turning from' and a 'turning to' (e.g., 14:15–16, turning from idols to the living God; 26:18, turning from darkness to light, from Satan to God).[18] This, of course, fits A. D. Nock's definition of conversion: an experience that involves belief that the old was wrong and the new is right. According to Nock, this is different from 'adhesion' in which one turns toward a deity and an accompanying lifestyle without ever breaking off from another prior deity or lifestyle. In Nock's view, Judaism, Christianity, and pagan philosophy demanded conversion while cultic paganism expected only adhesion.[19] What the ancient textual evidence shows, however, is that there is a 'turning away' and a 'turning towards' not only in Judaism and in philosophy but also surprisingly in some forms of cultic paganism.

1) *Jewish*. The Hellenistic-Jewish romance, *Joseph and Aseneth*, tells the story of a pagan girl, Aseneth, who converts to Judaism as a condition for marrying Joseph. In 9:2, we hear that she "repented of her (infatuation with the) gods whom she used to worship, and spurned all the idols." In 13:11–12, she cries out to the God of Joseph:

> Behold now, all the gods whom I once used to worship in ignorance: I have now recognized that they were dumb and dead idols, and I have

---

[17] Ibid., 50.
[18] The language of turning (ἐπιστρέφειν and cognates) is shared by pagans, Jews, and Christians.
[19] A. D. Nock, *Conversion* (London: Oxford University Press, 1933), 7, 14, 134, 179.

caused them to be trampled underfoot by men, ... And with you I have taken refuge, O Lord my God.[20]

Aseneth turns from idols to the living God of Joseph. This conversion from idolatry to the living God is characteristic of all five of the post-biblical narratives of Gentile conversion to Judaism that I have mentioned above.

2) *Pagan.* On the one hand, in philosophical conversions there is the same double turning that we have seen in conversions of Gentiles to Judaism.[21] For instance, in *Nigrinus*, Lucian (or another) turns from luxury to the simplicity of the philosophic way. The case is similar with Polemo. Lucian says that, once exposed to the Academy's discourse, Polemo "repented of his past life," he "renounced his former mistress," and he "entered my service" (*Bis acc.* 17).[22] In Philostratus's *Vita Apollonii*, a youth is converted from skepticism to belief in the immortality of the soul by an appearance of Apollonius to him after the philosopher's departure from this life (8.31). On the other hand, in the type of cultic paganism reflected in Apuleius's *Metamorphoses*, Lucius turns from hostile fate and magic as a way to manipulate that fate, to the goddess Isis for her protection.[23] Isis, not magic, saves, so Lucius comes to believe.

What is seldom recognized is that cultic paganism often involved the dual turning.[24] Two examples will suffice to show this to be the case. One example is found in Plutarch's *De defectu oraculum* (434.45d-f), which captures the conversation of Greeks about the decreased consultation and utilization of the country's oracles.

> "I do not know," said Demetrius, "the state of affairs there at present; for as you all know, I have been out of the country for a long time now. But when I was there, both the oracle of Mopsus and that of Amphilocus

---

[20] The translation is from James H. Charlesworth, ed., *The Old Testament Pseudepigrapha* (2 vols.; Garden City, N.Y.: Doubleday, 1983, 1985), 2:223.

[21] The origins of this dualism would be Plato, *Resp.* 518c–d where he speaks of the conversion of the soul as the movement from darkness to light.

[22] Not all stories of conversion to philosophy explicitly involve the double turning: e.g., Porphyry's *Vit. Plot.* 3 speaks only of his following Ammonius continuously for eleven years.

[23] This was regarded as an exception by Nock, *Conversion*, 138–55.

[24] This is not to deny that some conversion narratives tell only of adhesion, e.g., Ovid, *Metam.* 3.574–698, tells of the adhesion of one Acoetes to the worship of Dionysius.

were still flourishing. I have a most amazing thing to tell as the result of my visit to the oracle of Mopsus. The ruler of Cilicia was himself still of two minds toward religious matters. This, I think, was because his skepticism lacked conviction, for in all else he was an arrogant and contemptible man. Since he kept about himself certain Epicureans, who, because of their admirable nature studies, forsooth, have an arrogant contempt, as they themselves aver, for all things such as oracles, he sent in a freedman, like a spy into the enemy's territory, arranging that he should have a sealed tablet, on the inside of which was written the inquiry without anyone's knowing what it was. The man accordingly, as is the custom, passed the night in the sacred precinct and went to sleep, and in the morning reported a dream in this fashion: it seemed to him that a handsome man stood beside him who uttered just one word 'Black' and nothing more, and was gone immediately. The thing seemed passing strange to us, and raised much inquiry, but the ruler was astounded and fell down and worshipped; then opening the tablet he showed written there the question: 'Shall I sacrifice to you a white bull or a black?' The result was that the Epicureans were put to confusion, and the ruler himself not only duly performed the sacrifice, but ever after revered Mopsus." (LCL)

Here a pagan person turns from skeptical philosophy to traditional religion.

A second example of the dual turning in the conversion to cultic paganism is found in the first book of Horace's *Carmina* (ca. 23 B.C.). *Carmina* 34 describes the poet's renunciation of skeptical philosophy and his return to the traditional state religion:

> My religious devotions were mean and infrequent.
> I strayed, a foolish man of wisdom,
> But now I set my sails
> in reverse, compelled to trace
>
> abandoned routes; for Jove who normally
> parts the clouds by fire crossed
> the empty sky with his thundering
> horses and aerial chariot
>
> by which the solid earth and wandering
> rivers, the dreaded Taenaran cave,
> the Atlantic shore, and the Styx
> are shaken. God can raise

the depths, diminish distinction, reveal
the obscure. Rapacious Fortune on whirring
wings delights in moving
crowns from head to head.[25]

Here Horace claims he moved from religious skepticism back to traditional religion because of his experience of the inexplicable phenomenon of thunder on a clear day. He remains within a pagan frame of reference, but he has been converted from one form of paganism to another.[26]

Since both Jewish and pagan persons had knowledge of conversion as a 'turning from' and as a 'turning to,' they would have felt little formal discontinuity if and when they heard the narrative of Acts with its depiction of conversion in these terms.

Miracles and Preaching as Catalysts

Third, Dupont contends that in Acts the catalysts of conversion are preaching (e.g., 2:37–38; 4:3; 10:44; 11:19–21) and miracles (e.g., 4:33; 9:32–34; 9:36–43; 14:3). This fits nicely into the ancient Greco-Roman context of both Jewish and pagan persons.[27]

1) *Jewish.* On the one hand, Josephus (*A.J.* 20.2.3–4 §34–48) tells of the conversion of the royal house of Adiabene. It happened because a certain Jewish merchant, whose name was Ananias, taught the women who belonged to the king to "worship God according to the Jewish religion." Ananias also persuaded Izates, the king's son, to embrace Judaism as well. Here conversion is prompted by teaching. On the other hand, in Judith, the conversion of Achior, an officer in the Ammonite

---

[25] Translation from David Mulroy, *Horace's Odes and Epodes* (Ann Arbor: University of Michigan Press, 1994), 93–94.

[26] This evidence demands a rather severe revision of Nock's categories. This is important because Nock's distinction between Jewish and Christian conversion and cultic pagan adhesion underlies most New Testament scholarship today. See, e.g., Meeks, *The Origins of Christian Morality*, 28; John E. Stambaugh and David L. Batch, *The New Testament in Its Social Environment* (LEC; Philadelphia: Westminster, 1986), 45–46; and Martin Goodman, *Mission and Conversion: Proselytizing in the Religious History of the Roman Empire* (Oxford: Clarendon, 1994), 27.

[27] Ramsay MacMullen, 'Two Types of Conversion to Early Christianity,' *VC* 37 (1983): 174–92 and elsewhere, contends that early Christianity grew mainly through demonstrations of divine power/miracles. There would have been a cultural predisposition in this direction apart from Christianity.

army, is effected when he hears that Judith has slain the Assyrian general, Holofernes. "And when Achior saw all that the God of Israel had done, he believed in God with all his heart, and accepted circumcision and was adopted into the household of Israel" (Jdt 14:10). Both teaching and marvels functioned as catalysts for conversion in ancient Judaism.

2) *Pagan*. On the one hand, conversion to philosophy was usually due to hearing the teaching of the philosopher. So Polemo is brought from drunkenness to sobriety by exposure to the words of Xenocrates. Diogenes Laertius says that, in spite of the young man's intrusion, Xenocrates "without being at all disturbed went on with his discourse as before, the subject being temperance. The lad, as he listened, by degrees was taken in the toils" (*Vit. phil.* 4.3.16–18). Also, Lucian (or another) becomes enraptured and transformed as a result of hearing the words of Nigrinus in Rome. Lucian, speaking of Nigrinus, says: "Beginning to talk on these topics and to explain his position, ... he poured enough ambrosial speech over me to put out of date the famous sirens ... and the nightingales and the lotus of Homer. A divine utterance!" (*Nigr.* 17). On the other hand, conversion within cultic paganism was usually linked to a miracle. Lucius becomes a devotee of Isis when she effects his transformation from a donkey to human form. The ruler of Cilicia becomes a worshipper of Mopsus as a result of a miracle of knowledge. Horace changes orientation from skeptical philosophy to traditional religion because of an unprecedented event that was, to him, best explained in terms of traditional mythology.[28]

Whether one was Jewish or pagan, preaching/teaching and miracle were the normal catalysts of conversion in antiquity. If and when such people of antiquity heard the narrative of Acts, they would have felt at home in its religious world, at least in respect to the forces which it depicts as the catalysts of conversion.

Divine Grace

Fourth, Dupont argues that in Acts the roots of conversion are in divine grace. God grants salvation (5:31; 11:18; 13:48; 15:9, 14; 16:14). The same assumptions are found in non-messianic Jewish and pagan traditions.

---

[28] The Christian Apocryphal Acts express the conviction that more than anything else miracles initiate the process of conversion. Cf. Eugene V. Gallagher, 'Conversion and Salvation in the Apocryphal Acts of the Apostles,' *Sec Cent* 8 (1991): 13–30.

1) *Jewish.* In the *Testament of Job* 2–5 we hear of the conversion of Job from idolatry to faith in the living God, the creator. The process involves two steps. First there is a time of reasoning in which Job's critical faculties undermine the status of idols. Then there is a divine disclosure which grants Job the true knowledge he seeks. This act of divine grace enables Job to make the transition from idolatry to true faith. In the *Apocalypse of Abraham* 1–7, the patriarch's conversion follows the same two steps noted in the case of Job. Abraham is initially involved in a rational critique of idols (1–6); he then is the recipient of a divine disclosure which enables the transition to faith in the living God (6–7). In both of these Jewish documents, the process of conversion is possible only because divine grace grants an individual what is needed.

2) *Pagan.* The same emphasis may be found in pagan sources as well. Shumate's study of Apuleius's *Metamorphoses* shows how the preparation for Lucius's conversion operates on an almost entirely passive subject. In theological terms, this conversion occurs because of grace.[29] Furthermore, just as in the cases of Job and Abraham, Lucius's transition to devotion to Isis is made possible only by her self-disclosure to him. This comes on the beach, in her actions on his behalf to restore him to human form, and by her later invitation to him to be initiated. Lucius's conversion is by grace from first to last. In the accounts of conversion to philosophy one does not normally hear such an explicit emphasis on divine grace. Nevertheless, Dio Chrysostom says that "whatever wise and true words about the gods and the universe there are to be found among men, none have ever lodged in human souls except by the divine will" (*1 Regn.* 57). The assumptions of pagan philosophy allowed for the possibility of belief in the graced nature of conversion.

Once again, the ancient Mediterranean auditors who heard the Acts of the Apostles would sense continuity between the larger cultural expectations about conversion and those depicted in Acts. Non-messianic Judaism and Greco-Roman paganism allowed for a common belief in deity as the ultimate author of change.[30]

---

[29] Shumate, *Crisis and Conversion*, 121–22.
[30] Finn, *From Death to Rebirth*, 240.

A Continuing Change of Life

Fifth, the final aspect of Dupont's portrayal of conversion in Acts is that Christian conversion involves a continuing change of life. This belief was not alien to Mediterranean antiquity generally.

1) *Jewish*. The account of the conversion of Achior, which we introduced earlier, emphasized the ongoing significance of his newfound faith and circumcision by closing with the note that he remained committed to Judaism "unto this day" (Jdt 14:10). There was permanence to the conversion. In the *Testament of Job*, the hero makes his commitment to renounce idols and worship the creator. He says to God: "Till death I will endure: I will not step back at all" (5:1).[31] Subsequent events depict Job as showing endurance, as not growing weary, and as finally triumphing over Satan (27:4–5). Thus, his conversion also apparently involved a continuing commitment to the convert's change of life-orientation.

2) *Pagan*. On the one hand, a continuing change of life-orientation was characteristic of a true conversion to philosophy, Diogenes Laertius says of Polemo who was converted by listening to Xenocrates' words about temperance: "He became so industrious as to surpass all the other scholars, and rose to be himself head of the school in the 116th Olympiad" (*Vit. phil.* 3.16–18), Seneca claimed that what is stated in the conversion narrative itself is typical of the life of philosophy:

> I understand, Lucilius, that I am not only being improved but that I am being transformed. I do not already promise or hope that nothing is left in me that needs change. ... The very fact that the soul sees failings in itself which it previously ignored is a proof of its change to a better state. (*Ep.* 6.1, LCL)

Plutarch speaks to the same issue:

> What possible form of argument, my dear Sosius Senecio, will keep alive in a man the consciousness that he is growing better in regard to virtue, if it is a fact that the successive stages of his progress produce no abatement of his unwisdom. ... [I]n the study of philosophy, neither progress nor any sense of progress is to be assumed, if the soul does not put aside any of its gross stupidity and purge itself thereof, and if ... it is wedded to the evil. (*Virt. prof.* 75.1b-d, LCL)

---

[31] Translation is from Charlesworth, *The Old Testament Pseudepigrapha*, 1:841.

The argument moves on the assumption that conversion to philosophy involves a change of life by degrees and in stages during one's entire lifetime.

On the other hand, the persistent effects of a change can be found in cultic paganism as well. Plutarch's account of the conversion of a ruler of Cilicia to belief in the oracle of Mopsus ends with the statement that "the Epicureans were put to confusion, and the ruler himself not only duly performed the sacrifice, but ever after revered Mopsus" (*Def. orac.* 434.45d-f).

Whether it be a Jewish or pagan person in Mediterranean antiquity, conversion was believed to involve a change of orientation that continued throughout one's lifetime.[32] Once again, the ancient auditors who heard the Acts narrative and reflected on its depiction of Christian conversion would have sensed little formal discontinuity in the way conversion was described.

This essay began with a slightly modified form of Jacques Dupont's description of Christian conversion as depicted in the Acts of the Apostles. It then sought to determine whether or not auditors from non-messianic Judaism, on the one hand, and pagan philosophy and cultic paganism, on the other, would have heard continuities or discontinuities in the depiction of conversion in the narrative of Acts. This brief comparison has enabled us to see that, insofar as the formal components of conversion are concerned, non-Christian auditors in antiquity would have sensed enough continuities with the depiction of Christian conversion in Acts to be able to understand it.[33] Their difficulty,

---

[32] Both Jews and pagans were aware of and concerned about conversions away from their positions to others. 1 Macc (1:10–15, 41–50; 2:15–22) tells of Jewish conversion in Palestine to pagan ways under Antiochus Epiphanes. Cf. Harry A. Wolfson, *Philo: Foundations of Religious Philosophy in Judaism, Christianity, and Islam* (2 vols.; Cambridge, Mass.: Harvard University Press, 1948), 1:73–85, who identifies at least three reasons for Jewish conversion to paganism in Alexandria. Aulus Gellius, *Noct. att.* 3.13.1–5 tells of Demosthenes' leaving Plato for Callistratus, 5.3 tells how Protagoras forsook philosophy for rhetoric.

[33] An obvious question to be raised at this point has to do with whether or not pagans and non-messianic Jews engaged in aggressive proselytizing as did the messianists and Christians. The issue is focused especially on non-messianic Judaism. Since the work of Schurer and Juster at the beginning of this century, most scholars have subscribed to the view that Jewish proselytizing reached a peak of intensity in the first century A.D. In recent years there has been some dissent (e.g., J. Munck, D. Rokeah, E. Will, and C. Orrieux, and most recently, Martin Goodman and Scott McKnight). James Carleton Paget, 'Jewish Proselytism at the Time of Christian Origins: Chimera or Reality?' *JSNT* 62 (1996): 65–103, surveys the evidence and argu-

if they felt one, would have been with the object/content of the Christian conversion experience (that is, Christ), not with its formal components.

---

ments and concludes that some Jews proselytized, contra Goodman and McKnight. Shaye J. D. Cohen, *From the Maccabees to the Mishnah* (LEC; Philadelphia: Westminster, 1987), 57, draws a similar conclusion: "There is no evidence of an organized Jewish mission to the Gentiles, but individuals seem to have engaged in this activity on their own."

CHAPTER TEN

ACTS 20:7–12 AS EARLY CHRISTIAN APOLOGETIC

In the narrative flow, Acts 20:1–21:26 carries out Paul's resolution in 19:21 to go to Jerusalem after having passed through Macedonia and Achaia. The functions of the large thought unit within the overall plot are three: (1) to depict Paul's care of his churches as he is leaving them, as a model for ministry (20:2; 20:7–12; 20:17–35); (2) to parallel Jesus' journey to Jerusalem in Luke 9:51–19:44 and his acceptance of God's will in Luke 22:42 with the experience of Paul, as a way of interpreting Paul's sufferings; and (3) to show Paul's spirit of accommodation in his quest for church unity (21:18–26).[1] Our passage, 20:7–12, fits within the first function. It shows concretely the truth of Paul's assertions in Acts 20:20, 27, 31 (e.g., v. 31—"I did not cease *night or day* to admonish everyone with tears," RSV).

It is possible, moreover, that an additional aim is operative in this passage, an apologetic one. If so, this would not be the only place in Acts where apologetic purposes are being served.[2] The possibility of an apologetic function for Acts 20:7–12 is raised by two sets of details in the pericope: (1) the reference to the 'many lamps' in verse 8, and (2) the reference to the fall, death, and resuscitation of the boy, Eutychus, in the context of Christian worship (vv. 9, 10, 12). The purpose of this essay will be to explore how an ancient auditor might have heard Acts 20:7–12, given these details. We begin with the reference to 'many lamps.'

The Many Lamps

The reference to the 'many lamps' in verse 8 has been variously interpreted in the past.

---

[1] Charles H. Talbert, *Reading Acts: A Literary and Theological Commentary on the Acts of the Apostles* (New York: Crossroad, 1997).
[2] A. J. Malherbe, 'Not in a Corner: Early Christian Apologetic in Acts 26:26,' in *Paul and the Popular Philosophers* (Minneapolis: Fortress, 1989), 147–63.

1) Some think that the presence of lamps serves no discernible purpose. In antiquity, for example, the Western witness, D, has not 'lamps' (λαμπάδες) but rather 'windows' (ὑπολαμπάδες). In the modern period, Jürgen Roloff says merely that it is unclear why the lamps are mentioned.[3] A confession of ignorance is an honest response by an interpreter but it leaves open the door for others to explore additional possibilities.

2) Others think that the reference to 'lamps' has an historical function. The many lamps, which depleted the oxygen in the air, were the cause of Eutychus's drowsiness and his falling asleep.[4] Even if one assumes the narrative is historical, however, the text does not make any explicit cause and effect connections between the lamps and Eutychus's falling asleep.

3) Still others think Acts 20:7–12 has a novelistic function. The lamps are an incidental detail—like mention of the time of night, the length of the discourse, the number of stories in the house, and the name of the youth—included by a good fictional imagination in a story designed to portray the power of the risen Jesus at work in Paul.[5] A judgment about the genre of the material and the lack of the historicity of the material, however, does not thereby exclude a 'meaning function' for the details in the narrative of Acts.

4) Yet others think that Acts 20:7–12 has a symbolic function.[6] The story depicts the church with the word and sacrament as the sphere of light and life, outside of which is darkness and death, and warns believers to remain awake lest they fall into the darkness and perish. Whereas Luke would doubtless have agreed with the proposed theological statements associated with the symbolic interpretation (e.g., Luke 22:45–46), it is not characteristic of Luke to allegorize his narratives.

---

[3] Jürgen Roloff, *Die Apostelgeschichte* (NTD 5; Göttingen: Vandenhoeck & Ruprecht, 1981), 298.

[4] E.g., F. F. Bruce, *The Book of Acts* (NICNT; Grand Rapids: Eerdmans, 1956), 408.

[5] Luke T. Johnson, *The Acts of the Apostles* (SP 5; Collegeville, Minn.: Liturgical Press, 1992), 356, 358.

[6] B. Tremel, 'A propos d'Actes 20:7–12: Puissance du thaumaturge ou du temoin?' *RTP* 112 (1980): 359–69. Both Gerhard Schneider, *Die Apostelgeschichte, Teil 2* (HTKNT; Freiburg: Herder, 1982), 284–85, and Robert Tannehill, *The Narrative Unity of Luke-Acts*, (2 vols; Minneapolis: Fortress, 1990), 2:249–50, are sympathetic with Tremel's thesis.

5) A final group of scholars regard Acts 20:7–12 as having an apologetic function.[7] The many lights prove the nonsubversive and moral nature of the worship assemblies of Christians, defending against charges that Christians engaged in subversive activities and immorality in the darkness of their gatherings. The major argument against this reading is that the evidence for such charges against Christians is later than Acts.[8]

It is the thesis of this part of this essay that the suspicion of night meetings, especially religious ones, was so pervasive in Mediterranean culture that an auditor of Acts would automatically have heard the way the story was told as a legitimation of Christian worship and as protection against past, present, or potential charges against Christian assemblies. The evidence that follows shows this to be the case.

1) *Pagan charges against other pagans.* Romans feared night meetings for two reasons: conspiracy and immorality. On the one hand, conspiracy was associated in the Roman mind with night meetings. (a) Cicero's speech against Cataline reflects the mindset. He asks the accused:

> Do you not see that your conspiracy is held fast by the knowledge of all these men? Do you not think that there is a man among us who does not know what you did last night or the night before last, where you were, whom you summoned to your meeting, what decision you reached? (*Cat.* 1.1, LCL)

Later Cicero describes in detail the association of the conspiracy with nocturnal activity.

> As it was growing dark, they (Cataline's conspirators) went secretly to the Mulvian Bridge and there divided their party into two groups in the near-by houses, so that the Tiber and the bridge lay between them. ... At about three o'clock in the morning when the envoys of the Allobroges with a large retinue and accompanied by Volturicius were beginning to cross the Mulvian Bridge, these men fell upon them, and both sides drew their swords. (*Cat.* 3.5–6, LCL)

(b) Juvenal continues the comment on the conspiracy of Cataline in his *Satirae*.

> Where can be found, O Cataline, nobler ancestors than thine, or than thine, Cethegus? Yet you plot a night attack, you prepare to give our

---

[7] E.g., Ernst Haenchen, *The Acts of the Apostles* (Philadelphia: Westminster, 1971), 585.
[8] Hans Conzelmann, *Acts of the Apostles* (Hermeneia; Philadelphia: Fortress, 1987), 169.

> houses and temples to the flames as though you were the sons of trousered Gauls, or sprung from the Senones, daring deeds that deserved the shirt of torture. (*Sat.* 8.231–35, LCL)

The connection of conspiracy with night meetings was ingrained in the Roman consciousness.

On the other hand, sexual immorality was associated by Mediterranean peoples with night meetings. First, in the 5th century B.C., Euripides has Pentheus voice the Greeks' concern about Bacchic night-time excesses.

> It chanced that, sojourning without this land,
> I heard of strange misdeeds in this my town,
> How from their homes our women have gone forth
> Feigning a Bacchic rapture, and rove wild o'er wooded hills,
>   in dances honouring
> Dionysus, this new-God—whoe'er be. (*Bacch.* 215–220, LCL)

Second, Cicero, writing in the first century B.C., mentions in passing a concern about "the performance of sacrifices by women at night" (*Leg.* 2.35). Marcus proposes to Atticus:

> Assuredly we must make most careful provision that the reputation of our women be guarded by the clear light of day, when they are observed by many eyes, and that initiation into the mysteries of Ceres be performed only with those rites which are in use in Rome. ... And, that we may not perchance seem too severe, I may cite the fact that in the very centre of Greece, by a law enacted by Diagondas of Thebes, all nocturnal rites were abolished for ever; and furthermore that Aristophanes, the wittiest poet of the Old Comedy, attacks strange gods and the nightly vigils which were part of their worship. (*Leg.* 2.37, LCL).

Third, Livy also speaks about such nighttime immorality connected with religious rites.

> A nameless Greek came first to Etruria, ... a priest of secret rites performed by night. There were initiatory rites which at first were imparted to a few, then began to be generally known among men and women. To the religious elements in them were added the delights of wine and feasts, that the minds of a larger number might be attracted. When wine had inflamed their minds, and night and the mingling of males and females, youth with age, had destroyed every sentiment of modesty, all varieties of corruption first began to be practiced. (39.8, LCL)

2) *Pagan charges against Jews.* Plutarch makes reference to the nocturnal festivals of the Jews.

> The time and character of the greatest, most sacred holiday of the Jews clearly befit Dionysus. When they celebrate their so-called Fast, at the height of the vintage, they set out tables of all sort of fruit under tents and huts plaited for the most part of vines and ivy. They call the first of the days the feast of Tabernacles. A few days later they celebrate another festival, this time identified with Bacchus not through obscure hints but plainly called by his name, a festival that is a sort of "Procession of Branches" or "Thyrsus Procession," in which they enter the temple each carrying a thyrsus. What they do after entering we do not know, but it is probable that the rite is a Bacchic revelry, for in fact they use little trumpets to invoke their god as do the Argives at their Dionysia. (*Quaest. conv.* 4.6.2, Stern).

3) *Jewish charges against pagans.* The Wisdom of Solomon from the 1st century B.C. accuses pagans of the same type of immorality in association with their night meetings.

> For whether they ... celebrate secret mysteries or hold frenzied revels with strange customs, they no longer keep either their lives or their marriages pure. (14:23–24, NRSV)

4) *Pagan charges against Christians.* During the 2nd and 3rd centuries A.D., the charge of loving the dark and practicing immorality therein is explicitly levelled against Christians.

(a) Justin in his *Dialogus cum Tryphone* asks his Jewish debate partners if they believe the pagan charge that after their banquets Christians extinguish the lights and indulge in unbridled sensuality (10). Trypho says that he does not believe the charges of nocturnal immorality made by the rabble (10).

(b) Theophilus of Antioch also echoes the charge.

> They (the unintelligent people who falsely accuse Christians) said that our wives are the common property of all and live in promiscuity, that we have intercourse with our own sisters. (*Autol.* 3.4, Grant)

(c) Athenagoras refers to the same thing in his *Legatio pro Christianis* 3.

(d) Tertullian also knows the charges that a Christian, before the light is extinguished, checks to see where his mother or sister may be so as to be able at least to avoid them in the sexual excesses which will follow (*Apol.* 7.13–8.5).

(e) Minucius Felix offers the fullest statement of the charges, as expressed by the pagan, Marcus Cornelius Fronto:

> They have thus formed a rabble of blasphemous conspirators, who with nocturnal assemblies ... seal their pact not with some religious ritual but with desecrating profanation; they are a crowd that furtively lurks in hiding places, shunning the light. (*Oct.* 8.4, Clarke)
>
> We all know, too, about their banquets; they are on everyone's lips. ... On a special day they gather for a feast with all their children, sisters, mothers—all sexes and all ages. There, flushed with the banquet after such feasting and drinking, they begin to burn with incestuous passions. They provoke a dog tied to the lampstand to leap and bound towards a scrap of food which they have tossed outside the reach of his chain. By this means the light is overturned and extinguished, and with it common knowledge of their actions; in the shameless dark with unspeakable lust they copulate in random unions, all equally being guilty of incest, some by deed, but everyone by complicity. (*Oct.* 9.6–7, Clarke)

(f) Origen reports a similar charge levelled by Celsus that Christians extinguish lamps to do the works of darkness (*Cels.* 6.27). This includes indulging in unrestrained sexual intercourse with the women among them (6.40).

Given the trajectory of pagan criticism of Christians about night meetings, the correspondence between Pliny and Trajan in the early 2nd century takes on new meaning. Pliny writes to the emperor about the "Christian problem" in Bithynia (*Ep. Traj.* 10.96). He says those who had formerly been Christians said that the sum of their guilt amounted only to their meeting before daybreak on an appointed day to sing hymns to Christ as to a god and then to depart until evening when they would meet again to partake of ordinary and harmless food. They had, moreover, ceased the evening meetings after Pliny's edict forbidding secret societies. Whether the governor's concern was about conspiracy or immorality, Roman suspicion of Christians' night meetings existed in the early 2nd century A.D.

5) *Jewish charges against Christians.* Origen, *Contra Celsum* 6.27, criticizes Celsus for his hatred of Christians. He compares the pagan critic to a group of Jews who

> when the teaching of Christianity began to be proclaimed, spread abroad a malicious rumour about the gospel, to the effect that ... when the followers of the gospel want to do the works of darkness they turn out the lights and each man has sexual intercourse with the first woman he meets. (Chadwick)

6) *Christian charges against pagans.* Eph 5:11–12 addresses converted Gentiles with an exhortation not to engage in the behavior of their pagan past (cf. 1 Pet 4:3–4), including nocturnal excesses.

> Take no part in the unfruitful works of darkness, but instead expose them. For it is a shame even to speak of the things that they do in secret. (RSV)

7) *Christian charges against other Christians.* Mainline Christians criticized certain fringe groups in terms of the cultural stereotype.

(a) Jude 12–13 is too general for certainty but its concerns are similar to those expressed elsewhere.

> These are blemishes on your love-feasts, while they feast with you without fear, feeding themselves. They are waterless clouds carried along by the winds; autumn trees without fruit, twice dead, uprooted; wild waves of the sea, casting up the foam of their own shame; wandering stars, for whom the deepest darkness has been reserved.

(b) Justin, *Apologia i* 26 is explicit about the matter. He says:

> All who follow these men (e.g., Simon of Samaria, Menander, and Marcion) are, as we said above, called Christians, just as those who do not share the same doctrines share among philosophers the name of philosophy. We do not know whether they are guilty of those disgraceful and fabulous deeds, the upsetting of the lamp, promiscuous intercourse. ... (Falls)

What does this evidence indicate? It shows that hostility to night meetings because of their associations with conspiracy and/or immorality was commonplace among and within a wide variety of groups in the ancient Mediterranean world. This hostility existed before Christianity ever came on the scene and on a scope far broader than later pagan critiques of Christians. Given the cultural mindset, it would have been almost impossible for an auditor of Acts 20:7–12 not to have heard these overtones being addressed by the text. The reference to the 'many lights' would have served an apologetic purpose. Christian assemblies may be at night but they do not take place in the darkness. They are no cover for immorality. Having said this, it is now time to turn to a second set of details that has the potential to be understood in terms of apologetic.

The Fall, Death, and Resuscitation of a Boy

The fall (v. 9), death (v. 9—ἤρθη νεκρός refers to real death, cf. *T. Jud.* 9:3[9]), and resuscitation (vv. 10,12) of the lad, Eutychus, are integral to the miracle story. The fall and death constitute the problem, while the resuscitation is the miracle cure. The reaction to the miracle comes in verse 12.

These particular details in the story have been variously interpreted. (1) Some interpreters note that Acts 20:7–12 follows the model of similar stories of Elijah (1 Kgs 17:21–23) and Elisha (2 Kgs 4:34).[10] (2) Others see the similarities with the story about Peter in Acts 9:36–43.[11] (3) Still others say Acts 20:7–12 reflects a link with Jesus' raising of a young man (Luke 7:11–15).[12] It seems to me that all three of these readings are correct, as far as they go. The same power that worked in the prophets, Jesus, and Peter is now at work in Paul. Having said that, however, there is more to be noted.

In Mediterranean culture, reference to a night meeting involving a boy who is killed in a cultic context immediately poses a problem that must be addressed. The association of infanticide and cannibalism with deviant religious/magical practices was so widespread in Mediterranean antiquity that any mention of a lad's death in connection with a cultic observance would automatically evoke suspicion in people's minds. The following evidence shows this to be the case.

1) *Pagan charges against other pagans.* Cannibalism in the Greco-Roman mind was associated either with groups on the geographical fringes of the civilized world that tended towards bestiality (Aristotle, *Pol.* 1.1.9) or with deviant religious/magical practices.[13] On the one hand, eating humans was deemed typical of the uncivilized. Herodotus is a storehouse of examples: the Massagetae (1.216), certain Indians called Callatiae (3.38), other Indians called Padaei (3.99), Isedones (4.26), Sythians (6.64), neighbors of the Sythians, the maneaters (4.106; also referred to

---

[9] Haenchen, *Acts*, 585, n. 6; Conzelmann, *Acts*, 169.
[10] Haenchen, *Acts*, 585.
[11] F. C. Baur and the Tübingen School made much of this.
[12] R. B. Rackham, *The Acts of the Apostles* (Westminster Commentaries, 14th ed.; London: Methuen, 1951), 380.
[13] Andrew McGowan, 'Eating People: Accusations of Cannibalism against Christians in the Second Century,' *JECS* 2 (1994): 413–41.

by Philostratus, *Vit. Apoll.* 6.25). In addition, Strabo mentions the men who inhabit the Caucasus (15.1.56).

On the other hand, infanticide/cannibalism was associated with deviant cultic practices. (a) Livy's comments about the undesirability of the Bacchanalia focus not only on the sexual immorality but also on the practices of murder and dismemberment (39.8–19). (b) Diodorus Siculus tells of Apollodorus, the leader of a proletarian revolution in Cassandreia in the 3rd century B.C., who invited a young lad, a friend, to a sacrifice, then slew him as an offering to the gods, gave his conspirators the lad's vitals to eat, and when he had mixed his blood with wine, bade them drink it (22.5.1). (c) Ovid speaks about Lycaon's disbelief that his visitor was a god, so in order to test him killed a hostage, cooked his limbs, and set the food on the table for Jupiter to eat. Being a deity, Jupiter knew what was done. In anger he brought the house crashing down and changed Lycaon into a wolf (*Metam.* 1.198–239). (d) Achilles Tatius's *Leucippe et Clitophon* 3.15, tells of a band of robbers who sacrifice a young girl, roast her bowels, and then eat them. (e) Fragment B1 of Lollianus's *Phoinikika* speaks about a band of robbers who kill a boy, cut his heart out, roast it, and then distribute it to the gang members who swear an oath of loyalty over it. (f) Philostratus, *Vita Apollonii*, tells of certain false charges against the philosopher. He allegedly sacrificed an Arcadian boy to divine the secrets of the future as part of a conspiracy (7.11, 20; 8.5). Reference is made to his alleged eating of the sacrifice (8.5). Apollonius denies the false charges and is freed.

2) *Pagan charges against Jews.* Josephus, *Contra Apionem* 2.89–102, says that Apion told the tale that Jews used to catch a Greek, fatten him up, kill him, eat his entrails, and swear an oath upon this sacrifice that they would ever be at enmity with the Greeks.

3) *Jewish charges against pagans.* Wisdom of Solomon 14:23–24 accuses pagans not only of sexual immorality but also of infanticide in their cultic observances.

> For whether they kill children in their initiations, or celebrate secret mysteries, or hold frenzied revels ... , they no longer keep either their lives or their marriages pure. (NRSV)

4) *Pagan charges against Christians.* In the second and third centuries A.D., pagans charged Christians with infanticide/cannibalism as part of their

worship assemblies. (a) Justin, *Apologia i* 26, presupposes the charge of cannibalism. His *Apologia ii* 12, refers to the charge against Christians that they "feast on human flesh." (b) Tatian, *Oratio ad Graecos* 25, also mentions the charge. (c) Theophilus, *Ad Autolycum* 3.4,15, defends against the charge that Christians eat human flesh. (d) Athenagoras, *Legatio pro Christianis* 3, refutes the charge that Christians engage in Thyestean feasts. (e) Minucius Felix, *Octavius* 9, deals with the charge that in Christian worship an infant is slain by the initiate.

> A young baby is covered with flour, the object being to deceive the unwary. It is then served before the person to be admitted into their rites. The recruit is urged to inflict blows onto it—they appear to be harmless because of the covering of flour. Thus the baby is killed with wounds that remain unseen and concealed. It is the blood of the infant—I shudder to mention it—it is this blood that they lick with thirsty lips; these are the limbs they distribute eagerly; this is the victim by which they seal their covenant; it is by complicity in this crime that they are pledged to mutual silence; these are their rites, more foul than all sacrileges combined (9.5, Clarke)

(f) Tertullian refers to and refutes the charge that Christians in their rites kill a little child and eat it (*Apol.* 7–8; *Praescr.* 1.7,15).

5) *Jewish charges against Christians*. Origen, *Contra Celsum* 6.27, speaks about those Jews who early in Christian history spread the false report that "Christians offered up an infant in sacrifice and partook of its flesh."

6) *Christian charges against pagans*. The Christian apologists of the second and third centuries not only tried to refute the charges that Christians were guilty of infanticide/cannibalism in their rites but also levelled such charges against the pagan world. (a) Tatian, *Oratio ad Graecos* 25, contends:

> It is not we who eat human flesh ... it is among you that Pelops is made a supper for the gods, although beloved by Poseidon; and Kronos devours his children; and Zeus swallows Metis. (*ANF* 2)

(b) Theophilus of Antioch, *Ad Autolycum*, both castigates Greco-Roman theater for portraying cannibalism in depicting the eating of the children of Thyestes and Terens (3.15) and critiques Greek philosophy for its teachings.

> What is your opinion of the precepts of Zeno and Diogenes and Cleanthes which their books contain, inculcating the eating of human flesh:

that fathers be cooked and eaten by their own children? Diogenes ... teaches children to bring their own parents in sacrifice and devour them. (3.5 [*ANF* 2])

(c) Minucius Felix, *Octavius* 30, contends that Saturn did not expose his children but devoured them; Jupiter, moreover, taught Bellona to steep her sacred rites with a draught of human gore.

7) *Christian charges against other Christians.* Justin, *Apologia* i 26, says that Simon Magus, Menander, Marcion, and those who take their names from these men are called Christians even though they are rejected by mainstream believers. These heretics may very well be guilty of "eating human flesh."

The charges of cannibalism and/or infanticide are so pervasive in Mediterranean antiquity from pre-Christian times until well into our era among so many different groups that anyone in that culture who heard about a night meeting, associated with cultic practices, that involved the death of a child would automatically be suspicious. The story in Acts 20:7–12 would almost certainly have been heard in the context of these associations.

Already in pre-Christian times, the two charges of the practice of sexual immorality in the dark and the killing of children in religious rites were associated as part of a total picture of undesirable practices. Livy 39 and Wis 14:23 show this to be the case for both pagans and Jews. The link between the two charges continued into the second and third centuries of our era (e.g., Justin, *Dial.* 10; Origen, *Cels.* 6.27). It can with justification be said that there was a Mediterranean mindset that linked night meetings having religious overtones with immorality and the killing of children.

The miracle story of Acts 20:7–12 had among its ingredients the death of a boy in the context of Christian worship. The reference to the 'many lights' in verse 8 would say to the auditor that the Christian assembly was not doing anything under cover of darkness. The circumstances surrounding the death of Eutychus (an accident due to his falling asleep) and his resuscitation by the leader of the assembly say that the Christian assembly neither intended nor tolerated his death. He left alive! A story told in the terms given it in Acts 20:7–12 would dispel an auditor's suspicions and allay an auditor's fears. Its apologetic overtones would defend Christian assemblies against the hostile stereotypes described in this essay. Given the cultural milieu,

Acts 20:7–12 would function in this way whether or not explicit charges were at that moment being made against Christians and whether or not its author intended it to do so.[14]

---

[14] I am indebted to Daniel Hilty who in the summer of 1994 worked with me on an independent research project that included a study of ancient Mediterranean views of 'night meetings.'

CHAPTER ELEVEN

ONCE AGAIN: THE GENTILE MISSION IN LUKE-ACTS

This paper deals with two problems, one major and one minor, related to the depiction of the Gentile mission in Acts. (1) How is the origin of the Gentile mission in Acts to be understood theologically? (2) Why is there a disproportionate amount of attention given to Jewish rejection of the gospel in Acts? These two questions will be treated in order. We begin with the first.

Luke-Acts is a narrative account in two parts: part one, the life of the founder of the Christian community; part two, a sketch of the Christian community from its beginnings in Jerusalem to its expansion to Rome. The story is about a Jewish founder and a community of Jewish followers in Palestine that ultimately becomes a predominantly Gentile Christian community in lands outside Palestine. How did a Palestinian Jewish movement become a non-Palestinian Gentile one? That is the historical question. What justification was there for a Palestinian Jewish movement becoming a non-Palestinian Gentile one? That is the religious question. It is on the latter question that this essay focuses.[1]

How is the origin of the Gentile mission understood by the author of Luke-Acts? Research offers us two options. On the one hand, some scholars contend that Luke thinks the Gentile mission originated because of Jewish rejection of the gospel.

> It was to the Jews that salvation was first offered, and offered again and again. It was not until they refused it by their vilification of Jesus that the emissaries of Christianity turned to the Gentiles.[2]

At three points in the Pauline mission, in Asia Minor, in Greece, and in Rome, there are statements to this effect.

---

[1] Dixon Slingerland, 'The Jews in the Pauline Portion of Acts,' *JAAR* 54 (1986): 305–21, argues that Acts is not historical either in its picture of Paul or its portrayal of the Jews. Whatever one makes of such a claim, it is irrelevant for our purposes. This article is concerned solely with Acts' theology.

[2] Ernst Haenchen, *The Acts of the Apostles* (trans. R. McL. Wilson; Philadelphia: Westminster, 1971), 101; Jack T. Sanders, *The Jews in Luke-Acts* (Philadelphia: Fortress, 1987).

1) Acts 13:46–47 indicates that when the Jews in Antioch of Pisidia rejected Paul's preaching, Paul and Barnabas spoke out boldly, saying:

> It was necessary that the word of God should be spoken first to you. Since you thrust it from you, and judge yourselves unworthy of eternal life, behold, we turn to the Gentiles. (RSV)

The turning to the Gentiles is depicted as a fulfillment of scripture (Isa 49:6):

> I have set you to be a light for the Gentiles, that you may bring salvation to the uttermost parts of the earth.

2) Acts 18:6 tells how, when Paul preached to Jews in Corinth and experienced their rejection of his message that the Christ was Jesus, the apostle said:

> Your blood be upon your heads! I am innocent. From now on I will go to the Gentiles. (RSV)

3) Acts 28:25–28 relates how in Rome, after the Jewish response to Paul's preaching was divided, he made two points. First, the Jewish failure to respond properly fulfilled the prophecy of Isa 6:9–10 (Acts 28:26–27). Second, "let it be known to you then that this salvation of God has been sent to the Gentiles; they will listen" (Acts 28:28, RSV).

J. C. O'Neill has also contended that the Stephen episode marks the same point in the mission to the city of Jerusalem signaled by the threefold refrain in Paul's mission in the Diaspora.[3] By the end of the Stephen episode, the city as a whole has lost its chance, though individual Jews might still repent. Furthermore, the spread of the gospel ultimately to Gentiles results from the city's rejection (8:4–5; 11:19–21; 13:1–3). If so, then there is a motif in Acts that portrays the Gentile mission as originating because of Jewish rejection of the gospel. Both the rejection by the Jews and the turning to the Gentiles, moreover, are seen as fulfillments of scripture.

On the other hand, other scholars argue that in Lukan theology the Gentile mission originated because of Jewish acceptance of the gospel.[4] Their argument unfolds in several stages.

---

[3] J. C. O'Neill, *The Theology of Acts in Its Historical Setting* (London: SPCK, 1961), 81.

[4] Jacob Jervell, *Luke and the People of God* (Minneapolis: Augsburg, 1972), 41–74; Gerhard Lohfink, *Die Sammlung Israels. Eine Untersuchung zur lukanischen Ekklesiologie* (StANT 34; München: Kösel-Verlag, 1975), 55; Augustin George, 'Israël dans l'oeuvre de Luc,' *RB* 75 (1968): 481–525.

1) Israel did not reject the gospel but became divided over the issue. Some were repentant (Acts 2:41; 4:4; 5:14; 6:1, 7; 12:24; 13:43; 14:1; 17:10–11; 21:20; 28:24–25); others were unrepentant (Acts 4:1–3; 5:17, 27–28; 13:45; 14:2, 4–5; 17:5–7; 17:13; 28:24–25).

2) The repentant Jews are the restored, purified, true Israel. The unrepentant portion of the People has forfeited its membership in the people of God (Acts 3:23).

3) The presupposition of Gentile inclusion does not consist in Israel's rejection of the gospel *en bloc*, but in the fulfillment of the promises to Israel. As Acts 15:16–18 (= Amos 9:11–12 LXX, influenced by Jer 12:15) puts it:

> After this I will return, and I will rebuild the dwelling of David, which has fallen; I will rebuild its ruins, and I will set it up, that the rest of men may seek the Lord, and all the Gentiles who are called by my name, says the Lord, who has made these things known from of old. (RSV)

According to this text, it is the repentant Israel that is the theological presupposition for the inclusion of the Gentiles. Because Israel has thus been restored, the Gentiles seek out salvation (10:5, 8, 17–22, 32–33). There is here a motif of Jewish acceptance of the gospel which leads to Gentile inclusion with believing Jews in God's people (15:14). This is also regarded as a fulfillment of scripture.

Current research is stalemated on the issue of which explanation is to be preferred because both options have a basis in the text of Acts. Neither is capable of displacing the other.[5] How is this apparent contradiction to be explained? Should one take a tradition history approach and argue that one explanation represents the perspective of the author and the other is but undigested tradition? Or should one take the position that the author is but a primitive individual who happens to be confused and perhaps does not recognize the apparent contradiction he has created? Neither of these options is worthy of respect because each violates the integrity and intelligence of the author. If an explanation is to be offered, it should be one that respects the final form of the text of Luke-Acts and that gives the author the benefit of the doubt on

---

[5] The same two points of view lie side by side in the Pseudo-Clementines, *Recogn.* 1:42.1 and 1.64.2—the Gentile mission results from unbelief of Jews; *Recogn.* 1.63—the Gentile mission follows belief of Jews.

his intelligence. This essay will argue that the apparent contradiction can be resolved if read in light of Luke's overall perspective regarding the divine plan.[6]

According to Luke-Acts, there is a divine purpose that stands behind the events of history. It is spoken of as the βουλὴ τοῦ θεοῦ in Luke 7:30; Acts 2:23; 4:28; 5:38–39; 13:36; 20:27. It is referred to as God's θέλημα in Luke 22:42; Acts 21:14; 22:14. It is described as God's ἐξουσία in Acts 1:7.

Events of history happen according to this divine plan in Luke-Acts. This is sometimes described with the term δεῖ as in Luke 2:49; 4:43; 9:22; 13:33; 17:25; 21:9; 22:37; 24:7; 24:26; 24:44; Acts 1:16; 1:21; 3:21; 4:12; 9:16; 17:3; 23:11; 27:24. It is referred to by κατὰ τὸ ὡρισμένον in Luke 22:22; by ὁ ὡρισμένος ὑπὸ τοῦ θεοῦ in Acts 10:42; and by ᾧ ὥρισεν in Acts 17:31. In Acts 26:16 the term used is προχειρίσασθαι; in Acts 22:14 it is προεχειρίσατο. The expression is ἦν ἀναγκαῖον in Acts 13:46. In Luke 9:31; 9:44; 24:21; Acts 17:31; 26:22–23, it is μέλλει that refers to the fact that events happen according to the divine plan.

The realization of the divine plan is often spoken of in terms of fulfillment. Luke 1:20; 4:21; 21:24; Acts 1:16; 3:18; 13:27, all use πληροῦν. Luke 9:51 uses συμπληροῦσθαι. Luke 18:31 and 22:37 employ τελεῖν.

This divine plan or will of God can be known by humans. The scriptures of Israel make it known: for example, Luke 4:18–19; 24:45–47; Acts 13:23, 32–33, 37; 15:15; 28:25–27. Angelic announcement reveals it as well: for example, Luke 1:13–17; 1:30–33; Acts 10:3–8, 22, 30–33; 27:23–25. Living humans prophesy in ways that make the divine will known: for example, Luke 1:29–32, 34–35; Acts 21:10–11. Both the pre-Easter Jesus (for example, Luke 9:22, 44; 18:31–33; 11:13) and the risen Christ (for example, Luke 24:49; Acts 1:4–5; 1:8) express the divine purpose for others to know. Sometimes God's purpose is manifest by special appointment, as in Acts 22:14. In various ways, the will of God which lies behind and determines the course of history is made known to humans.

When God's plan is made known to humans, it often explains the meaning of events: for example, Acts 1:15–22; 2:12–21; 4:25–28; 13:32–37; 15:13–21. It also may evoke an active response to something that needs doing: for example, Acts 15:13–21; 22:14–16. This latter fact shows

---

[6] John T. Squires, 'The Plan of God in Luke Acts,' (Ph.D. diss., Yale University, 1987). Robert C. Tannehill, 'Israel in Luke-Acts,' *JBL* 104 (1985): 69–85, regards it as the unifying element in Luke-Acts.

beyond any shadow of a doubt that the Lukan understanding of the divine plan does not carry with it ideas of inexorability but rather those of contingency. There is here no determinism that undermines human freedom.[7]

What has been said so far about the Lukan understanding of the divine plan for history would have been intelligible to a Mediterranean hearer of Luke-Acts. The belief that a divine necessity controls human history, shaping the course of its events, was a widespread assumption in Mediterranean antiquity. A pagan like Polybius reflects this conviction. Early in his career he saw that Roman power was irresistible. As a Stoic, he believed that the Roman order of things was part of a divine providence that ruled the world. This belief he expounded in his *Historiae*. In 1.4.1–2 he says:

> Fortune (ἡ τύχη) having guided almost all the affairs of the world in one direction and having forced them to incline towards one and the same end, a historian should bring before his readers under one synoptical view the operations by which she has accomplished her general purpose.

A Jew like Josephus shared this cultural belief. As a Jew, however, he viewed the divine necessity as deriving from the personal will of God who is a living person and not a neutral necessity. So in *Antiquitates judaicae* 10.8.2–3 §142 he tells of Jeremiah's prophecy of the fall of Jerusalem being fulfilled and says that these events manifest the nature of God, "which foretells all which must (δεῖ) take place, duly at the appointed hour." Pagan and Jew alike believed that history unfolded according to a divine necessity or compulsion that could be expressed in terms of δεῖ or δέον ἐστί. A Jew would have heard it in terms of his belief in a personal deity, but the cultural context was agreed that history unfolded according to a divine necessity. It was in these terms that Luke's language about the divine plan would have been heard.

It was also believed in Mediterranean antiquity that the divine will could be disclosed to and known by humans. This was often connected with oracles in the pagan sphere and prophecy in the Jewish culture. Indeed, oracles/prophecy not only revealed the divine plan but advanced it. History moved along its appointed course as a fulfillment of oracles/prophecy.

---

[7] As Charles Cosgrove, 'The Divine δεῖ in Luke-Acts,' *NT* 26 (1984): 168–90, correctly argues, disagreeing with S. Schulz, 'Gottes Vorsehung bei Lukas,' *ZNW* 54 (1963): 104–16.

166   CHAPTER ELEVEN

Three examples from the pagan world give one a feel for that segment of the culture.

1) Lucian's *Alexander (Pseudomantis)* tells of one Alexander who wanted to start a new religion. As a first step to this end, he and a companion went to Chalcedon and buried bronze tablets which stated that in the near future Asclepios and his father, Apollo, would migrate to Pontus. These tablets were found and, as a result, the people set about building a temple. Alexander, dressed like Perseus, then went to Abonutichus, declaiming an oracle which said he was a scion of Perseus. A Sybilline prophecy of his activity was then produced. As a result of two written prophecies and one oral prophecy, the stage was set for the emergence of a new religion. Events follow oracles.

2) Suetonius's *Vespasianus* contains a section of omens that prophesy his ascendancy as emperor. Among these references are not only Josephus's declaration that he would soon be released by the same man who would then be emperor but also mention of antique vases dug up by soothsayers which had on them an image of Vespasian. History develops along lines indicated by prophecy/oracles.

3) Apuleius's *Asinus aureus* moves to its climax with Lucius trapped in the form of a donkey as a result of his experimentation with magic. Despairing over his plight, he cries out to Isis to save him. The goddess appears to him by night and gives an oracle (11.7). The next day Lucius does exactly as Isis had said. He eats the roses that are a part of the procession in Isis's honor and is miraculously changed back into a human being. Having been saved from his fate, Lucius is initiated into the Isis cult. He says, "I was not deceived by the promise made to me" (11.13). In all three of these examples from the pagan world, the fulfillment of the oracle legitimates the religious or political authority of the person referred to by the prophecy or the deity that gave it. What happened in each case was in line with what the divine realm had allegedly revealed before the fact.

Three examples from the Jewish milieu should also suffice.

1) The Deuteronomy history uses the device of prophecy and fulfillment. For example, in Deut 28 Moses says that if Israel does not keep the covenant and obey the commandments, then she will go away into exile (vv. 25, 36–37). In 2 Kgs 17 the northern kingdom falls to the

Assyrians and the Israelites are taken into bondage. Verse 7 says the exile was because of Israel's sins; verse 23 says what was done was "as the Lord spoke by all his servants the prophets." In 2 Kgs 25 the southern kingdom is taken away into Babylonian exile. Moses' prophecy in Deut 28 about what would happen if Israel proved disobedient is shown to have been fulfilled in the subsequent narrative of 2 Kings. History moves according to the divine plan as disclosed and effected through prophecies.

2) At Qumran one finds a religious community that believed its own history was the fulfillment of the prophecies of the Jewish scriptures. In the commentaries on Isaiah, Micah, Ps 37, and especially Habakkuk, there are statements of their position. When they interpret the prophets and Psalms as prophecies that are fulfilled in the wickedness of Qumran's enemies and in the righteousness of Qumran's covenanters, they are saying not only that the time of fulfillment has come but also that they are heirs of the promises of Israel, the true people of God. Again, what happens in history is the fulfillment of the divine plan for history as revealed and effected by prophecies.

3) In his *Antiquitates judaicae* Josephus uses the motif of prophecy and fulfillment as evidence of the providence of God (2.16.5 §33). In 8.4.2 §109–110 the fact that the prophecy of David was fulfilled makes clear the providence of God. In 10.11.7. §278–281 the fulfillment of Daniel's prophecies of the destruction of the temple by Antiochus Epiphanes and later the Romans is said to demonstrate, against the Epicureans, the providence of God. The pattern of prophecy-fulfillment in the history of Israel constitutes evidence for the providence of God. Again, history moves according to the divine purpose as revealed and effected by prophecies.

Of course, in Luke-Acts there is a major motif of the fulfillment of prophecy.[8] The prologue speaks of "the things fulfilled (πεπληροφορημένων) among us" (Luke 1:1). There follows a narrative that is literally

---

[8] Charles H. Talbert, 'Excursus A: The Fulfillment of Prophecy in Luke-Acts,' in *Reading Luke: A Literary and Theological Commentary* (New York: Crossroad, 1984), 234–40; idem, 'Promise and Fulfillment in Lucan Theology,' in *Luke-Acts: New Perspectives from the Society of Biblical Literature Seminar* (ed. C. H. Talbert; New York: Crossroad, 1984), 91–103.

controlled by a prophecy-fulfillment pattern. Prophecy is given by the scriptures of Israel, by living prophets, and by heavenly beings. The prophecies disclose the divine will and the fulfillment of the prophecy moves the story along to another stage. In this regard, the Lukan writings would have been perfectly intelligible to the Mediterranean hearer whether pagan or Jewish.

It was also a part of the Mediterranean mind-set that viewed history as the fulfillment of oracles/prophecies to hold that an oracle could be misunderstood as well as understood. The very act of misunderstanding could be the means by which the oracle/prophecy was fulfilled. Herodotus's *Historiae* are a storehouse of examples. The classic example is the story of Croesus, who, after acknowledging the Delphic oracle to be the only true place of divination, asked it if he should send an army against the Persians. The oracle replied that if he should send an army, he would destroy a great empire. Mistaking the meaning of the oracle, Croesus went to war against the Persians and lost. Sending his chains to Delphi, Croesus asked if it were the manner of Greek gods to be thankless. The priestess replied that the oracle was right. Croesus should have sent to ask whether the god spoke of Croesus's or Cyrus's empire. "But he understood not that which was spoken, nor made further inquiry: wherefore now let him blame himself" (1.91). When Croesus received the answer, he confessed that the sin was not the god's but his own.

The similarity of this way of thinking to Acts 13:27 would not be lost on Luke's original hearers:

> those who live in Jerusalem and their rulers, because they did not recognize him nor understand the utterances of the prophets which are read every sabbath, fulfilled these by condemning him. (RSV)

Here, in a speech of Paul to the synagogue in Pisidian Antioch, the claim is made that the death of Jesus, which was a part of the divine plan (Luke 9:22, 44; 18:31–33; 24:26–27, 46; Acts 2:23; 3:18), happened according to divine plan because of the people's failure to understand the oracles/prophecies of scripture. A similar note is sounded in Peter's speech in Acts 3:17–18:

> And now, brethren, I know that you acted in ignorance, as did also your rulers. But what God foretold by the mouth of all the prophets, that his Christ should suffer, he thus fulfilled. (RSV)

In Luke-Acts, as in Mediterranean culture generally, the divine purpose for history can be effected by human misunderstanding and ignorance as well as by human understanding and cooperation. Once this fact is grasped, the impasse in New Testament research over whether the Gentile mission originated because of Jewish unbelief or belief can be resolved.

Since Mediterranean culture assumed a divine plan behind the events of history which was moved along in terms of oracles/prophecies and their fulfillment, and since the divine purpose could be accomplished both by human understanding and cooperation with prophecy and by human misunderstanding/ignorance of it, it ought not to be difficult to believe that in Acts both streams of evidence for why the Gentile mission originated are part of the Lukan mind.

It is indisputable that Gentiles were included in God's people in Acts after some in Israel believed the gospel and because they believed it. The believing Jews interpreted their inclusion of Gentiles as action in line with the revelation of the divine will in scriptural prophecy (Acts 15:13–21). Inclusion of Gentiles after Jewish belief is understood as part of the divine plan. It is something that is done and approved by those who know the meaning of scripture and, therefore, cooperate with the divine will revealed in it. History moves along according to the will of God because of human understanding and cooperation.

It is also indisputable that Gentiles were included in God's people after Jewish rejection of Jesus and the gospel and because of such rejection (Acts 13:27–29; 13:46; 18:6; 28:24–28). The missionaries interpreted their inclusion of the Gentiles as action in line with the revelation of the divine will in scriptural prophecy (Acts 13:46–47—going to the Gentiles is in line with the prophecy of Isa 49:6; Acts 28:25–27—Jewish rejection is in line with the prophecy of Isa 6:9–10). Inclusion of the Gentiles after Jewish unbelief is interpreted as part of the divine plan. The very rejection of Jesus and the gospel by certain Jews, though done in ignorance and out of misunderstanding of the meaning of scriptural prophecies, served but to advance the divine will's accomplishment in history. Ignorance of God's intent and failure to cooperate with his will serve to advance his purposes just as understanding and cooperation do.

For Acts to assert that the Gentile mission had originated both because of Jewish belief and in accordance with the meaning of scriptural prophecy and because of Jewish unbelief due to failure to understand scriptural prophecy properly is something that Mediterranean hearers would have understood. It was a common cultural conviction that the divine purpose behind history that determined history's movement was effective not only in connection with human understanding and cooperation but also in spite of human misunderstanding and opposition. Both dimensions of the matter would have been expected by the readers. As so often is the case in Luke-Acts, the author does not disappoint cultural expectations.

Having dealt with the major question, it is now necessary to focus on the minor issue with which this essay is concerned. Why is there a disproportionate amount of attention given to Jewish rejection of the gospel in Acts? A cursory reading of Acts reveals that when Jews are approached with the gospel, some believe and some disbelieve. The same phenomenon is present in the Gentile mission. Some believe and some do not. Both audiences become divided when confronted with the Christian message. Yet the narrative of Acts makes much of the Jewish rejection and little of the Gentile disbelief. Why is this the case? Is it, as has been recently suggested, that the Christian author of Acts is anti-Semitic?[9] Or are there other concerns that are involved?

In the Third Gospel there is a general theme of status reversal.[10] The New Age will overturn the values and structures of the Present Evil Age. We meet this motif in the birth narratives (1:51–53) and in the Sermon on the Plain (6:20–26), for example. In the central section of Luke (9:51–19:44), Jesus' teaching anticipates this eschatological reversal by overturning the common estimate of what is virtue and what is vice. Consider 10:29–37 (good Samaritan—bad priest and levite); 10:38–42 (good inactive Mary—bad active Martha); 11:37–41 (good unclean—bad clean); 12:13–34 (good poor—bad rich); 14:7–11 (good humble—bad exalted); 15:11–32 (good prodigal—bad elder brother); 16:19–31 (good beggar—bad rich man); 18:9–14 (good tax collector—bad Pharisee); 18:18–30 (good poor—bad rich). This essay will suggest that the Lukan focus on Jewish rejection and Gentile acceptance of the gospel, in spite of the fact that both groups were divided in their response, is yet another part of the general theme of reversal connected with eschatological fulfillment and its inauguration.

The positions taken in Luke that we describe as reversal are rarely explicitly described as such by the author of Luke-Acts. The Magnificat (Luke 1:51–53) is explicit.

---

[9] Jack Sanders, 'The Parable of the Pounds and Lucan Anti-Semitism,' *TS* 42 (1981): 667, says of the Lukan scheme: "we recognize it for the anti-Semitic lie that it is."

[10] Talbert, *Reading Luke*, 171.

He has shown strength with his arm, he has scattered the proud in the imagination of their hearts, he has put down the mighty from their thrones, and exalted those of low degree; he has filled the hungry with good things, and the rich he has sent empty away. (RSV)

The same is true of the beatitudes and the woes (Luke 6:20–23, 24–26). That the Evangelist is explicit in places like these enables the reader to say for certain that the reversal theme is intended and to anticipate it later in the narrative when it is not explicitly signaled.

What enables the reader to say that various passages that have no explicit designation as such reflect the reversal motif is a knowledge of the common cultural assumptions that lie behind a given text. Only because the reader knows the general Jewish cultural estimate of priests, levites, and Samaritans can she hear the parable of the Good Samaritan as a reversal of values (bad priest and levite—good Samaritan). It is not spelled out explicitly in the text. Yet because of the reversal motif that is explicit elsewhere and because of a knowledge of general cultural assumptions not spelled out in the text, one does not hesitate to read or hear the parable in terms of the reversal motif.

It was common Jewish conviction that when the Law was revealed at Sinai, it was offered to all nations. When the nations refused it, God gave it to Israel. Three examples illustrate the position, (1) *Mekilta*, 'Bahodesh,' 1, on Exod 19:2, says that although God gave the Torah openly, the nations were unwilling to accept it. So He declared his word unto Jacob. (2) *Sifre* on Deuteronomy §343, says that when God revealed himself he did so not only to Israel but to all the nations. They rejected his revelation. So when the Lord saw that, he gave the Law to Israel. (3) *Pesikta Rabbati* 30:4, says that before the Lord gave the Torah to Israel, he went around offering it to all the seventy nations. Since no one of them would accept it, it was finally offered to Israel. G. F. Moore contends that this position was "the teaching of both great schools of the second century, the schools of Ishmael and Akiba, and is therefore presumably part of the earlier common tradition from which they drew."[11] We are dealing, then, with a belief of at least the late first century. It was Jewish convention that God's revelation had been offered first to the Gentiles; after their rejection of it, God had turned to Israel who accepted it.

---

[11] George F. Moore, *Judaism* (3 vols.; Cambridge: Harvard University Press, 1958), 1:277.

Acts 2 tells of a new communication from God analogous to the Sinai events that is intended to be understood by all.[12]

1) Philo's comments show how the Sinai theophany was understood in Hellenistic Judaism prior to Luke-Acts. In *De decalogo* 9.33, he writes:

> God wrought on this occasion a miracle ... by bidding an invisible *sound* to be created in the air ... which giving shape and tension to the air and changing it to *flaming fire*, sounded forth like the breath through a trumpet.

2) In addition to the sound and fire, Philo speaks of the speech that could be understood by all the audience.

> Then from the midst of the *fire* ... there sounded forth to their utter amazement a *voice*, for the flame became *articulate speech in the language familiar to the audience* (*Decal.* 11.46).

We have already seen that part of the Jewish conviction about Sinai was that it was offered to the nations. *Midrash* Tanhuma 26c says it went into seventy languages so that all could understand (cf. *t Sotah* 8:6). Sound, fire, and speech understood by all were characteristic of the Sinai theophany. The same ingredients are found in Luke's narration of the Pentecostal events of the New Covenant. Taken together with the fact that *Jubilees* 6 regards Pentecost as the day associated with the renewal of the covenant made with Moses and the fact that at least by the second century rabbinic Judaism regarded Pentecost as the day the law was given at Sinai, it seems that Acts 2 intends to understand the Christan Pentecost in terms of the events that took place at Sinai. Just as a revelation of God was disseminated from Sinai, so a new communication goes forth at Pentecost. This is the key signature for the composition that follows.

Unlike the events at Sinai where God goes first to the Gentiles and only after their rejection of his revelation turns to Israel, the new divine disclosure goes first to Israel and only after her rejection of the gospel do the messengers turn to the Gentiles who listen. The narrative of Acts continues the Lukan reversal theme. In connection with the inauguration of the New Age, there is a status reversal. Whereas it was formerly rejection by Gentiles/acceptance by Israel, now it is rejection

---

[12] Gerhard Schneider. *Die Apostelgeschichte* (2 vols.; Freiburg: Herder, 1980, 1982): 1:246–47.

by Jews/acceptance by Gentiles. Just as in the Third Gospel's use of the reversal motif, so here too reversal is ironic. The disproportionate attention given to Israel's rejection of the gospel is not a manifestation of anti-Semitism but an expression of the irony of reversal of status in connection with the End times.

CHAPTER TWELVE

THE THEOLOGY OF SEA STORMS IN LUKE-ACTS

This essay deals with the theology, implicit and explicit, in the narratives about sea storms in Acts 27 and Luke 8:22–25.[1] It attempts to answer two questions: (1) What theological content would ancient Mediterranean listeners have heard in these narratives? and (2) How do the theological implications of these two stories fit into the Lukan whole?[2]

Theological Content in Acts 27 and Luke 8:22–25

Acts 27

We begin with Acts 27. What theological content would an ancient listener have heard in this narrative? The attempted answer to this question will be developed in three stages: (1) composition, (2) comparative materials, and (3) context.

Composition

Acts 27 belongs to a large thought-unit dealing with Paul's journey from Caesarea to Rome. It consists of introductory (27:1–8) and concluding (28:11–16) itineraries enclosing three episodes (27:9–20; 27:21–44; 28:1–10).

INTRODUCTORY ITINERARY (27:1–8)

1. To Myra in a ship of Adramyttium (1–5)
2. To Fair Havens on a ship of Alexandria (6–8)

---

[1] This essay was co-authored by Talbert and his student, John Herbert Hayes, and is used with the latter's permission.
[2] This way of framing the aim of the paper relegates to irrelevance much secondary literature which either focuses on the question of sources or treats the text of Luke-Acts as something other than a religious document (e.g., a secular narrative).

EPISODE ONE (27:9–20)

1. Paul's prediction (27:10) based on the time of year (27:9) is disregarded because of greed (27:11) and an unsatisfactory harbor (27:12)
2. Paul's prediction is fulfilled in three paragraphs:
   (a) the south wind blew gently (27:13)
   (b) a tempestuous wind struck (27:14–17)
   (c) they were violently storm-tossed so that all hope was abandoned (27:18–20)

EPISODE TWO (27:21–44)

1. Paul's prediction (27:21–22, 26) is based on an angelic message (27:23–25)
2. Paul's prediction is fulfilled in three paragraphs:
   (a) about midnight, Paul gives a warning (27:27–32)
   (b) as day was about to dawn, Paul gives encouragement (27:33–38)
   (c) when it was day, all escaped to land (27:39–44)

EPISODE THREE (28:1–10)

1. Paul is protected from the effects of snakebite (28:1–6)
2. Paul prays effectively for healing (28:7–10)

CONCLUDING ITINERARY (28:11–16)

1. To Puteoli on a ship of Alexandria (28:11–14)
2. To Rome via the Appian Way (28:15–16)

Acts 27 comprises the introductory itinerary and the first two episodes of the larger thought unit.

Comparative Materials

Acts 27 is an example of the type-scene involving sea storm and shipwreck.[3] Narratives of storm and shipwreck are widespread in Mediterranean antiquity. Among the extensive remains we may mention the following:[4]

---

[3] The language of type-scene is that of Pamela Thimmes, *Studies in the Biblical Sea-Storm Type-Scene* (San Francisco: Mellen, 1992).

[4] The following accounts of sea storms and shipwrecks were collected by J. H. Hayes as part of a project sponsored by the Spire for Individualized Research at Wake

1) *Greek*. Homer, *Odyssea* 4.499–511; 5.291–453; 12.403–28; Aeschylus, *Agamemnon* 647–66; Herodotus, *Historiae* 7.188–92; 8.12–14; Euripides, *Troades* 77–86; *Iphigenia taurica* 1391–1498; *Helena* 400–413; Apollonius Rhodius, *Argonautica* 2.1093–1121; Polybius, *Historiae* 1.37; *Ninus* C; Chariton, *De Chaerea et Callirhoe* 3.3; Chion of Heraclea, 4; a fragment of the romance, *Herpyllis*; Dio Chrysostom, *Orationes* 7.2–7; Xenophon of Ephesus, *Ephesiaca* 2.11; 3.2; 3.12; Lucian, *Toxaris* 19–21; *Navigium* 7–9; Aelius Aristides, Ἱερῶν λόγοι 2.12–14; 2.64–68; Achilles Tatius, *Leucippe et Clitophon* 1.1; 3.15; the anonymous romance, *Historia Apollonii regis Tyri* 11–12; Heliodorus, *Aethiopica* 1.22; 5.27; Quintus of Smyrna, *Posthomerica* 14.359–527.

2) *Roman*. Plautus, *Rudens* 62–78; Virgil, *Aeneid* 1.122–252; 3.253–75; 5.14–43; Ovid, *Metamorphoses* 11.477–574; *Tristia* 1.2.1–110; Curtius, *Historiae Alexandri Magni* 4.3.16–18; Phaedrus, *Fabulae* 4.23; Petronius, *Satyricon* 114; Seneca, *Agamemnon* 456–578; Lucan, *Bellum civile* 4.48–120; 5.560–677; 9.319–47; 9.445–92; Statius, *Thebais* 5.360–421; Valerius Flaccus, *Argonautica* 1.614–58; Silius Italicus, *Punica* 17.244–90; Tacitus, *Annales* 2.23–24.

3) *Jewish*. Jonah 1:3–17; *Testament of Naphtali* 6:1–10; Josephus, *Bellum judaicum* 1.19.1–2 + 279–80; *Vita* 13–16.

4) *Christian*. *Acts of Philip* 3.33–36; Pseudo-Clementine *Homilae* 1.8.

Practice in composing such narratives was part of the rhetorical training in the Roman imperial period.[5] Such stories shared numerous elements: for example,[6] (a) a warning not to sail (Polybius; Chion; *Herpyllis*; Aelius Aristides); (b) sailing in a bad season (Polybius; Chion; Dio Chrysostom; Lucian); (c) unusually chaotic winds (Homer; Herodotus; Apollonius Rhodius; *Herpyllis*; Lucian; Aelius Aristides; Achilles Tatius; *Hist. Apoll. reg. Tyr.*; Virgil; Ovid; Petronius; Seneca; Lucan; Statius); (d)

Forest University in the summer of 1994.

[5] M. P. O. Morford, *The Poet Lucan: Studies in Rhetorical Epic* (New York: Barnes and Noble, 1967), 32–36; Susan Marie Praeder, 'The Narrative Voyage: An Analysis and Interpretation of Acts 27–28,' (Ph.D. diss., Graduate Theological Union, 1980), 243. The Elder Seneca, *Controv.* 7.1.4 and 8.6, illustrates the use of stylized sea-storm episodes in his declamations.

[6] The list that follows is a part of a larger collection compiled by J. H. Hayes, summer, 1994, as part of his individualized research project.

darkness during the storm (Homer; Herodotus; Apollonius Rhodius; Chariton; *Herpyllis*; Aelius Aristides; Achilles Tatius; *Hist. Apoll. reg. Tyr.*; Heliodorus; Virgil; Ovid; Curtius; Petronius; Seneca; Lucan; Juvenal); (e) horrendous waves (Herodotus; *Herpyllis*; Lucian; Achilles Tatius; Virgil; Ovid; Lucan); (f) sailors scurrying about (Aelius Aristides; Achilles Tatius; Heliodorus; Virgil; Curtius; Petronius; Tacitus; Jonah); (g) cargo or tackle thrown overboard (Lucian; Achilles Tatius; Heliodorus; Tacitus; Juvenal; Jonah; Josephus; *Acts Phil.*); (h) control of the ship given up and its being driven by the winds and waves (Homer; Herodotus; Apollonius Rhodius; Chariton; *Herpyllis*; Lucian; Achilles Tatius; Heliodorus; Virgil; Ovid; Petronius; Lucan; Juvenal; *T. Naph.*); (i) the ship's frame or hull breaking up (Homer; Aeschylus; Euripides; Apollonius Rhodius; Xenophon; Lucian; Achilles Tatius; *Hist. Apoll. reg. Tyr.*; Virgil; Ovid; Petronius; Jonah; *T. Naph.*); (j) passengers abandoning all hope (Homer; Herodotus; Apollonius Rhodius; *Herpyllis*; Lucian; Achilles Tatius; Virgil; Ovid; Petronius; Lucan; Valerius Flaccus; *Acts Phil.*); (k) the ship wrecking on rocks or a shallow beach (Homer; Aeschylus; Herodotus; Euripides; Apollonius Rhodius; Polybius; *Ninus*; Dio Chrysostom; Xenophon; Lucian; Achilles Tatius; Heliodorus; Plautus; Virgil; Seneca; Lucan; Tacitus); (l) survivors drifting on planks (Homer; Euripides; Apollonius Rhodius; Xenophon; Lucian; Achilles Tatius; *Hist. Apoll. reg. Tyr.*; *T. Naph.*); (m) swimming to shore or to another ship (Homer; *Ninus*; Xenophon; Lucian; Achilles Tatius; Phaedrus; Josephus); (n) helpful, simple folk on shore (Dio Chrysostom; Petronius).

The common elements justify one's calling such accounts type-scenes (i.e., a literary convention with recurring elements and functions). So predictable were these accounts that they became the object of satire (Juvenal, *Sat.* 12.1782; Lucian, *Merc. cond.* 1–2) and parody (Lucian, *Ver. hist.* 1.5–6).

Some of these sea stories functioned merely as a record of historical events (e.g., Tacitus, *Ann.* 2.23–24); others served primarily as entertainment (e.g., Petronius, *Satyr.* 114). Certain narratives, however, taught either theological or moral lessons. Examples of moral lessons taught by sea narratives include:[7] (a) reckless pride leads to destruction (Polybius, *Hist.* 1.37; cf. Acts 27:9–12); (b) wealth is a burden and is a transient possession (Phaedrus, *Fab.* 4.23; cf. Acts 27:18, 38); (c) a true friend is willing to risk his life for the other (Lucian, *Tox.* 19–21; cf. Acts 27:31–32); (d)

---

[7] Luke T Johnson, *The Acts of the Apostles* (Collegeville, Minn.: Liturgical Press, 1992), 451, recognizes some of these moral lessons.

only the true philosopher is calm in a crisis (Lucian, *Peregr.* 43–44; the story of Pyrrho in Diogenes Laertius, *Vit. phil.* 9.68; cf. Acts 27:33–36); (e) when in crisis, pray (*T. Naph.* 6:1–10; cf. Acts 27:23–26). Most of these moral points function in subsidiary roles in Acts 27.

The theological functions of sea narratives, viewed in terms of causality,[8] fall into four categories:[9]

1) Storm caused by gods or God and outcome also due to gods or God, whether deliverance or death (Homer, *Od.* 4.499–511; 5.291–453; Aeschylus, *Ag.* 647–66; Herodotus, 7.188–92; Euripides, *Tro.* 77–86; *Iph. taur.* 1391–1489; Apollonius Rhodius, 2.1093–1121; Chariton, 3.3; Virgil, *Aen.* 1.122–252; Seneca, *Ag.* 456–578; Statius, *Theb.* 5.360–421; Valerius Flaccus, 1.614–58; Silius Italicus, 17.244–90; Jonah 1:3–17).

2) Storm caused by gods or God and outcome due to mortals on the ship (Euripides, *Hel.* 400–413; Plautus, *Rud.* 62–78).

3) Storm due to other than a divine cause and outcome due to gods or God (*Herpyllis*; Lucian, *Merc. cond.* 1–2; *Nav.* 7–9; Aelius Aristides, Ἱερῶν λόγοι 2.12–14; Achilles Tatius, 1.1; 3.15; Virgil, *Aen.* 3.253–75; Ovid, *Trist.* 1.2.1–110; *T. Naph.* 6:1–10; Josephus, *Vita* 13–16; *Acts Phil.* 3.33–36).

4) Storm due to other than a divine cause and outcome due to natural or human agents (Apollonius Rhodius, *Argon.* 4.1228–47; Polybius, 1.37; *Ninus* C; Chion, 4; Dio Chrysostom, *Orat.* 7.2–7; Xenophon of Ephesus, *Ephes.* 2.11; 3.2; 3.12; Lucian, *Tox.*19–21; *Ver. hist.* 1.5–6; 2.47; Aelius Aristides, Ἱερῶν λόγοι 2.64–68; *Hist. Apoll. reg. Tyr.* 11–12; Heliodorus, 1.22; 5.27; Virgil, *Aen.* 5.14–43; Ovid, *Metam.* 11.472–574; Quintus Curtius, *Hist. Alex. Magn.* 4.3.16–18; Phaedrus, *Fab.* 4.23; Petronius, *Satyr.* 114; Lucan, 5.560–677; 9.319–47; Tacitus, *Ann.* 2.23–24; Josephus, *B.J.* 1.279–80).

---

[8] Ancient Mediterranean peoples debated various theories of causation. Sometimes the categories 'natural' and 'divine' were used. See R. M. Grant, *Miracle and Natural Law in Graeco-Roman and Early Christian Thought* (Amsterdam: North Holland Publishing, 1952).

[9] This typology was suggested by C. H. Talbert and developed by J. H. Hayes during the summer of 1994 as part of the Spires Program for Individualized Research at Wake Forest University.

The first of these categories of narratives of sea storms has received attention of late. Gary Miles and Garry Trompf in 1976[10] and David Ladouceur in 1980[11] have called attention to the Mediterranean assumption that nature is a vehicle of divine justice and, if so, then storm and shipwreck can be understood as divine judgment on the wicked; and conversely, the absence of storm and shipwreck can be seen as evidence of absence of guilt. It is against this background, they claim, that Acts 27 is to be understood.

The Elder Seneca, in his stylized declamations written in the early first century A.D., includes one that is relevant to our concerns (*Controv.* 7.1, LCL). A son is unjustly convicted of parricide (the attempted murder of his father). As punishment, he is put on a boat whose rigging was removed. He immediately finds himself in a storm. Seeing this, his brother says: "The sea ... is waiting for a parricide" (i.e., to punish the criminal). Then he prays: "I commend him to you, Fortune—if he is innocent" (7.1.4). "The seas roll savagely, hurricanes press the ship's sides with the rush of their spray, the boat is beaten on every side by dangers; but innocence is safe" (7.1.10). The boat is "equipped by heaven; suddenly sails have appeared, suddenly the ship begins to ride higher and right itself. Innocence is a great shield in danger" (7.1.10). This vindication by heaven is met with wonder: "O seas that are more fair than trials" (7.1.11). In the first century A.D. the assumption that divine justice sometimes acts through the sea is common enough that it can be used in the teaching of declamation. If this is really the backdrop of Paul's shipwreck scene, in what way does this cultural assumption serve as the key to Acts 27?

Acts 27 belongs to category 3 of ancient sea-storm type-scenes: the storm is due to natural causes, the outcome is due to the divine will. In Acts 27 the narrator makes no mention of divine action in sending the storm. Rather there are references that indicate the natural causes of the storm: (a) the time of year (27:9—"the time of the fast had already gone by,[12] so Paul warned them," NAB); (b) the apparent greed of the

---

[10] Gary Miles and Garry Trompf, 'Luke and Antiphon,' *HTR* 69 (1976): 259–67.

[11] David Ladouceur, 'Hellenistic Preconceptions of Shipwreck and Pollution as a Context for Acts 27–28,' *HTR* 73 (1980): 435–49.

[12] The fast refers to the Day of Atonement, 10th Tishri. For Jews, the Feast of Booths five days after the fast marked the end of the season for sailing. Generally, from May 27 (?) until September 14 was regarded by Mediterranean people as the safe season for sea travel.

pilot and owner of the ship who want to sail despite the bad time of the year[13] (27:11—"the centurion paid more attention to the pilot and the owner of the ship than to what Paul said," NAB); (c) the search for a suitable harbor in which to spend the winter (27:12—"Since the harbor was unfavorably situated for spending the winter, the majority planned to put out to sea ... in the hope of reaching Phoenix, a port in Crete," NAB); (d) the fact that other ships had spent the winter in a safe harbor (28:11—"Three months later we set sail on a ship that had wintered at the island," NAB). All of these details make the same point. The storm and shipwreck were not due to divine judgment but rather to a natural cause, namely, the time of the year. Such a depiction of Paul's experience of storm and shipwreck could be understood as a protection against possible misunderstanding in terms of category 1: since one cannot escape divine justice, the storm is caused by God as a judgment on a guilty party, Paul. That the narrator was aware of such a possibility is evidenced by the views espoused by his characters in 28:4b: "This man must certainly be a murderer; though he escaped the sea, justice has not allowed him to remain alive."

Over against any impression that Paul was judged guilty by God because he was involved in a storm and shipwreck, Acts 27 makes explicit that the storm and shipwreck were due to the time of the year (27:9). Over against any claim that Paul's escape from the dangers of the deep was due to human prowess, Acts 27 makes explicit that the deliverance was in accord with the divine plan (27:23–25; 19:21–22; 23:11). The effect of the former is to declare that Paul's involvement in storm and shipwreck was not evidence of his guilt. The effect of the latter is to say that Paul's preservation is part of the divine plan to carry the gospel to Rome by means of this innocent man. You cannot stop the divine plan! This seems likely to be the way an ancient Mediterranean listener would have heard the narrative, given the cultural conventions about sea storms and shipwrecks.

---

[13] Since grain was needed in Rome, Claudius had instituted a policy to secure a regular supply. Suetonius, *Claud.* 18.2, says Claudius assumed the expense of any loss suffered by ship owners due to winter storms. Pliny the Elder, *Nat.* 2.47.125, says that not even the fury of storms closed the sea, because of avarice (David W J. Gill and Conrad Gempf, eds., *The Book of Acts in Its Graeco-Roman Setting* [Grand Rapids, Mich.: Eerdmans, 1994], 22).

Context

The reading suggested above on the basis of comparative material is reinforced by an examination of the immediate contexts of Acts 27. Two contexts should be considered: (1) Acts 28:1–10, the narrative which follows chapter 27 and which goes together as part of the larger thought-unit of 27:1–28:16, and (2) Acts 23:12–26:32, the large thought-unit which precedes chapter 27.

Acts 28:1–10 constitutes Episode Three in the thought-unit of 27:1–28:16 and consists of two parts: 28:1–6 and 28:7–10. In the first part, Paul is bitten by a viper (v. 3) which causes the natives to think he is a murderer who, though he escaped from the sea, has now been caught by divine justice (v. 4). When he is not affected by the snakebite, the natives change their opinion (v. 5). He is not a murderer; he is a god. Two observations emerge from verses 3–4. First, there is an explicit statement by the characters of the Mediterranean assumption that the animal kingdom, often a serpent, functioned as a vehicle of divine justice. Second, the serpent bite is explicitly understood as a corollary to involvement in storm and shipwreck. Both are believed by the natives to function in the same way, as divine judgment.

Three examples from the Greco-Roman world illustrate one or both dimensions of the case. (a) In *Anthologia Graeca* 7.290, we read:

> The shipwrecked mariner had escaped the whirlwind and the fury of the deadly sea, and as he was lying on the Libyan sand not far from the beach ... naked and exhausted by the unhappy wreck, a baneful viper slew him. Why did he struggle with the waves in vain, escaping then the fate that was his lot on the land? (LCL)[14]

Here both dimensions are combined: snakebite and shipwreck as vehicles of divine destiny.

(b) Heliodorus, *Aethiopica* 2.20, tells of a brigand, Themouthis, making his escape, who lay down to sleep, "but the sleep he slept was the final sleep, the brazen sleep of death, for he was bitten by a viper."[15]

(c) An Egyptian papyrus of the fourth to fifth centuries A.D., cited by Cadbury, reads:

---

[14] Sometimes a villain escaped judgment by the sea because he was destined for a further punishment (e.g., Caesar escapes by being hurled to shore by a miraculous tenth wave [Lucan, *Bell. civ.* 5.672–677] because the parricide was being saved for the death he deserved). See Morford, *The Poet Lucan*, 34.

[15] B. P. Reardon, ed., *Collected Ancient Greek Novels* (Berkeley: University of California Press, 1989), 392.

A son having murdered his own father and fearing the laws fled into the desert. As he passed through the mountains he was pursued by a lion; and being pursued by a lion he went up into a tree, and finding a snake as he went up into a tree and being unable to go up on account of the snake he came down again. Wrong doing does not escape the attention of god. The divine always brings the wicked into Dike.[16]

Similar assumptions are expressed in Jewish sources as well.[17] (a) In the Tosefta, *Sanhedrin* 8:3 [E], R. Simeon ben Shatah (ca. A.D. 80) said he saw a man with a sword running after a fellow. The two ran into a deserted building. When Simeon entered, he saw the one slain and the other with the sword dripping blood. The rabbi comments: "But He who knows the thoughts of man will exact punishment from the guilty. He did not move from the spot before a snake bit him and he died."[18] (b) The Jerusalem Talmud, *Berakhot* 5:1 [XIVD], contains a tradition about R. Haninah ben Dosa (before A.D. 70) who, when praying, was bitten by a snake but did not interrupt his prayers. Not only was the rabbi not affected by the bite but the snake died at the entrance to its den. In the Babylonian Talmud, after these events Haninah is reported to have said: "It is not the snake that kills, but sin" (*b. Berakhot* 33a).[19] A righteous man is unaffected by snakebite, just as a wicked man is punished by it.

This latter point corresponds to the Jewish mind-set found in Dan 6:22, in which Daniel says to the king: "My God sent his angel and shut the lions' mouths ... *because* I was found blameless before him." That this idea is not limited to a Jewish context is evidenced by the Greco-Roman tradition found in Horace, *Carmina* 1.22. There the poet proves his righteousness with the news that while he was strolling unprotected through the woods, a wolf fled from him, leaving him unharmed. The animal kingdom, like the sea, punishes the wicked as the agent of divine justice. It does not, however, harm the righteous.

The same cultural mind-set is reflected in Christian sources as well. In the *Acts of John* a villain lusted in vain after the married Drusiana. When she died, he bribed the steward of her husband to open the tomb so he could have his way with the corpse. When they entered, but before the act could occur, a serpent appeared and slew the steward

---

[16] Henry J. Cadbury, *The Book of Acts in History* (London: Black, 1955), 27.
[17] L. H. Silberman, 'Paul's Viper: Acts 28:3–6,' *Forum* 8 (1992): 247–54.
[18] *The Tosefta: Neziqin* (trans. Jacob Neusner; New York: KTAV, 1981), 223.
[19] *The Babylonian Talmud: Seder Zera'im* (ed. I. Epstein; trans. M. Simon; London: Soncino Press, 1948), 204.

with a single bite. The narrator describes this judgment as "such as they deserve to suffer who do such deeds" (70–71). The apostle John, however, who then entered the tomb, was unharmed by the serpent (75).[20]

There seems to be no other way to read Acts 28:1–6 in a Mediterranean context. The natives think Paul guilty when he is bitten; they change their minds when he is unaffected. So Paul is declared innocent by God! Neither storm nor serpent bite is to be taken as God's judgment on Paul. Quite the contrary, God protects and vindicates his upright one.

Acts 28:7–10 functions in two ways. First, it refutes the natives' wrong belief that Paul is a god (v. 6). How? In verse 8, in connection with the healing of Publius's father, Paul "prays" for the healing. A god does not pray for a healing but heals out of himself (cf. Luke 8:46). Likewise, a magician with pretensions to deity would not pray but would regard the miracle as his own doing. This is made clear by Philostratus, *Vita Apollonii* 8.7.9. In Apollonius's defense before Domitian, he contends that he is no magician even though he has eradicated the disease causing a plague in Ephesus. Why? Because he "prayed" to Hercules for the healing. A magician would not do this because he would consider it his own achievement. Contrary to the natives' opinion, Paul is neither a god nor a pretender to divine honors (= a magician; cf. Acts 8:10).

Second, the four-verse unit indicates that Paul is a righteous man. James 5:16b-18, in the context of prayers for healing, uses Elijah as an example to indicate that "the fervent prayer of a righteous person is very powerful" (NAB). John 9:31, again in the context of healing, has the formerly blind man declare: "We know that God does not listen to sinners, but if one is devout and does His will, He listens to him" (NAB). That Paul's prayer is answered is an indication that he is regarded as righteous by God. Paul is not a god but he is a righteous man. Acts 28:1–10 declares Paul innocent by God's decree. This declaration parallels the same point in chapter 27. Acts 27 says Paul is not guilty even if he was in a storm and shipwreck. Acts 28 says Paul is not guilty even if he was bitten by a serpent. Both affirm that Paul is God's servant, a righteous man whose prayers are answered. By God's decree, Paul is innocent.

---

[20] M. R. James, *The Apocryphal New Testament* (Oxford: Clarendon, 1955), 245–46.

Acts 23:12–26:32 forms the second part of chapter 27's immediate context as the immediately preceding large thought-unit. This unit is subdivided into four scenes, each dealing with Paul's status before Roman authorities.

SCENE ONE (23:12–35)

> The plot (23:12–15)
> The plot is discovered (23:16–22)
> The plot is foiled (23:23–35) and Paul is declared innocent (23:29)

SCENE TWO (24:1–27)

> Felix hears charges against Paul (24:1–9)
> Felix hears Paul's defense (24:10–21)
> Felix disposes of Paul's case by delay, putting off the Jews (24:22–23) and Paul (24:24–27)

SCENE THREE (25:1–12)

> Festus hears charges against Paul (25:1–7)
> Festus hears Paul's defense (25:8) and appeal to Caesar (25:9–11)
> Festus disposes of Paul's case by agreeing to send him to Caesar (25:12)

SCENE FOUR (25:13–26:32)

> Agrippa hears charges against Paul: privately (25:13–22) and publicly (25:23–27), including a statement of Paul's innocence by Festus (25:25)
> Agrippa hears Paul's defense (26:1–23)
> Agrippa and others, after dialogue with him (26:24–29), give their judgment that Paul is innocent (26:30–32)

The thrust of the large thought-unit, 23:12–26:32, is that Paul is declared innocent by human authorities (Acts 23:29; 25:25; 26:31, 26:32). This means that the last sections of Acts are concerned to declare Paul's innocence. His innocence is recognized and declared by both human authorities (23:12–26:32) and divine authority (27:1–28:10). The storm and shipwreck function as part of this overall design. At the same time, the deliverance from the storm and shipwreck are understood as part of God's vindication of God's messenger, enabling Paul to carry the gospel to Rome (Acts 19:21–22; 23:11).

Luke 8:22–25

It is time to turn to Luke 8:22–25 to ask what theological overtones an ancient listener would have heard. Again, remarks that follow will be developed in terms of composition, comparative materials, and context.

Composition
This is a miracle story with the usual three parts: problem (vv. 22–24a), miracle (v. 24b), and reaction to the miracle (v. 25). Its obvious point is that Jesus has power over the wind and the sea.

Comparative Materials
Ancient listeners might have heard a range of implications.

1) When Luke 8:25b gives as the reaction to the miracle the question, "Who then is this, who commands even the winds and the sea, and they obey him?" (NAB) echoes from the LXX could have been heard. Ps 88:9 (LXX; MT 89:9) reads: "Thou rulest the power of the sea, and thou calmest the tumult of its waves." Ps 106:29–30 (LXX; MT 107:29–30) reads: "And he commands the storm, and it is calmed into a gentle breeze, and its waves are still. And they are glad, because they are quiet; and he guides them to their desired haven." Of course, the one about whom the LXX speaks is Yahweh. The story, then, applies to Jesus the attributes of the Lord. Who is Jesus? Jesus is one with Yahweh's power.

2) The question, 'Who is this?' might have evoked other echoes as well. Two biographies of Pythagoras offer relevant data about the popular belief that would have been 'in the air' in Luke's time. Porphyry, *Vita Pythagorae* 29, says of the philosopher that "he calmed storms on rivers and seas, for the comfort and safe passage of his friends."[21] Similar feats were performed by his followers Empedocles, Epimenides, and Abaris. Iamblichus, *Vita Pythagorae* 28, says that one sign of the philosopher's divinity were his "tranquilizations of the waves of rivers and seas, in order that his disciples might the more easily pass over them."[22] Among others who did such things was Empedocles of Agrigentum, surnamed the 'wind-stiller.' In *Vita Pythagorae* 3, moreover, a story is

---

[21] Kenneth Sylvan Guthrie, ed., *The Pythagorean Sourcebook and Library* (Grand Rapids, Mich.: Phanes Press, 1987), 129.
[22] Ibid., 91.

recounted of a shipboard journey Pythagoras took during the time for travel to be suspended. "The sailors considered that contrary to their expectations, the voyage had proceeded without interruptions, as if some deity had been on board."[23] Again, echoes that might have been heard in Luke 8:22–25 relate to one who had the marks of divinity.

3) It is even possible that the question of the identity of Jesus, the stormstiller, could have had apologetic overtones. Plutarch, in *Caesar* 38.2–4, tells the story of how Caesar, disguised as a slave, went on board a ship. When a strong wind arose so that the ship could make no progress, the captain was about to turn around. Caesar then disclosed himself and said: "Come, good man, be bold and fear naught; thou carryest Caesar and Caesar's fortune in thy boat" (LCL). The sailors forgot the storm and tried to force their way through the waves with the oars. The project proved impossible, and Caesar reluctantly allowed the captain to put about and return to port. In such a story, one hears that Caesar is only a man, although he tries to act like a god. In his pretensions to divinity, he is an impostor—unlike Jesus.[24] Such stories about Caesar were likely to have circulated long before Plutarch wrote.

"Who is this that commands the wind and the sea and they obey him?" An ancient listener would have heard in the story a claim for Jesus' divine authority. Luke 8:22–25, like Acts 27, belongs to category 3 of sea-storm type-scenes: the cause of the storm may be other than the divine (here, actually the demonic), but the outcome is due to divine power. The divine power in Luke 8:22–25 is located in the person of Jesus. Contrast Acts 27:1–28:10 in which divine power is located outside of Paul. Indeed, that Paul is delivered from storm and shipwreck in Acts 27 is due to the divine power of the Lord, a power demonstrated in Luke 8:22–25.

---

[23] Ibid., 60.

[24] It is possible that Acts 28:11 reflects the same type of polemic in its context: "Three months later we set sail on a ship that had wintered at the island, an Alexandrian ship with the Twin Brothers as its figurehead" (NRSV). While Paul and his company were tossed about on the sea and finally delivered by the God to whom Paul belonged, the Twin Brothers, those famed deliverers of travelers in peril at sea, spent the winter in the safe harbor at Malta (so J. H. Hayes).

Context

Luke 8:22–25 is part of a large thought-unit, 8:22–9:6, in which four miracle stories demonstrate Jesus' power (8:22–25; 8:26–39; 8:43–48; 8:40–42, 49–56). These stories are followed by 9:1–6, in which Jesus gives power and authority to the Twelve for their mission work.[25] Luke 8:22–25's function in this thought-unit is to say that Jesus' power includes authority over the sea. His 'sent ones' are, therefore, not outside the sphere of his control and protection when they travel on the sea. Moreover, the exorcism story in 8:26–39, set in Gentile territory, in which demons, resident in unclean swine, try to escape Jesus' power by rushing into the waters of the lake, functions in part to say that demons are by no means eluding the authority of the one to whom even wind and water hearken. Jesus is Lord of the sea and its storms. His 'sent ones' may have faith that they are safe in his power for the assigned tasks that lie before them.

Do Acts 27 and Luke 8:22–25 Fit into the Lukan Whole?

The theological perspectives of Acts 27 and Luke 8:22–25 fit nicely into the Lukan whole. Three dimensions of the overall vision of Luke-Acts can be employed to demonstrate this claim: (1) the divine plan, (2) the use of foreshadowing in Luke-Acts, and (3) the use of correspondence between events in Luke and those in Acts.

The Divine Plan

According to Luke-Acts there is a divine plan that stands behind the events of history.[26] It is spoken of as the βουλὴ τοῦ θεοῦ in Luke 7:30; Acts 2:23; 4:38; 5:38–39; 13:36; 20:27. It is referred to as God's θέλημα in Luke 22:42; Acts 21:14; 22:14. It is described as God's ἐξουσία in Acts 1:7.

Events of history happen according to this divine plan in Luke-Acts. This is sometimes described with the term δεῖ as in Luke 2:49; 4:43; 9:22; 13:33; 17:25; 21:9; 22:37; 24:7; 24:26; 24:44; Acts 1:16; 1:21; 3:21; 4:12; 9:16; 17:3; 23:11; 27:24. It is referred to by κατὰ τὸ ὡρισμένον in Luke 22:22; by ὁ ὡρισμένος ὑπὸ τοῦ θεοῦ in Acts 10:42; and by ᾧ

---

[25] Charles H. Talbert, *Reading Luke* (New York: Crossroad, 1982), 95–97.
[26] For what follows, see chapter 11, 'Once Again: The Gentile Mission in Luke-Acts.' John T. Squires, *The Plan of God in Luke-Acts* (Cambridge: Cambridge University Press, 1993), offers the fullest treatment of the Mediterranean backgrounds of the concept.

ὥρισεν in Acts 17:31. In Acts 26:16 the term used is προχειρίσασθαι; in Acts 22:14 it is προεχειρίσατο. The expression is ἦν ἀναγκαῖον in Acts 13:46. In Luke 9:31; 9:44; 24:21; Acts 17:31; 26:22–23, the word μέλλει refers to the fact that events happen according to the divine plan.

The realization of the divine plan is often spoken of in terms of fulfillment. Luke 1:20; 4:21; 21:24; Acts 1:16; 3:18; 13:27, all use πληροῦν. Luke 9:51 uses συμπληροῦσθαι. Luke 18:31 and 22:37 employ τελεῖν.

The divine plan can be known by humans. The scriptures of Israel make it known, as in Luke 4:18–19; 24:45–47; Acts 13:23, 32–33, 37; 15:15; 28:25–27. Angelic announcement reveals the plan as well, as in Luke 1:13–17; 1:30–33; Acts 10:3–8, 22, 30–33; 27:23–25. Living humans prophesy in ways that make the divine will known, as in Luke 1:29–32, 34–35; Acts 21:10–11. Both the pre-Easter Jesus (Luke 9:22, 44; 18:31–33; 11:13) and the risen Christ (Luke 24:49; Acts 1:4–5, 8) express the divine purpose. Sometimes God's purpose is made manifest by special appointment, as in Acts 22:14. The will of God, which lies behind and determines the course of history, is made known to humans in various ways.

What has been said about the Lukan understanding of the divine plan for history would have been intelligible to a Mediterranean hearer. The belief that divine necessity controls human history, shaping the course of events, was a widespread assumption in Mediterranean antiquity.

A pagan like Polybius reflects this conviction. Early in his career, Polybius saw that Roman power was irresistible and, as a Stoic, he believed the Roman order was part of a divine providence that ruled the world. This belief he expounded in his *Historiae*.

> Fortune (τύχη) having guided almost all the affairs of the world in one direction and having forced them to incline towards one and the same end, a historian should bring before his readers under one synoptical view the operations by which she has accomplished her general purpose. (1.4.1–2, LCL)

A Jew like Josephus shared this cultural belief. As a Jew, however, he believed that the divine necessity derived from the personal will of God, who is a living person and not a neutral necessity. So in *Antiquitates judaicae* 10.8.2–3 §142, for example, he tells of the fulfillment of Jeremiah's prophecy of the fall of Jerusalem, and says that these events manifest the nature of God, "which foretells all which must (δεῖ) take place, duly at the appointed hour" (LCL). Pagan and Jew alike believed that history unfolded according to a divine necessity or compulsion that could be expressed in terms of δεῖ or δέον ἐστί. A Jew would have heard the idea in terms of his belief in a personal deity, but the cultural context was agreed that history unfolded according to a divine necessity. It was in these terms that Luke's language about the divine plan would have been heard.

It was also believed in Mediterranean antiquity that the divine will could be disclosed to and known by humans. This idea was often connected with oracles in the pagan sphere and with prophecy in the Jewish culture. Indeed, oracles and prophecy not only revealed the divine plan but advanced it. History moved along its appointed course as a fulfillment of oracles and prophecy. This was true for pagan (e.g., Lucian, *Alex.*; Suetonius, *Vesp.*; Apuleius, *Asin. aur.*) and for Jewish settings (the Deuteronomic history; Qumran; Josephus, *A.J.*).

A major motif of fulfillment of prophecy exists in Luke-Acts. The prologue speaks of "the things fulfilled (πεπληροφορημένων) among us" (Luke 1:1). There follows a narrative that is literally controlled by a prophecy-and-fulfillment pattern. Prophecy is given by the scriptures of Israel, by living prophets, and by heavenly beings. The prophecies disclose the divine will and the fulfillment of prophecy moves the story to another stage. In this regard the Lukan writings would have been perfectly intelligible to the Mediterranean hearer, whether Jewish or pagan.

Within this scheme, the narrative of Acts 23:12–28:16 fits nicely. In Acts 23:11 a prophecy of the risen Christ controls the rest of the book: "The following night the Lord stood by him and said, 'Take courage. For just as you have borne witness to my cause in Jerusalem, so you must (δεῖ) also bear witness in Rome'" (NAB). In Acts 27:23–26 Paul speaks to the terrified sailors and passengers on board the storm-driven ship:

> I urge you now to keep up your courage; not one of you will be lost, only the ship. For last night an angel of the God to whom I belong and whom I serve stood before me and said, "Do not be afraid, Paul. You are destined (δεῖ) to stand before Caesar; and behold, for your sake, God has granted safety to all who are sailing with you." Therefore, keep up your courage, men; I trust in God that it will turn out as I have been told. We are destined (δεῖ) to run aground on some island. (NAB)

If the storm and shipwreck of Paul's journey to Rome are due to natural causes and not divine judgment, his deliverance is part of the divine plan that he preach the gospel in Rome before Caesar. In this regard, Acts 27 fits into the scheme of Luke-Acts.

Foreshadowing in Luke-Acts

In Luke-Acts, as in other texts of Mediterranean antiquity, there is frequent use of foreshadowing. In Greek and Roman epics, for example, one finds devices to forecast the future, both the future that finds fulfillment within the narrative and the future whose fulfillment is beyond the narrative.[27] Sometimes the foreshadowing is done by the author, sometimes by a divine being within the narrative, and sometimes by a mortal character (all of which are found in Luke-Acts). These foreshadowings frequently take the form of prophecies of the future: for example, in the *Aeneid* 7.652–53, the author hints that Lausus will meet his death; in the *Aeneid* 11.587–94, the goddess Diana's words to Opis foreshadow the later death of Camilla with the attendant death of her slayer; and in the *Aeneid* 12.725–38, Andromache foresees the future fate of Astyanax and of the Trojans in general. A Greco-Roman hearer of Luke-Acts, therefore, would have understood the evangelist's use of foreshadowing.

The closest parallels to the Lukan use of foreshadowing by prophecy, however, are from the LXX. Luke's repeated use of prophecy fulfillment, for example, functions as foreshadowing by divine forecast, sometimes within a dream or vision, sometimes apart from a dream or vision.[28] This reflects the same practice in the LXX.

1) Take the matter of foreshadowing by divine forecast. In 2 Sam 11 David sins against Uriah. In chapter 12, Nathan the prophet confronts David. In 12:10–12, 14, there is a prophecy of the consequences of David's sin (foreshadowing by divine forecast): (a) the sword will never depart from David's house (v. 10); (b) God will raise up evil against David out of his own house (v. 11a) and will take David's wives and give them publicly to another (vv. 11b-12); (c) the child to be born of the illicit union with Bathsheba will die (v. 14).

This foreshadowing serves as a focusing technique, enabling the reader to know what to look for in the narrative that follows.[29] (c) The child dies (2 Sam 12:15b-19). (a) Absalom has his brother Amnon killed (2 Sam 13:28–29, 32). Absalom is killed by Joab and his men

---

[27] George E. Duckworth, *Foreshadowing and Suspense in the Epics of Homer, Apollonius, and Virgil* (New York: Haskill House, 1966).

[28] Meir Sternberg, *The Poetics of Biblical Narrative* (Bloomington: Indiana University Press, 1987), 105, 285–308.

[29] Ibid., 115.

(2 Sam 18:14–15). Solomon has his brother and rival, Adonijah, killed (2 Kgs 2:23–25). (b) Absalom goes in to his father's concubines in the sight of all Israel (2 Sam 16:21–22). The foreshadowing allows the narrator to dispense with continual enactment of divine intervention that might overschematize the plot, and to benefit from the artistic gains of "omnipotence behind-the-scenes."[30]

This foreshadowing is much like the divine forecast of Acts 23:11: "Just as you have borne witness to my cause in Jerusalem, so you must also bear witness in Rome" (NAB). What follows throughout the trials before authorities may seem like a secular narrative devoid of divine intervention, but the action is controlled by the foreshadowing of divine forecast. Following biblical models, it is a theological narrative with omnipotence behind the scenes.

2) Consider also the matter of foreshadowing through dreams or visions in the LXX. In Gen 37:5–7, Joseph tells his brothers of his dream that they would bow down to him and that he would rule over them (v. 8). The wellknown events of Joseph's sale into slavery in Egypt follow. Then because of famine the brothers are forced to come to Egypt to seek food. In 42:9, Joseph remembers the dream. Then when events take a turn for the worse with the brothers, in 43:23 they bow down before Joseph, in 43:28 they do obeisance before Joseph, and in 44:11 they fall to the ground before Joseph. Again the story is told in terms of divine omnipotence behind the scenes, much like Acts 27, in which Paul tells fellow travelers of the previous night's dream/vision that all would be saved (vv. 23–26). The apparently secular narrative that follows is very much a theological narrative.

Luke 8:22–25, together with its companion pieces in the large thought-unit (8:22–9:7), also functions as foreshadowing. In this case, it is not foreshadowing by prophecy but foreshadowing by demonstration. One hears both that Jesus' power controls the sea and that he has authority over demons, even in Gentile territory. Acts works out that foreshadowing both in terms of the Lord's protection of the Lord's servants on the sea (Acts 27) and in terms of authority over the demonic in Gentile territory (Acts 16:16–18; 19:13–20).

This usage resembles the LXX's use of foreshadowing by demonstration in the Elijah-Elisha cycles of 1 and 2 Kings. The first cycle

---

[30] The language is that of ibid., 106.

dealing with Elijah tells stories of his accomplishments. Then the reader learns that Elisha is anointed as prophet in his stead (1 Kgs 19:16), and that the Spirit of Elijah rests on Elisha (2 Kgs 1:15). Following that, a series of events connected with Elisha depicts his deeds, which have similarities with deeds of Elijah. For example, Elisha parts the water (2 Kgs 2:13–14) as Elijah had done (2 Kgs 2:8); Elisha promises a gift of water (2 Kgs 3:20) as Elijah had done (1 Kgs 18:45); Elisha multiplies the oil (2 Kgs 4:1–7) as Elijah had done (1 Kgs 17:8–16); and Elisha raises a child (2 Kgs 4:18–37) as Elijah had done (1 Kgs 17:17–24). In these two cycles, the deeds of Elijah function as foreshadowing by demonstrating what will be accomplished by Elisha, who has the Spirit of Elijah's hero. Demonstrations of the Spirit in the Elijah cycle foreshadow events worked out in the Elisha cycle. Whether it be foreshadowing by divine forecast, by dream, or by demonstration, Acts 27 and Luke 8:22–25 fit nicely into the overall Lukan literary and theological design.

Correspondence between Luke and Acts

Recognition of correspondences between persons and events in Luke and Acts has a long history. Given the evidence, such claims seem reasonable. Luke-Acts comes from a time and place in which Virgil could organize the *Aeneid* into two halves, Books 1–6 and Books 7–12, with each book of the second half balancing the corresponding book of the first.[31] Correspondence between Jesus' last journey to Jerusalem and Paul's final journey to Jerusalem is especially persuasive.[32] Examples include the following.

Luke 9:51–19:46	*1. Acts 19:21–21:17*
Jesus makes a final journey to Jerusalem (9:31, 51; 12:50; 13:33; 18:31–33)	Paul makes a last journey to Jerusalem (20:3; 20:22–24, 37–38; 21:4, 10–11, 21:13)
under divine necessity (13:33)	under divine necessity (20:22; 21:14)
involving disciples' lack of understanding (9:45; 18:34)	involving friends' lack of understanding (21:4, 12–13)
Luke 19:37	*2. Acts 21:17–20*
Jesus receives a good reception and the people praise God.	Paul receives a good reception and God is glorified.

---

[31] George E. Duckworth, *Structural Patterns and Proportions in Virgil's 'Aeneid'* (Ann Arbor: University of Michigan Press, 1962), 2–10.

[32] C. H. Talbert, *Literary Patterns, Theological Themes, and the Genre of Luke-Acts* (Missoula, Mont.: Scholars Press, 1974), 15–23, gives a fuller discussion.

Luke 19:45–48
Jesus goes into the Temple.

Luke 22:54
Jesus is seized.

Luke 22:26; 23:1; 23:8; 23:13
The four trials of Jesus (Sanhedrin, Pilate, Herod, Pilate).

Luke 23:4, 14, 15, 22
Jesus is declared innocent.

Luke 24
Jesus is raised from the dead.

3. Acts 21:26
Paul goes into the Temple.

4. Acts 21:30
Paul is seized.

5. Acts 23, 24, 25, 26
The four trials of Paul (Sanhedrin, Felix, Festus, Herod).

6. Acts 23:9; 25:25; 26:31, 32
Paul is declared innocent.

7. Acts 27:1–28:10
Paul is saved from death by God.

It is the last two sets of parallel events that concern us here. If Acts 23:12–26:32 functions as a declaration of Paul's innocence by human authorities, parallel to the declarations of Jesus' innocence by human authorities in Luke 23:4, 14, 15, 22, can his deliverance from storm, shipwreck, and from snakebite be seen as a parallel to Jesus' resurrection?[33]

Jesus' death in Luke raises the question whether, from a human point of view, he is a guilty criminal and, from the divine perspective, is accursed. Declarations of his innocence by human authorities make it clear that his death is not the execution of the guilty but the innocent sufferings of a martyr. The vindication of his resurrection and exaltation reveals that he is not accursed of God but is Lord and Christ. Similarly, after Paul is taken into custody he is kept a prisoner, possibly indicating that, from a human vantage point, he is wicked. Moreover, he experiences shipwreck and snakebite, events that might convey that he was a wicked man receiving his just deserts from God. Declarations by human authorities of his innocence make it clear that he is no criminal, and the circumstances of his shipwreck and snakebite speak forcefully of his innocence and righteousness before God. Both Luke and Acts end with declarations of their respective heroes' innocence by both human and divine authority. In the Third Gospel, Jesus' vindication takes the form of his resurrection and exaltation; in Acts, Paul's

---

[33] M. D. Goulder, *Type and History in Acts* (London: SPCK, 1964), 61, describes the events of Acts 27 as Paul's "death" and those of Acts 28:1–10 as Paul's "resurrection," paralleling Jesus' death in Luke 23 and his resurrection in Luke 24.

vindication takes the form of deliverance from shipwreck and snakebite, and the fact that his prayers for healing were answered.[34]

The foregoing remarks have attempted to answer the two questions with which we began: (1) What theological content would the hearers of Luke-Acts have derived from sea-storm narratives in Luke 8:22–25 and Acts 27? and (2) How do these sea-storm narratives fit into the Lukan whole? At least a tentative answer can be given to both queries. Jesus possesses divine power over wind and storm, an authority he uses for the benefit of his 'sent ones,' both before and after Easter. That Paul was caught in a storm and shipwreck and was bitten by a serpent do not mean he was deemed guilty by God. The sea-storm narrative says the storm was due to natural causes, not divine justice. His deliverance was due to the divine plan, not Paul's own human prowess. The Malta narrative states that Paul is not a guilty man because he was bitten by a serpent. Rather he is a righteous man who is untouched by snakebite and whose prayers are answered by God. Acts 27:1–28:10 says, therefore, that Paul is deemed not guilty by God, but rather as righteous. God has pronounced Paul innocent in this thought-unit as human authorities did in 23:12–26:32. These conclusions, moreover, fit nicely into the larger Lukan literary and theological landscape.

---

[34] This interpretation hardly qualifies as a candidate for Luke Johnson's scorned "allegorical" reading of Acts 27 in terms of Jesus' death and resurrection (*Acts*, 457).

CHAPTER THIRTEEN

WHAT IS MEANT BY THE HISTORICITY OF ACTS?

Of what value is the Acts of the Apostles for the study of early Christianity? This question demands answers on two levels: (1) Of what value is Acts for our knowledge of Christianity near A.D. 100 (i.e., for the time when the book was written)? and (2) Of what value is Acts for our knowledge of Christianity during the apostolic age (i.e., for the time of the events narrated, before A.D. 64)? The latter is the focus of this chapter. Our query is about the historicity of Acts, that is, Acts' value for our knowledge of Christianity up through Paul.

The question of the historicity of Acts has been neglected since the early years of this century.[1] Two reasons for this neglect seem to be primary: (1) There has been in this century a shift of focus in the study of Acts from historical to theological concerns, and (2) the complexity of the problems and the extent of the knowledge from multiple fields required to deal with the issues are so threatening as to make scholars look to less demanding areas of study.

If one agrees that such neglect should be remedied, one then faces the further question: *What* do we really mean by the historicity of Acts? One's answer to this question determines *how* one goes about arguing either for or against the historicity of Acts. So *what* and *how* are two sides of the same coin. In fact, one can see the *what* assumed by noting the *how* of the argument.

A survey of the secondary literature reveals three levels of argument about *what* and *how*, plus three specific issues crucially related to the matter of the historicity of Acts. The purpose of this chapter is to describe these three levels and three issues in order to define as precisely as possible what one means when one speaks about the historicity of Acts. Until the nature of the problem is clearly defined, progress toward the larger matter of the value of Acts for the study of early Christianity is delayed.

---

[1] Colin J. Hemer, *The Book of Acts in the Setting of Hellenistic History* (ed. C. H. Gempf; Tübingen: J. C. B. Mohr, 1989), 1.

We begin with an overview of the three levels of argument about the historicity of Acts: (1) contemporary color, (2) historical sequence, and (3) individual events and episodes. These three levels of argument will be taken up in the order mentioned here.

Contemporary Color

The argument from contemporary color assumes that a document is not historically accurate if it contains errors and anachronisms.[2] By inference, a document must be historically accurate if one does not find errors and anachronisms. Hence, the quest to show or to deny the historicity of Acts involves the search for signs of the presence or absence of contemporary color, that is, the fitness of details in Acts to our knowledge of its environment.

Let us begin with a few representative examples of Acts' congruence with its milieu.

1) *Titles of officials.* (a) The title 'proconsul' (ἀνθύπατος) is correctly used for the two governors of senatorial provinces named in Acts: Sergius Paulus, governor of Cyprus (Acts 13:7–8), and Gallio, governor of Achaea (Acts 18:12). (b) Inscriptions confirm that the city authorities in Thessalonica in the first century A.D. were called politarchs (πολιτάρχης, Acts 17:6, 8). (c) According to inscriptions, γραμματεύς is the correct title for the chief executive magistrate (town clerk) in Ephesus (Acts 19:35). (d) Felix (Acts 23:24, 26) and Festus (Acts 24:27; 25:1) are correctly called procurators (ἡγεμών) of Judea. (e) Acts correctly refers to Cornelius (10:1) and Julius (27:1) as centurions (ἑκατοντάρχης) and to Claudius Lysias (Acts 21:31; 23:26) as a tribune (χιλίαρχος).

2) *Administrative divisions.* Unlike other provinces, Macedonia was divided into four administrative districts. If one follows the Greek text of the Nestle 26th edition (πρώτης μερίδος instead of πρώτη τῆς μερίδος, assuming dittography of τη), Acts 16:12 reflects this division when it calls Philippi a colony and a city of the first district of Macedonia.

---

[2] E. Mary Smallwood, *The Jews under Roman Rule: From Pompey to Diocletian* (Leiden: Brill, 1976), 312, gives an example of this type of argument in denying historicity to a purported letter from Hadrian to his brother-in-law about the emperor's visit to Egypt in A.D. 130.

3) *Town assemblies.* Acts 19:29–41 and (possibly) 17:5 describe the function of town assemblies in the operation of a city's business. This is characteristic of the first and perhaps early second centuries. In the second century A.D., however, these town assemblies were replaced by town councils.

4) *Details about the administration of affairs associated with the Jewish temple in Jerusalem.* (a) Both inscriptions[3] and literary sources (e.g., Philo, *Legat.* 212; Josephus, *A.J.* 14.11.5 §417; *B.J.* 5.5.2 §193–94; 6.2.4 §125–26) speak about the prohibition against Gentiles in the inner areas of the temple. Acts 21:27–36 presupposes this. (b) A Roman tribune had to possess Roman citizenship. During the reign of Claudius citizenship could be bought with a sufficient number of bribes (e.g., Dio Cassius 60.17.5–6). The tribune in Acts 21:28, Claudius Lysias, who had bought his citizenship, apparently had gained it during the time of Claudius, when bribes were in fashion. (c) Roman soldiers were permanently stationed in the tower of Antonia with the responsibility of watching for and suppressing any disturbances at the festivals of the Jews (e.g., Josephus, *B.J.* 5.5.8 §244). To reach the affected area they would have had to come down a flight of steps into the Temple precincts (Josephus, *B.J.* 5.5.8 §243). The events of Acts 21:31–37 reflect these details precisely.

5) *Synchronization of historical details.* R. P. C. Hanson gives an example.

> He (Luke) tells us that Paul encountered the high priest Ananias shortly before he met the procurator Felix (Acts 23:2, 33; 24:2, 3); that Felix was at that time married to Drusilla (24:24); that some time afterwards (whether as long as two years or not is uncertain) Felix was superseded by Festus, who shortly after reaching Palestine attended to Paul's case and gave him, among other measures, a hearing before King Agrippa II, with whom the King's sister Bernice was at that time living (25:1–27).[4]

Hanson concludes, "This is a very remarkable piece of synchronization on the part of the author."[5] It would have been easy to miss the fact that Ananias was priest at just that time. He was deposed sometime during the procuratorship of Felix. It would have been difficult to get Drusilla rightly related to Felix. She had already been married to one husband,

---

[3] Cf. C. K. Barrett, *The New Testament Background: Selected Documents* (New York: Harper, 1961), 50, for an example.
[4] R. P. C. Hanson, *The Acts* (Oxford: Clarendon, 1967), 8.
[5] Ibid.

and even more so to get Bernice correctly associated with Festus. She lived with her brother, Agrippa, for only a limited time during Festus's procuratorship.

This type of evidence has been assembled carefully by a host of scholars. One of them, the Roman historian A. N. Sherwin-White, concludes,

> For Acts, the confirmation of historicity is overwhelming. Yet Acts is, in simple terms and judged externally, no less of a propaganda document than the Gospels, liable to similar distortion. But any attempt to reject its basic historicity even in matters of detail must now appear absurd. Roman historians have long taken it for granted.[6]

There are those, however, who believe the same type of evidence argues against the historicity of Acts. A few typical examples should suffice.

1) *Gamaliel's speech.* Acts 5:33–39 gives an account of a speech by the first-century Pharisee Gamaliel, in which he refers to two movements other than the Way: one led by Theudas (v. 36), and "after him" (v. 37) one led by Judas the Galilean. Josephus places Judas about A.D. 6 (*A.J.* 18.1.1 §4–10; 20.5.2 §102; *B.J.* 2.8.1 §118; 2.17.8 §433; 7.8.1 §253). He places Theudas under the procurator Fadus, A.D. 44–46 (*A.J.* 20.5.1 §97–98). Two problems emerge. First, the order of Judas and Theudas is reversed in Acts 5. Second, Theudas's movement comes after the time when Gamaliel is speaking. There is not much to be said about this unless Josephus is wrong or there was an earlier Theudas.

2) *Geography of Palestine.* First, Acts 9:31, which says, "So the church throughout all Judea and Galilee and Samaria had peace and was built up" (RSV), has been taken to mean that Judea was understood to have been directly connected to Galilee. If so, then Luke had an incorrect understanding of Palestinian geography. In response, one must note first that Luke does not always use Judea in the same way. (a) Sometimes Judea refers to the Roman province which, in contrast to Galilee, was subject to Roman procurators (Luke 3:1; 23:6). (b) At other times it refers to the whole of Palestine (Luke 1:5; 7:17; 23:5; Acts 10:37). (c) In still other places Judea refers to the part of Palestine inhabited by Jews, excluding Samaria (Acts 1:8) and Galilee (Acts 9:31) and even Caesarea (Acts 12:19). (d) Sometimes Luke distinguishes between Judea

---

[6] A. N. Sherwin-White, *Roman Society and Roman Law in the New Testament* (Grand Rapids: Baker, 1978), 189.

and Jerusalem (Acts 1:8; 8:1). In Acts 9:31 Judea is used as in instance (c). One must note secondly, given Acts 8:1 ("scattered throughout the region of Judea and Samaria," RSV) and 15:1–3 (which has the journey pass from Antioch through Phoenicia and Samaria to Jerusalem), that Luke knows the proper arrangement of Palestine's component regions. The order of the regions mentioned in 9:31 must be due to other than geographical reasons.[7]

A second example is Acts 23:31, which says the soldiers brought Paul from Jerusalem to Antipatris, a distance of some forty-five miles, overnight. Thirty miles constituted a suitable day's journey whether by land or by sea. Both the numbers involved (two hundred soldiers, seventy horsemen, two hundred spearmen) and the speed of the journey (thirty-eight to forty-five miles in a night) are exaggerated to emphasize the importance of the person being accompanied and the extent of the danger.

There are certainly points at which the contemporary color of Acts can be challenged, but they are few and insignificant compared to the overwhelming congruence between Acts and its time and place. What is one to make of such evidence?

There is widespread agreement that an exact description of the milieu does not prove the historicity of the event narrated. Henry J. Cadbury's *The Book of Acts in History* makes two points: (1) Acts fits beautifully into its contemporary setting (Greco-Roman, Jewish, and early Christian), and (2) accurate local color in no way proves general historical accuracy.[8] This has prompted a strong response from Ward Gasque.

> Cadbury's statement ... that Greek and Latin novels are often as full of accurate local and contemporary color as are historical writings is misleading. ... Whereas the author of Acts is carefully accurate in his representation of the time and places of which he writes, the local and contemporary color contained in the writers of fiction is that of the time and places in which they write.[9]

One level on which the argument about the historicity of Acts is carried on is that involving the quest for contemporary color. Taken alone, however, its results are indecisive.

---

[7] Martin Hengel, *Between Jesus and Paul* (Philadelphia: Fortress, 1985), 99.
[8] Henry J. Cadbury, *The Book of Acts in History* (London: Adam & Charles Black, 1955), 120.
[9] Ward Gasque, *A History of the Criticism of the Acts of the Apostles* (Tübingen: Mohr, 1975), 193, n. 94.

Historical Sequence

The argument from historical sequence assumes that a document is not historically reliable if it lacks a correct sequence of the events narrated. By inference, a document must be historically trustworthy if the events it relates are given in their proper chronological order. Scholars involved in this type of argument, therefore, look for evidence to corroborate or correct the historical sequence given by Acts. This evidence comes from Greco-Roman and Jewish sources on the one hand and the Pauline epistles on the other.

Greco-Roman and Jewish sources speak about certain events also mentioned by the narrative of Acts. They enable one to check the relative chronology of the events in Acts. Five such events are usually noted.[10]

1) The reference to the death of Herod Agrippa I in Acts 12:23 has a counterpart in Josephus (*A.J.* 19.8.2 §343–51). From Josephus, Herod's death can be dated to A.D. 44.

2) Acts 11:28 and 12:25 speak of a famine under Claudius (A.D. 41–54). The famine is mentioned in Acts before the death of Herod (12:20–23). Josephus (*A.J.* 20.2.5 §51–53; 20.5.2 §100–101) mentions a famine in Jerusalem relieved by the good graces of Queen Helena of Adiabene connected with the procuratorship of Tiberius Julius Alexander (A.D. 46–48) and possibly with that of his predecessor, Fadus. Josephus, however, locates the famine after the death of Herod. Assuming Josephus's accuracy, Agabus's prophecy is, therefore, not precisely placed in the sequence of Acts (11:28). It may belong to the period when the signs of trouble were first apparent in Egypt.[11] Or the order of the two events may have been inverted due to some Lucan tendency.[12]

3) Acts 18:2 mentions an edict of Claudius expelling the Jews from Rome. Suetonius (*Claud.* 25.4) mentions the same event. The fifth-

---

[10] E.g., Donald L. Jones, 'Luke's Unique Interest in Historical Chronology,' in *SBL Seminar Papers, 1989* (SBLSP 28; Atlanta: Scholars Press, 1989), 378–87; Karl P. Donfried, 'Chronology,' *ABD* 1:1016–22; G. B. Caird, 'Chronology of the New Testament,' *IDB* 1:603–7.

[11] Hemer, *The Book of Acts*, 6; K. S. Gapp, 'The Universal Famine under Claudius,' *HTR* 28 (1935): 258–65.

[12] Charles H. Talbert, 'Again: Paul's Visit to Jerusalem,' *NovT* 9 (1967): 26–40.

century historian Orosius (7.6.15–16) places the edict in the ninth year of Claudius (A.D. 49), citing Josephus as an authority. Two matters cause some pause. First, we know of no such reference by Josephus in his extant materials. Second, Dio Cassius (60.6.6) mentions Claudius's embargo on Jewish meetings in Rome in A.D. 41, but there is no hint of actual expulsion. As a result, some have wanted to identify the embargo on public meetings with the expulsion and regard them as two references to the same event and then to date the event to A.D. 41. If so, then the relative chronology of Acts at this point is problematic. If, however, as seems preferable, one takes the references to be to two different events and accepts Orosius's date of A.D. 49, the relative chronology is correct.

4) The proconsulship of Gallio is mentioned in Acts 18:12. On the basis of an inscription found at Delphi, Gallio's stay in Corinth can be dated to about A.D. 51–52.[13] This fits the relative chronology of Acts.

5) The procuratorship of Festus mentioned in Acts 24:27 is also referred to by Josephus (*A.J.* 20.8.9 §182). Eusebius in his chronological tables places the arrival of Festus in the tenth year of Agrippa II. Josephus (*B.J.* 2.14.4 §284) places the beginning of Agrippa's reign in A.D. 50. His tenth year would have been A.D. 59.[14] If so, then the relative chronology of Acts is appropriate.

In addition to these five points in the relative chronology of Acts corroborated or corrected by Greco-Roman and Jewish sources, scholars who work at this level seek further clarification from a comparison of Acts with Paul's letters.

T. H. Campbell, in a rarely noticed article of 1955,[15] argues that the sequence of Paul's missionary activities that can be inferred from his letters is remarkably compatible with the information from Acts.[16] His schema as developed from the letters runs as follows:

---

[13] Klaus Haacker, 'Gallio,' *ABD* 2:901–3.

[14] Contra Kirsopp Lake, 'The Chronology of Acts,' in *The Beginnings of Christianity* (ed. F. J. Foakes-Jackson and Kirsopp Lake; 5 vols.; Grand Rapids: Baker, 1966), 5:464–67, who puts the date at 55.

[15] T. H. Campbell, 'Paul's Missionary Journeys as Reflected in His Letters,' *JBL* 74 (1955): 80–87.

[16] His schema is approved by W. G. Kümmel, *Introduction to the New Testament* (Nashville: Abingdon: 1966), 179, and J. A. Fitzmyer, 'The Pauline Letters and the Lucan Account of Paul's Missionary Journeys,' in *SBL Seminar Papers, 1988* (SBLSP 27; Atlanta: Scholars Press, 1988), 83.

persecution of Christians (Gal 1:13–14; cf. Acts 9)
conversion (Gal 1:15–17a; cf. Acts 9)
to Arabia (Gal 1:17b; cf. Acts makes no mention)
to Damascus (Gal 1:17c; cf. Acts 9)
to Jerusalem (Gal 1:18–19; cf. Acts 9)
to regions of Syria and Cilicia (Gal 1:21; cf. Acts 11:25)
to Jerusalem after fourteen years (Gal 2:1–10; cf. Acts 11 or 15?)
to Philippi (1 Thess 2:1–2; Phil 4:15–16; cf. Acts 16)
to Thessalonica (1 Thess 2:1–2; Phil 4:15–16; cf. Acts 17)
to Athens (1 Thess 3:1–3; cf. Acts 17)
to Corinth (2 Cor 11:7–9; cf. Acts 18)
to Ephesus (1 Cor 16:8–9; cf. Acts 19)
to Troas (2 Cor 2:12; Acts does not mention)
to Macedonia (2 Cor 8–9; cf. Acts 20)
to Corinth (2 Cor 12; cf. Acts 20:2b-3)
to Jerusalem (Rom 15:22–25; cf. Acts 21)
to Rome (Rom 15:22–25; cf. Acts 28)

When the sequence of Paul's movements as revealed by his letters is put side by side with that recorded in Acts, there is a correspondence which is very striking, especially in view of the probability that the author of Acts had not read Paul's letters.[17]

There are, of course, some details Acts does not mention just as there are some things the epistles do not mention. The most serious gap in the sequence is that in Paul's letters one finds no clue as to when his work in the province of Galatia should be placed. We learn only that Paul had been among the Galatians twice when he wrote them (Gal 4:13). In spite of these gaps, the overall correspondence between the relative order of events in Acts and in Paul's letters is remarkable.

The major problem in any attempted correlation between Paul's letters and Acts is that of Paul's visits to Jerusalem. The situation can be simply stated. In Paul's letters one hears explicitly about three visits of the apostle to Jerusalem: (a) Gal 1:18–19; (b) Gal 2:1–10; (c) Rom 15:25–32. In Acts there are five such visits described: (a) Acts 9:26–29; (b) Acts 11:27–30; 12:25; (c) Acts 15:1–29; (d) Acts 18:22; and (e) Acts 21:15–17. The first visits mentioned in Paul's letters and in Acts are usually thought to be the same, in spite of certain difficulties. It is Paul's first visit to Jerusalem after his conversion. The last visits in Paul's letters and in Acts are usually thought to be the same, in spite of certain differences. It is his visit to deliver the collection, at which time

---

[17] Campbell, 'Paul's Missionary Journeys,' 84.

he is arrested and eventually sent to Rome. The problem lies in the attempted correlation between the second visit mentioned in Galatians (2:1–10) and the three visits in Acts (chs. 11; 15; 18).

There are multiple solutions proposed. A partial list is instructive.

(a) Galatians 2 = Acts 15[18]
(b) Galatians 2 = Acts 11[19]
(c) Galatians 2 = Acts 11 = Acts 15[20]
(d) Galatians 2 = Acts 18[21]
(e) Galatians 2 = a visit nowhere mentioned in Acts[22]

If one assumes the first solution, the implications about the historical sequence of Acts are negative. Acts is not simply silent about events; it is simply wrong about a certain key event (Acts 11). If one assumes the second solution, the implications are more favorable for Acts. The first two visits dovetail nicely. A certain later visit merely goes unmentioned in the epistles. At present the entire discussion is stalemated.

At this point one needs to become aware of an assumption that controls virtually the entire discussion. It is decisive in the evaluation of the data. This assumption runs as follows: Paul's letters are primary sources for a knowledge of Paul; Acts is a late secondary source. Of the two sources, Paul's letters are obviously the more trustworthy. This is true not only for Paul's ideas but also for Paul's career.[23] So one starts from Gal 1–2. The trustworthiness of the narrative outline of Paul's career in this autobiographical section is underscored by his oath of truthfulness in 1:20 ("In what I am writing to you, before God, I do not lie!" RSV).

In spite of its apparent truth (a primary source is to be preferred over a secondary source), this assumption is in need of careful reconsideration given the nature of autobiography in antiquity.[24] George Lyons states the case:

---

[18] J. B. Lightfoot, *Saint Paul's Epistle to the Galatians* (10th ed.; London: Macmillan, 1890), 123–28.

[19] A. M. Ramsey, 'What Was the Ascension?' in *Historicity and Chronology in the New Testament* (ed. D. E. Nineham: London, SPCK, 1965), 57–59.

[20] Morton S. Enslin, *Christian Beginnings* (New York: Harper, 1938), 228–29.

[21] John Knox, *Chapters in the Life of Paul* (Nashville: Abingdon, 1950).

[22] T. W. Manson, *Studies in the Gospels and Epistles* (Philadelphia: Westminster, 1962), 176–78.

[23] Knox, *Chapters in the Life*.

[24] George Misch, *A History of Autobiography in Antiquity* (2 vols.; Cambridge: Harvard University Press, 1951).

> Caution is in order in reaching historical conclusions on the basis of ancient autobiographical literature. ... Persuasion, not truth, was its overriding concern. ... The emphasis upon ethical characterization and idealization permitted exaggeration and/or suppression of certain aspects of the real life as legitimate autobiographical devices. Protests of truthfulness often were made precisely at the point where truth was most seriously compromised. ... Autobiographical documents scarcely ever have the value of truthful records or objective narratives.[25]

Scholes and Kellog take the same line. "First person narrative in antiquity seems to have been used mainly not for factual representation but for highly unreliable and one sided *apologiae*."[26] For this reason, Jack Sanders can say that Paul's remarks in Gal 1–2 should be considered suspect and so unreliable as to the sequence of events and details of the apostolic council.[27] If one operates out of expectations conditioned by ancient autobiography (e.g., Cicero *Ep.* 5.12—"An autobiographer must needs ... pass over anything that calls for censure"), there must be much less certainty about the absolute reliability of the sequence of events derived from Gal 1–2, especially as regards Paul's visits to Jerusalem. The implications of this consideration have yet to be worked out in terms of Paul's visits to Jerusalem in Acts.

From the point of view of Greco-Roman and Jewish history, the relative sequence of events in Acts is sound. The one possible exception is the date of the famine. From the perspective of Paul's letters, the relative sequence of events is also generally sound. The one sticking point is the possible correlation of Paul's visits to Jerusalem in Galatians and Acts, especially Gal 2:1–10's counterpart in Acts (11? or 15?). This is not to claim historicity for every detail; it is to claim soundness for the overall sequence of events in Acts with rare exception, insofar as comparative materials allow one to check.

Nevertheless, the ongoing debate about the correlation of Paul's visits to Jerusalem in Galatians and in Acts prevents decisive conclusions from this level of argument.

---

[25] George Lyons, *Pauline Autobiography* (Atlanta: Scholars Press, 1985).
[26] Robert Scholes and Robert Kellog, *The Nature of Narrative* (New York: Oxford University Press, 1966), 244.
[27] Jack T. Sanders, 'Paul's Autobiographical Statements in Galatians 1–2,' *JBL* 85 (1966): 335.

Confirmed Facts and Episodes of Integrity

It is assumed that a document cannot be regarded as historically reliable if its individual events cannot be confirmed by external evidence and if its individual episodes do not manifest integrity/unity. By inference, a document whose events can be confirmed by external means and whose episodes can be shown to possess integrity must be considered historically reliable. Scholars who argue at this level search for external confirmation for individual facts in Acts' narrative and seek to show that the individual episodes of the account do, in fact, possess integrity/unity. The two sides of this argument need explanation.

1) Excursus I of Adolf Harnack's *The Acts of the Apostles* is entitled 'Survey of the narratives of St. Luke concerning the Primitive Community and the earlier history of St. Paul (Acts i–xiv), which are confirmed by the Pauline Epistles.'[28] In this appendix, Harnack gives thirty-nine examples of facts in Acts 1–14 that can be confirmed from the Pauline epistles. A few examples suffice.

(a) Jerusalem, not some town in Galilee, is the seat of the primitive community (Acts passim; Gal 2; Rom 15).
(b) Christian communities were also in existence outside Jerusalem, especially in Judea, at a very early date (Acts 9:31; 1 Thess 2:14; Gal 1:22).
(c) The churches of Jerusalem and Judea had to endure persecution at the hands of their compatriots (Acts passim; 1 Thess 2:14).
(d) Barnabas is an important missionary to the Gentiles from the Jerusalem church, especially as regards Antioch of Syria (Acts 11:22–26; Gal 2:13). He worked side by side with Paul (Acts 11:25–26; Gal 2:1, 13).
(e) Baptism was an act of entry into the Christian community (Acts 2:38; 8:12; 1 Cor 1:14; Rom 6:1–4). It was in the name of Jesus (Acts 2:38; 1 Cor 1:13)
(f) The resurrection of Jesus was at the core of Christian proclamation (Acts 1:22; 2:32; 3:15; 5:30; 1 Cor 15:14, 17).
(g) Paul fled secretly from Damascus after escaping over the wall (Acts 9:23–25; 2 Cor 11:32–33).

---

[28] Adolph Harnack, *The Acts of the Apostles* (New York: G. P. Putnam's Sons, 1909).

Harnack concludes,

> The agreement which in these numerous instances exists between the Acts (chs. i–xiv) and the Pauline epistles ... is so extensive and so detailed as to exclude all wild hypotheses concerning those passages of the Acts that are without attestation in those epistles. The Acts is an historical work that has nothing in common with the later 'Acts of the Apostles,' and is not to be judged by the standard nor criticized by the method which suits these.[29]

2) The second aspect of this level of work has to do with the challenges to the integrity of various episodes in the narrative of Acts. It is sometimes argued that a single episode in Acts is actually a combination of more than one event and hence is not to be taken as historically reliable.[30]

Acts 18, Paul's visit to Corinth, is a prime example. Does Acts 18 conflate two or more Pauline visits to Corinth into one? Jerome Murphy-O'Connor seems to think so.[31] On the one hand, Acts 18:2 says that Aquila and Priscilla had lately come to Corinth from Italy because Claudius had commanded all the Jews to leave Rome. As we have seen, this expulsion is confirmed by Suetonius (*Claud.* 25.4), who says, "Since the Jews were continually making disturbances at the instigation of Chrestus, he (Claudius) expelled them from Rome." The question about the expulsion relates to its date.

The fifth-century historian Orosius (7.6.15–16) says,

> Josephus refers to the expulsion of Jews by Claudius in his ninth year. But Suetonius touches me more in saying, "Claudius expelled from Rome the Jews constantly making disturbances at the instigation of Chrestus."

If Orosius is taken at face value, then the event is linked to A.D. 49.

Dio Cassius, a third-century historian, speaks of an event that happened in A.D. 41. He says,

> As for the Jews, who had increased so greatly by reason of their multitude that it would have been hard without raising a tumult to expel them from the city, he did not drive them out, but ordered them, while continuing their traditional mode of life, not to hold meetings. (60.6.6)

---

[29] Ibid., 272.

[30] Gerd Lüdemann, *Early Christianity according to the Traditions of Acts* (Minneapolis: Fortress, 1989), 130–33, 176, 178, 194, 200.

[31] Jerome Murphy-O'Connor, *St. Paul's Corinth* (Wilmington, Del.: Michael Glazier, 1983).

The question is, Are Orosius and Dio Cassius speaking about the same event or two separate events? Murphy-O'Connor contends they are referring to one and the same event: namely, as a result of a disturbance in a Roman synagogue concerning Christ, Claudius expelled the missionaries who were not Roman citizens and temporarily withdrew from that Jewish community the right of assembly.[32]

On the other hand, Acts 18:12 says that when Gallio was proconsul of Achaea, the Jews brought Paul before the tribunal. From an inscription found at Delphi, Gallio's presence in Corinth can be dated to A.D. 51–52.[33] If this is so, then Acts 18 actually contains in its narrative about Paul's coming to Corinth two separate visits of the apostle to the city, one in A.D. 41 and the other in A.D. 50–52. A document that conflates separate events into a narrative and treats them as one is obviously not historically reliable.

Stephen Benko, however, concludes that the accounts of Claudius's dealings with the Jews in Rome cannot be convincingly conflated into a single episode, but that trouble did arise on two occasions during his reign: A.D. 41 and A.D. 49.[34] The main reason for refusing to conflate the events is that the one denies what the other affirms. Dio Cassius says Claudius in 41 did not expel the Jews; Orosius agrees with Suetonius that Claudius did expel the Jews and dates it to 49. The most natural way to take accounts that are diametrically opposite is to regard them as referring to different events. If so, then the unity of Acts 18 is upheld. Priscilla and Aquila arrived in Corinth sometime after their expulsion from Rome in 49. Paul joined them and was there during Gallio's tenure in 51–52. A document that narrates episodes that have integrity has a high claim to historicity; one that conflates separate events into one does not.

From this cursory survey of the types of argument having to do with individual events and episodes one can see the nature of the issues. Regarding the evidence assembled by Harnack, an opponent might say, Yes, a number of details in Acts 1–14 are confirmed by Paul's letters, but what about those that are not? Is it legitimate to infer historicity for uncorroborated details because some details check out? Regarding the

---

[32] Ibid., 136.
[33] Adolf Deissman, *Paul: A Study in Social and Religious History* (New York: Harper, 1912), 261–86; Murphy-O'Connor, *St. Paul's Corinth*, 141–52.
[34] Stephen Benko, *Pagan Rome and the Early Christians* (Bloomington: Indiana University Press, 1984), 18.

debates about the unity of individual episodes, one can see that every issue is debatable and that what is probable appears different to various scholars.

This appendix so far has sought, by a hasty survey, to indicate the three levels on which the debates about the historicity of Acts are carried on. No one is sufficient to carry the day, either for or against the historical value of the Acts of the Apostles. Any successful argument must involve all three levels of evidence: accurate contemporary color, sound historical sequence, and confirmed facts and individual episodes with integrity. Even then the argument is incomplete. This is because the matter of Acts' historicity also involves three specific issues: (1) the speeches, (2) the portrait of Paul, and (3) the miracles. No argument for or against the historicity of Acts is adequate that omits even one of these issues. The second part of this paper, therefore, will survey these issues and how they play a role in the overall case one way or the other.

The Speeches of Acts

Since Dibelius[35] and Cadbury,[36] most scholars have regarded the speeches of Acts after the analogy of the speeches used in ancient historical writings. Thucydides (1.22.1) is most often quoted:

> As to the speeches that were made by different men, either when they were about to begin the war or when they were already engaged therein, it has been difficult to recall with strict accuracy the words actually spoken, both for me as regards that which I myself heard, and for those who from various other sources have brought me reports. Therefore, the speeches are given in the language in which, as it seemed to me, the several speakers would express, on the subjects under consideration, the sentiments most befitting the occasion, though at the same time I have adhered as closely as possible to the general sense of what was actually said.

Tacitus (*Ann.* 15.63) remarks on the occasion of Seneca's death that the farewell speech of that philosopher had been published literally so that the historian did not need to reproduce it in Seneca's own words. Pliny (*Ep.* 1.16) says regarding Pompeius Saturninus, "his histories will please you ... for the words he puts into the mouths of his characters

---

[35] Martin Dibelius, *Studies in the Acts of the Apostles* (ed. H. Greeven; New York: Scribner's, 1956).

[36] Henry J. Cadbury, 'The Speeches in Acts,' in *The Beginnings of Christianity* (ed. F. J. Foakes Jackson and Kirsopp Lake; 5 vols.; Grand Rapids: Baker, 1966), 5:402–26.

are as vivid as his own public speeches, though condensed into a simpler and terser style." Lucian (*Hist. conscr.* 58) says, "If a person has to be introduced to make a speech, above all let his language suit his person and his subject." Such statements from Thucydides to Lucian have been taken to mean that ancient speeches were an author's compositions based on what he deemed appropriate for the particular individual in his particular time, place, and circumstances.

This conclusion is reinforced by two additional strands of evidence. On the one hand, comparison of different versions of ancient speeches seems to confirm the conclusion reached. (a) Josephus (*A.J.* 1.6.3 §279–84) gives the farewell speech of Mattathias in a very different form from that in 1 Macc 2:50–68. (b) Also Herod's speech to his soldiers is found in two very different forms in two different places in Josephus (*A.J.* 15.5.3 §127–46 and *B.J.* 1.19.4 §373–79). (c) Plutarch (*Oth.* 15) and Tacitus (*Hist.* 2.47) manifest extensive agreement in their accounts of Otho but offer entirely different versions of his last address. (d) Dio Cassius's report of Caesar's speech to his soldiers (38.36–46) is very different from that reported by Caesar himself (*Bell. gall.* 1.40). On the other hand, recognition that biographers since the time of Xenophon,[37] as well as Jewish writers,[38] followed the same practice offers confirmation to the widely held conclusions of Cadbury and Dibelius. If so, what does this imply about the historicity of Acts?

A minority voice contends that it is "by no means true that all ancient historians felt free to put fictitious speeches in the mouths of historical characters."[39] Polybius is the example cited. In book 12, Polybius gives a contrast between history as he understands it and as one Timaeus practices it. Polybius is critical of Timaeus because his "pronouncements are full of dreams, prodigies, incredible tales, and to put it shortly, craven superstitions and womanish love of the marvelous" (12:24). His speeches are "untruthfully reported" and "on purpose" (12.25a). Timaeus "actually invents speeches," while it is the function of history to discover first of all what was actually spoken (12.25b). The brief speeches in Acts, moreover, bear no resemblance to the rhetorical compositions of Josephus. "This is not to say they are to be simply

---

[37] Patricia Cox, *Biography in Late Antiquity* (Berkeley: University of California Press, 1983), 63.
[38] Julius Kaplan, *The Redaction of the Babylonian Talmud* (New York: Bloch, 1933), 154.
[39] Hemer, *The Book of Acts*, 75.

fitted into a 'Polybian' alternative."[40] It does mean, however, that the possibility exists that some or all of the speeches of Acts are a digest or summary of what was actually said. The matter needs examination. In confronting this first specific problem, one meets yet again the divide between scholars about the historicity of Acts.

The Portrait of Paul

With the shift in focus from the historicity to the theology of Acts, certain scholars sharpened their descriptions of Lucan theology by contrasting it with Paul's as known from his epistles. Out of this emerged the contention that there is a discrepancy between the portrait of Paul in Acts and that in the genuine letters. Representative points in the comparison may be noted.[41]

1) In Acts, Paul is a great miracle worker. In the epistles, he is a suffering apostle (e.g., 2 Cor 12:10).
2) In Acts, Paul is an outstanding orator. In the epistles, he is called a feeble speaker (2 Cor 10:10).
3) In Acts, Paul is not on an equal footing with the Twelve. In the epistles, he is an apostle of equal standing with the Twelve (1 Cor 9:1; 15:1–11).
4) In Acts, Jewish opposition to Paul is due to his teaching about the resurrection from the dead. In the epistles, Jewish opposition is over the law (Gal 2:11–16).
5) In Acts, natural theology is used to portray Greco-Roman culture as a true preparation for Christianity. In the epistles, natural theology is used to hold the Gentiles responsible before God (Rom 1–3).
6) In Acts, Paul is pro Jewish law. In the epistles, he wages an anti Jewish polemic against the law.
7) In Acts, Paul's Christology is adoptionistic. In the epistles, Paul holds a Christology of preexistence.
8) In Acts, Paul does not hold to an imminent eschatology. In the epistles, there is an imminent expectation.

---

[40] Ibid., 78.
[41] Derived from Ernst Haenchen, *The Acts of the Apostles* (Philadelphia: Westminster, 1971), 112–16, and Philip Vielhauer, 'On the 'Paulinism' of Acts,' in *Studies in Luke-Acts* (ed. L. E. Keck and J. L. Martyn; Nashville: Abingdon, 1966), 33–50.

These contrasts are taken by scholars like Haenchen and Vielhauer as irreconcilable differences between the portrait of the historical Paul and the Lucan Paul. Given these discontinuities, the historical reliability of Acts is called into question.

These sharp distinctions between the picture of Paul gained from his genuine letters and that found in Acts have not gone unchallenged. Granted, there are at least three portraits of Paul found in the New Testament: that of the genuine epistles, that of the Deuteropaulines like the Pastorals, and that of Acts. Granted, each has its own distinctive elements. To call the discontinuities irreconcilable differences, however, is something many scholars will not accept. A typical response to Haenchen and Vielhauer runs something as follows.[42]

1) In Paul's letters, his ministry includes miracles (2 Cor 12:12; Rom 15:19; 1 Cor 2:1–4; Gal 3:1–5; 1 Thess 1:5). In Acts, Paul's ministry also involves suffering (Acts 14:5, 22; 16:19–40; 17:5–9, 13; 18:12–17; 20:1, 3; 21:4, 11–14, 27–36).

2) In Paul's letters, one finds evidences of rhetorical skills and techniques characteristic of the orators of his time (e.g., diatribe, *inclusio*, *chiasmus*). The specific charge in 2 Cor 10:10 refers to Paul's withdrawal at an earlier time rather than risk the loss of the church in Corinth.[43] It has nothing to do with his lack of rhetorical skill. Nor does 1 Cor 2:1–5 imply that Paul was oratorically deficient. It says rather that Paul's converts' confidence lay in the evidences of the Spirit in their midst rather than in Paul's verbal pretenses.

3) In Acts, the Twelve represent the true Jesus tradition while Paul stands for the vitality of religious experience of the risen Lord. Acts' schema makes the latter subservient to the former. In his letters, one also finds Paul subservient to the authentic tradition, which came down to him from the apostles before him (1 Cor 11:23–25; 1 Cor 15:1–11), at the same time that he claims his equal status based on his religious experience (Gal 1).

---

[42] A composite taken from Ulrich Wilckens, 'Interpreting Luke-Acts in a Period of Existentialist Theology,' in *Studies in Luke-Acts* (ed. L. E. Keck and J. L. Martyn; Nasville: Abingdon, 1966), 60–83; Peder Borgen, 'From Paul to Luke,' *CBQ* 31 (1969): 168–82; and Kümmel, *Introduction*.

[43] Charles H. Talbert, *Reading Corinthians* (New York: Crossroad, 1987), 111–12.

4) Jewish opposition to Paul in Acts is due not only to his teaching about the resurrection (Acts 23:6; 24:21; 26:6) but also because of Paul's perceived opposition to the law and Temple (15:5; 21:21; 21:28).
5) Both the Paul of Acts and of the genuine epistles hold to a natural theology or general revelation. The functions of this natural theology vary, depending upon the context in which it is used.
6) In Acts, Paul expresses reservations about the soteriological value of the Law (Acts 13:39) at the same time that he, as a Jewish Christian, lives by its rules amidst Jews (18:18; 21:23–24). This is similar to the Paul of the epistles who is critical of the law's soteriological role (Gal 2:19–21) at the same time that he lives by its tenets when necessary (1 Cor 9:19–23).
7) Paul's picture of Jesus in Acts 13:33 belongs not to preexistence Christology but rather to exaltation Christology; in Acts 17:30–31 it resembles two-foci Christology. In the epistles, an epiphany Christology (Gal 4:4) lies side by side with exaltation Christology (Phil 2:6–11) and probably a two-foci Christology (1 Thess 1:9–10).[44]
8) In the epistles, Paul sometimes seems to hold to an imminent expectation and believes he will be alive when the end arrives (1 Thess 4:15; 1 Cor 15:51–52); in other places he seems to reckon with his death before the parousia (Phil 1:19–26; 2 Cor 5:1–10?).

Two observations need to be made at this point. First, given these adjustments to the claims made for irreconcilable differences between Acts and the epistles in their portraits of Paul, Ulrich Wilckens can say that "it is Paul, interpreted existentially, who is so sharply set against Luke. ... But the existentially interpreted Paul is not the historical Paul."[45] Second, given the different historical situations of Paul and Acts, one should not expect theological identity. There would be continuity in doctrine, but the doctrines would be expected to function differently in different contexts.

If the discontinuities in the portraits of Paul in the genuine epistles and in Acts are taken to be irreconcilable differences, then the historicity of Acts may be called into question. If the discontinuities are seen

---

[44] The categories are those of R. H. Fuller, *The Foundations of New Testament Christology* (New York: Scribner's, 1965).
[45] Wilckens, 'Interpreting Luke-Acts,' 77.

merely as different shadings due to variation in historical contexts, then the historical reliability of Acts fares better.

Miracles

Since the nineteenth century the historical value of Acts has been called into question because of the presence of miracles in its narrative. This posture is still dominant. Gerd Lüdemann is a typical representative of this perspective in the current generation. Regarding the healing of the lame man in Acts 3, he writes,

> There is no historical nucleus to the tradition of the miracle story in vv. 1–10. Those who are lame from their childhood are (unfortunately) not made whole again. But the story reflects the existence of a Christian community which reported great things of Peter's activity in Jerusalem and/or miracles performed by him.[46]

Regarding the story of Peter's release from prison by an angel in Acts 12, Lüdemann writes,

> the miraculous release bears within itself its own historical refutation. However, we may still presuppose a historical nucleus in it, namely that Agrippa had Peter arrested.[47]

For someone with this presupposition about miracles, Acts is indeed a questionable entity.

Over against Lüdemann, one finds a scholar like the late Colin Hemer. Hemer says,

> I am content to operate in a framework where the possibility of miracle is accepted and its appearance is not an automatic cue for reinterpretation or special interpretation.[48]

> Within that framework we may still require reasonably rigorous testimony ... but their possibility may be accepted in principle.[49]

Are miracles possible? The possible is always a function of one's worldview. Worldviews are highly resistant to disconfirmation. The materialistic worldview, represented by Lüdemann, dictates that the world was and is ruled by iron physical laws that not even God could or can bend. Walter Wink comments:

---

[46] Gerd Lüdemann, *Early Christianity*, 54.
[47] Ibid., 145.
[48] Hemer, *The Book of Acts*, 443.
[49] Ibid., 443, n. 52.

In the last decade, advances in the understanding of the placebo effect, the functioning of the immune system, empirical studies of the control yogis can exercise over their internal organs, and above all, the shift from Newtonian lawfulness to Heisenberg's uncertainty principle have changed the way many people look at the possibility of healing. We simply no longer know for certain what is within the realm of possibility. Consequently, some scientists are beginning, *through* science, to jettison the materialistic worldview as reductionist.[50]

Wink points out that these changes in attitude are not based on a single scrap of new evidence from the ancient world but on shifting evaluations of what is possible. What one considers possible determines one's stance on the miraculous in the Acts of the Apostles.[51] On the matter of what is considered possible, scholars differ. These differences, of course, affect their evaluations of the historicity of Acts.

Having looked at the three levels of argument and the three specific issues associated with the question of the historicity of Acts, what can be concluded? What does one mean by the historicity of Acts? Judging from how the argument is conducted, it possible to say that an affirmation of the historical worth of the Acts of the Apostles can be given only if and when certain answers are possible on the levels of contemporary color, historical sequence, and individual episodes on the one hand, and to the issues of speeches, portrait of Paul, and miracles on the other. Confidence in the historicity of Acts requires a certain type of answer to be given in all six cases.

Even then the issue is not settled because of a final matter, namely, the burden of proof demanded. Lüdemann poses the problem. He says,

> The real question is whether Luke's information has to be proved to be true or rather whether it is only false if it can certainly be shown to be so.[52]

If one can show that external evidence confirms the accuracy of Acts' contemporary color at numerous points, does that give one the right to assume the accuracy of points that cannot be checked? If one can show that at a significant number of points the historical sequence of Acts' narrative checks out as sound, does that mean that one can assume the soundness of sequence at those points that cannot be checked? If

---

[50] Walter Wink, 'Our Stories, Cosmic Stories, and the Biblical Story,' in *Sacred Stories* (ed. Charles and Anne Simpkinson; San Francisco: Harper, 1993), 213.
[51] Ibid., 214.
[52] Gerd Lüdemann, *Early Christianity*, 51.

one can show that many individual matters of fact can be confirmed and the unity of a number of episodes can be established, should one infer that matters of fact that cannot be confirmed externally can be assumed to be accurate and that other episodes that are unverified by external data are indeed possessed of integrity?

One group of scholars believes it is responsible to infer the accuracy of unconfirmed material because of the accuracy of confirmed material. F. F. Bruce serves as spokesman for this position. He says,

> When a writer's accuracy is established by valid evidence, he gains the right to be treated as a reliable informant on matters coming within his scope which are not corroborated elsewhere.[53]

The other group thinks it is not responsible to accept anything in Acts as historically reliable unless it has been corroborated by other data, either external or internal. The former feel free to speak globally about the historicity of Acts; the latter are willing to speak about Acts' historical reliability in a much more limited sense. Martin Dibelius says, "the historical reliability of Acts must be measured in each individual case."[54] Assumptions matter.

Enough corroborating data has been assembled already by scholars to enable one to conclude that Acts is not mere fiction and that its record is reasonably reliable in areas where it can be checked. There are, however, enough unchecked areas and enough problems in areas that can be checked to keep professors and graduate students in work for the indefinite future.

Of what value is the Acts of the Apostles for the study of early Christian history, in particular the period prior to A.D. 64? That depends on what one thinks about Acts' historicity. How is the historicity of Acts determined? If the thesis of this essay is correct, the historical value of Acts is determined by an argument that includes the three levels and that addresses the three specific issues described above. Ultimately, the pervasiveness of one's argument will depend on the burden of proof demanded of it.

---

[53] F. F. Bruce, 'The Acts of the Apostles: Historical Record or Theological Reconstruction?' *ANRW* 25.3:2578.

[54] Dibelius, *Studies in the Acts*, 107; cf. Charles H. Talbert, 'Luke-Acts,' in *The New Testament and Its Modern Interpreters* (ed. E. J. Epp and G. W. Macrae; Atlanta: Scholars Press, 1989), 311.

BIBLIOGRAPHY

Alsup, J. E. *The Post-Resurrection Appearance Stories of the Gospel Tradition*. Stuttgart: Calver Verlag, 1975.
The Ante-Nicene Fathers. Edited by Alexander Roberts and James Donaldson. 1885–1887. 10 vols. Repr., Peabody, Mass.: Hendrickson, 1994.
Athanasskis, Apostolos A. *The Life of Pachomius*. Atlanta: Scholars Press, 1975.
Aune, D. E. *The New Testament in Its Literary Environment*. Library of Early Christianity. Philadelphia: Westminster, 1987.
———. 'The Problem of the Genre of the Gospels: A Critique of C. H. Talbert's *What Is a Gospel?*' Pages 9–60 in vol. 2 of *Gospel Perspectives*. Edited by R. T. France and David Wenham. 6 vols. Sheffield: JSOT Press, 1981.
The Babylonian Talmud: Seder Zera'im. Edited by I. Epstein. Translated by M. Simon. London: Soncino, 1948.
Barrett, C. K. *The New Testament Background: Selected Documents*. New York: Harper, 1961.
Bauckham, Richard. 'For Whom Were Gospels Written?' Pages 13–26 in *The Gospel for All Christians: Rethinking Gospel Audiences*. Grand Rapids: Eerdmans, 1998.
Baur, F. C. *Kritische Untersuchungen über die kanonischen Evangelien ihr Verhaltnis zu einander ihren Charakter und Ursprung*. Tübingen: LF Fues, 1847.
Bedae Venerabilis. *Corpus Christianorum. Series Latina 120, 121*. Turnholti: Typographi Brepols, 1953–.
Benko, Stephen. *Pagan Rome and the Early Christians*. Bloomington: Indiana University Press, 1984.
Borgen, Peder. 'From Paul to Luke.' *Catholic Biblical Quarterly* 31 (1969): 168–82.
Bouttier, M. 'L'humanite de Jesus selon Saint Luc.' *Recherches de science religieuse* 69 (1981): 33–43.
Bouyer, Louis. *The Spirituality of the New Testament and the Fathers*. Vol. 1 of *A History of Christian Spirituality*. New York: Seabury, 1963.
Bovon, Francois. *L'Evangile selon Saint Luc 9:51–14:35*. Commentaire du Nouveau Testament IIIb. Geneve: Labor et Fides, 1996.
———. *Luc le Theologien: Vingt-Cinq Ans de Recherches (1950–1975)*. Neuchatel: Delachaux & Niestle, 1978.
———. *Luke the Theologian: Thirty Three Years of Research (1950–1983)*. Translated by Ken McKinney. Allison Park, Pa.: Pickwick, 1987.
Brown, Raymond E. *The Birth of the Messiah*. Garden City, N.Y.: Doubleday, 1977.
Bruce, F. F. 'The Acts of the Apostles: Historical Record or Theological Reconstruction?' *ANRW* 25.3:2569–2603. Part 2, *Principat*, 25.3. Edited by H. Temporini and W. Haase. New York: de Gruyter, 1989.

———. *The Book of Acts*. New International Commentary on the New Testament. Grand Rapids: Eerdmans, 1956.
Brox, Norbert. *Zeuge und Märtyrer*. Munich: Kösel, 1961.
Bultmann, Rudolf. *Theologie des Neuen Testaments*. Tübingen: Mohr, 1948–53.
———. *Theology of the New Testament*. New York: Scribner, 1951–55.
Burridge, Richard A. *What Are the Gospels? A Comparison with Graeco-Roman Biography*. Society for New Testament Studies Monograph Series. Cambridge: Cambridge University Press, 1992.
Cadbury, Henry J. *The Making of Luke-Acts*. New York: Macmillan, 1927.
———. 'The Speeches in Acts.' Pages 402–26 in vol. 5 of *The Beginnings of Christianity*. Edited by F. J. Foakes-Jackson and Kirsopp Lake. Grand Rapids: Baker, 1966.
Caird, G. B. 'Chronology of the New Testament.' Pages 603–7 in vol. 1 of *Interpreter's Dictionary of the Bible*. Edited by George Arthur Buttrick. 4 vols. New York: Abingdon Press, 1962.
Calvin, John. *A Commentary on a Harmony of the Evangelists*. 3 vols. Grand Rapids: Eerdmans, 1949.
———. *A Commentary upon the Acts of the Apostles*. 2 vols. Grand Rapids: Eerdmans, 1949.
Camparetti, Domenico. 'Papro ercolanese inedito.' *Rivista di Fililogia* 3 (1875): 449–555.
Campbell, T. H. 'Paul's Missionary Journeys as Reflected in His Letters.' *Journal of Biblical Literature* 74 (1955): 80–87.
Cancik, Hubert. 'The History of Culture, Religion, and Institutions in Ancient Historiography: Philological Observations Concerning Luke's History.' *Journal of Biblical Literature* 116 (1997): 673–95.
Cardauns, Burkhart, ed. *M. Terentius Varro Antiquitates Rerum Divinarum*. 2 vols. Wiesbaden: Franz Steiner Verlag, 1976.
Carter, Warren. 'The Crowds in Matthew's Gospel.' *Catholic Biblical Quarterly* 55 (1993): 54–67.
———. 'Matthew 4:18–22 and Matthean Discipleship: An Audience-Oriented Perspective.' *Catholic Biblical Quarterly* 59 (1997): 58–75.
———. 'Recalling the Lord's Prayer: The Authorial Audience and Matthew's Prayer as Familiar Liturgical Experience.' *Catholic Biblical Quarterly* 57 (1995): 514–30.
Carter, Warren, and John Paul Heil. *Matthew's Parables: Audience-Oriented Perspectives*. Monograph Series. Washington, D.C.: Catholic Biblical Association, 1998.
Cassidy, Richard. *Jesus, Politics, and Society: A Study of Luke's Gospel*. Maryknoll, N.Y.: Orbis Books, 1978.
Charlesworth, James H. *The Old Testament Pseudepigrapha*. 2 vols. Garden City, N.Y.: Doubleday, 1983, 1985.
Chesnutt, Randall D. *From Death to Life: Conversion in Joseph and Aseneth*. Journal for the Study of the Pseudepigrapha: Supplement Series 16. Sheffield: Sheffield Academic Press, 1995.
Childs, Brevard S. *The New Testament as Canon: An Introduction*. Philadelphia: Fortress, 1985.

Cohen, Shaye J. D. *From the Maccabees to the Mishnah*. Library of Early Christianity. Philadelphia: Westminster, 1987.
Conzelmann, Hans. *Acts of the Apostles*. Translated by James Limburg, A. Thomas Kraabel, and Donald H. Juel. Hermeneia. Philadelphia: Fortress, 1987.
———. *Die Apostelgeschichte*. Tübingen: J.C.B. Mohr, 1963.
———. *Die Mitte der Zeit: Studien zur Theologie des Lukas*. Beiträge zur historischen Theologie 17. Tübingen: Mohr-Siebeck, 1954.
———. *An Outline of the Theology of the New Testament*. New York: Harper & Row, 1969.
———. *The Theology of St. Luke*. New York: Harper & Brothers, 1960.
Cosgrove, Charles H. 'The Divine δεῖ in Luke-Acts.' *Novum Testamentum* 26 (1984): 168–90.
———. 'The Justification of the Other: An Interpretation of Romans 1:18–4:25.' Pages 613–34 in *SBL Seminar Papers, 1992*. Society of Biblical Literature Seminar Papers 31. Missoula: Scholars Press, 1992.
Cox, Patricia. *Biography in Late Antiquity*. Berkeley: University of California Press, 1983.
Cyril of Alexandria. *Commentary on the Gospel of Luke*. Edited and translated by R. P. Smith. 2 vols. Oxford: Oxford University Press, 1859.
Danker, Frederick W. 'The Endangered Benefactor in Luke-Acts.' Pages 39–48 in *Society of Biblical Literature Seminar Papers, 1981*. Society of Biblical Literature Seminar Papers 20. Chico, Calif.: Scholars Press, 1981.
———. *Jesus and the New Age*. Philadelphia: Fortress, 1988.
Daube, David. *Collaboration with Tyranny in Rabbinic Law*. New York: Oxford University Press, 1966.
Deissman, Adolf. *Paul: A Study in Social and Religious History*. New York: Harper, 1912.
Dexter, Miriam Robbins. *Whence the Goddess?* New York: Pergamon Press, 1990.
Dibelius, Martin. *Aufsätze zur Apostelgeschichte*. Edited by H. Greeven. Göttingen: Vandenhoeck & Ruprecht, 1951.
———. *Studies in the Acts of the Apostles*. Edited by H. Greeven. New York: Scribner's, 1956.
———. 'Zur Formsgeschichte des Neuen Testament (ausserhalb der Evangelien).' *Theologische Rundschau* 3 (1931): 207–42.
Dillon, John, and Jackson Hershbell. *Iamblanchus, On the Pythagorean Way of Life*. Atlanta: Scholars Press, 1991.
Donfried, Karl P. 'Chronology.' Pages 1016–22 in vol. 1 of *Anchor Bible Dictionary*. Edited by David Noel Freedman. 6 vols. New York: Doubleday, 1992.
Dorandi, Titiano. *Storia dei Filosofi: La Stoa da Zenone a Panezio (P Herc 1018)*. Leiden: Brill, 1994.
———. *Storia dei Filosofi: Platone e L'Academia (P Herc 1021 e 164)*. Naples: Bibliopolis, 1991.
Doty, William G. 'The Concept of Genre in Literary Analysis.' Pages 413–48 in volume 2 of *SBL Seminar Papers, 1972*. 2 vols. Society of Biblical Literature Seminar Papers 8. Chico, Calif.: Scholars Press, 1972.

Downing, Christine. 'The Mother Goddess among the Greeks.' Pages 49–59 in *The Book of the Goddess: Past and Present*. Edited by Carl Olson. New York: Crossroad, 1983.
Dreyfus, F. 'Exegese en Sorbonne, Exegese en Eglise.' *Revue Biblique* 81 (1975): 321–59.
Drury, John. *Tradition and Design in Luke*. Atlanta: John Knox, 1976.
Duckworth, George E. *Foreshadowing and Suspense in the Epics of Homer, Apollonius, and Virgil*. New York: Haskill House, 1966.
———. *Structural Patterns and Proportions in Virgil's 'Aeneid.'* Ann Arbor: University of Michigan Press, 1962.
Dupont, Jacques. *The Salvation of the Gentiles*. New York: Paulist, 1979.
During, Ingemar. *Aristotle in the Ancient Biographical Tradition*. Goteborg: Goteborg Universitet Arsskrift, 1957.
Durkheim, Emile. *The Elementary Forms of Religious Life*. New York: Free Press, 1965.
Ellul, Jacques. *Violence*. New York: Seabury, 1969.
Enslin, Morton S. *Christian Beginnings*. New York: Harper, 1938.
The Fathers of the Church. Vol 15: Early Christian Biographies. Edited by Roy J. Deferrari. New York: Fathers of the Church, Inc., 1952.
Feuerbach, Ludwig. *The Essence of Christianity*. New York: Harper, 1957.
Finn, Thomas M. *From Death to Rebirth: Ritual and Conversion in Antiquity*. New York: Paulist, 1997.
———. Review of Wayne A. Meeks, *The Origins of Christian Morality: The First Two Centuries*. *Catholic Biblical Quarterly* 57 (1995): 602.
Fishel, H. A. 'Martyr and Prophet.' *Jewish Quarterly Review* 37 (1947): 265–80, 363–86.
Fitzmyer, Joseph A. *The Gospel According to Luke*. 2 vols. Word Biblical Commentary 28, 28a. Dallas: Word, 1981–85.
———. 'The Pauline Letters and the Lucan Account of Paul's Missionary Journeys.' Pages 82–89 in *SBL Seminar Papers, 1988*. Society of Biblical Literature Seminar Papers 27. Atlanta: Scholars Press, 1988.
Fowler F. G., and H. G. Fowler. *The Works of Lucian of Samosata*. 4 vols. Oxford: Clarendon, 1949.
Frend, W. H. C. *Martyrdom and Persecution in the Early Church*. Oxford: Blackwell, 1965.
Fuller, R. H. *The Foundations of New Testament Christology*. New York: Scribner's, 1965.
Gaiser, Konrad. *Philodems Academica: Die Berichte uber Platon und die Alte Akademie in zwei herkulanensischen Papyri*. Stuttgart: Frommann-Holzboog, 1988.
Gallagher, Eugene V. 'Conversion and Salvation in the Apocryphal Acts of the Apostles.' *Second Century* 8 (1991): 13–30.
Gapp, K. S. 'The Universal Famine under Claudius.' *Harvard Theological Review* 28 (1935): 258–65.
Garrett, Susan R. *The Demise of the Devil: Magic and the Demonic in Luke's Writings*. Minneapolis: Fortress, 1989.
Gasque, Ward. *A History of the Criticism of the Acts of the Apostles*. Tübingen: Mohr, 1975.

George, Augustin. *Études sur l'oeuvre de Luc*. Sources bibliques. Paris: Editions Gabalda, 1978.

———. 'Israël dans l'oeuvre de Luc.' *Revue biblique* 75 (1968): 481–525.

Gerstenberger, E. S., and W. Schrage. *Suffering*. Translated by J. E. Steely. Nashville: Abingdon, 1980.

Gigante, Marcello. 'Les Papyrus d'Herculanum aujourd'hui.' *Bulletin de la Société française de philosophie* 78 (1984): 1–30.

———. *Philodemus in Italy: The Books from Herculaneum*. Translated by Dirk Obbink. Ann Arbor: University of Michigan Press, 1990.

Gill, David W. J., and Conrad Gempf, eds. *The Book of Acts in Its Graeco-Roman Setting*. Grand Rapids: Eerdmans, 1994.

Goldin, Judah. *The Fathers According to Rabbi Nathan*. New Haven: Yale University Press, 1955.

Goodacre, Mark S. *Goulder and the Gospels: An Examination of a New Paradigm*. Journal for the Study of the New Testament: Supplement Series 133. Sheffield: Sheffield Academic Press, 1996.

Goodenough, E. R. *Jewish Symbols in the Greco-Roman Period*. 13 vols. New York: Pantheon Books, 1953–1968.

Goodman, Martin. *Mission and Conversion: Proselytizing in the Religious History of the Roman Empire*. Oxford: Clarendon, 1994.

Goulder, Michael D. *The Evangelists' Calendar: A Lectionary Explanation of the Development of Scripture*. London: SPCK, 1978.

———. *Luke: A New Paradigm*. 2 vols. Journal for the Studie of the New Testament: Supplement Series 20. Sheffield: Sheffield Academic Press, 1989.

———. *Type and History in Acts*. London: SPCK, 1964.

Gowler, David B. *Host, Guest, Enemy and Friend: Portraits of the Pharisees in Luke and Acts*. New York: Peter Lang, 1991.

Grant, R. M. *Miracle and Natural Law in Graeco-Roman and Early Christian Thought*. Amsterdam: North Holland Publishing, 1952.

Green, Joel B. *The Gospel of Luke*. New International Commentary on the New Testament. Grand Rapids: Eerdmans, 1997.

Gustafson, James M. 'The Relation of the Gospels to the Moral Life.' Pages 110–16 in vol. 2 of *Jesus and Man's Hope*. Pittsburgh: Pittsburgh Theological Seminary, 1970–1971.

Guthrie, Kenneth Sylvan, ed. *The Pythagorean Sourcebook and Library*. Grand Rapids: Phanes Press, 1987.

Haacker, Klaus. 'Gallio.' Pages 901–3 in vol. 2 of *Anchor Bible Dictionary*. Edited by David Noel Freedman. 6 vols. New York: Doubleday, 1992.

Haenchen, Ernst. *The Acts of the Apostles, A Commentary*. Translated by R. McL. Wilson. Philadelphia: Westminster, 1971.

Hanson, R. P. C. *The Acts*. Oxford: Clarendon, 1967.

Harnack, Adolph von. *The Acts of the Apostles*. New York: G. P. Putnam's Sons, 1909.

———. *Luke the Physician: The Author of the Third Gospel and the Acts of the Apostles*. Edited by W. D. Morrison. Translated by J. R. Wilkinson. NT Studies 1. New York: G. P. Putnam's Sons, 1907.

———. *The Sayings of Jesus: The Second Source of St. Matthew and St. Luke*. Translated by J. R. Wilkinson. NT Studies 2. New York: Putnam's, 1908.
Harstine, Stanley D. *Moses as a Character in the Fourth Gospel*. Journal for the Study of the New Testament: Supplement Series 229. Sheffield: Sheffield Academic Press, 2002.
Hauerwas, Stanley. 'The Politics of Charity.' *Interpretation* 31 (1977): 251–62.
———. *Vision and Virtue*. Notre Dame, Ind.: Fides, 1974.
Hays, Richard B. *Echoes of Scripture in the Letters of Paul*. New Haven: Yale University Press, 1989.
Hemer, Colin J. *The Book of Acts in the Setting of Hellenistic History*. Edited by C. H. Gempf. Tübingen: J. C. B. Mohr, 1989.
Hengel, Martin. *Between Jesus and Paul*. Philadelphia: Fortress, 1985.
Hood, Rodney T. 'The Genealogies of Jesus.' Pages 1–15 in *Early Christian Origins*. Edited by A. P. Wikgren. Chicago: Quadrangle Books, 1961.
Hornik, Heidi, and Mikeal Parsons. 'Ambrogio Lorenzetti's *Presentation in the Temple*: A 'Visual Exegesis' of Luke 2:22–38.' *Perspectives in Religious Studies* 28 (2001): 31–46.
Horsley, Richard A. *The Liberation of Christmas: The Infancy Narratives in Social Context*. New York: Crossroad, 1989.
Hubbard, Benjamin. 'Commissioning Stories in Luke-Acts: A Study of Their Antecedents, Form and Content.' *Semeia* 8 (1977): 103–26.
Iser, Wolfgang. *The Acts of Reading*. Baltimore: Johns Hopkins University Press, 1978.
———. *The Implied Reader: Patterns in Communication in Prose Fiction from Bunyan to Beckett*. Baltimore: Johns Hopkins University Press, 1974.
James, M. R. *The Apocryphal New Testament*. Oxford: Clarendon, 1955.
Jauss, Hans Robert. 'Literary History as a Challenge to Literary Theory.' *New Literary History* 2 (1970): 7–37.
Jervell, Jacob. *Luke and the People of God*. Minneapolis: Augsburg, 1972.
Johnson, Luke T. *The Acts of the Apostles*. Sacra pagina 5. Collegeville, Minn.: Liturgical Press, 1992.
———. *The Gospel of Luke*. Collegeville, Minn.: Liturgical Press, 1991.
———. 'Romans 3:21–26 and the Faith of Jesus.' *Catholic Biblical Quarterly* 44 (1982): 77–90.
Johnson, Roger A. et al. *Critical Issues in Modern Religion*. Englewood Cliffs, N.J.: Prentice-Hall, 1973.
Jones, Donald L. 'Luke's Unique Interest in Historical Chronology.' Pages 378–87 in *SBL Seminar Papers, 1989*. Society of Biblical Literature Seminar Papers 28. Atlanta: Scholars Press, 1989.
Jonge, Henk J. de. 'Sonship, Wisdom, Infancy: Luke 2:41–51a.' *New Testament Studies* 24 (1978): 317–54.
Justin Martyr. *The Writings of Justin Martyr*. Translated by Thomas B. Falls. Washington, D.C.: Catholic University of America, 1948.
Kaplan, Julius. *The Redaction of the Babylonian Talmud*. New York: Bloch, 1933.
Karris, Robert. 'Missionary Communities: A New Paradigm for the Study of Luke-Acts.' *Catholic Biblical Quarterly* 41 (1979): 80–97.

Keck, Leander E. 'The Spirit and the Dove.' *New Testament Studies* 17 (1970–71): 63–67.
Kee, H. C. *Christian Origins in Sociological Perspective*. Philadelphia: Westminster, 1980.
Kittel, G., and G. Friedrich, eds. *Theological Dictionary of the New Testament*. Translated by G. W. Bromiley. 10 vols. Grand Rapids: Eerdmans, 1964–1976.
Knox, John. *Chapters in the Life of Paul*. Nashville: Abingdon, 1950.
Koester, Craig. 'The Spectrum of Johannine Readers.' Pages 5–19 in *What Is John?* Edited by F. F. Segovia. Society of Biblical Literature Symposium Series 53. Atlanta: Scholars Press, 1996.
Krentz, Edgar. *The Historical-Critical Method*. Philadelphia: Fortress, 1975.
Kümmel, W. G. *Introduction to the New Testament*. Nashville: Abingdon: 1966.
Ladouceur, David. 'Hellenistic Preconceptions of Shipwreck and Pollution as a Context for Acts 27–28.' *Harvard Theological Review* 73 (1980): 435–49.
Lake, Kirsopp. 'The Chronology of Acts.' Pages 445–89 in vol. 5 of *The Beginnings of Christianity*. Edited by F. J. Foakes-Jackson and Kirsopp Lake. Grand Rapids: Baker, 1966.
Laistner, M. L. W., ed. *Bedae Venerabilis Expositio Actuum Apostolorum et Retractatio*. Medieval Academy of America Publication 35. Cambridge, Mass.: Medieval Academy of America, 1939.
———. *Venerable Bede: Commentary on the Acts of the Apostles*. Translated by L. T. Martin. Kalamazoo: Cistercian Publications, 1989.
Levine, L. I. 'R. Abbahu of Caesarea.' Pages 56–76 in *Christianity Judaism and Other Greco-Roman Cults, Part Four*. Edited by J. Neusner. Leiden: Brill, 1975.
Lightfoot, J. B. *Saint Paul's Epistle to the Galatians*. 10th ed. London: Macmillan, 1890.
Lohfink, Gerhard. *Die Sammlung Israels. Eine Untersuchung zur lukanischen Ekklesiologie*. Studien zum Alten and Neuen Testaments 34. München: Kösel-Verlag, 1975.
Lohfink, Norbert. 'The Deuteronomy Picture of the Transfer of Authority from Moses to Joshua.' Pages 234–47 in *Theology of the Pentateuch*. Translated by Linda M. Maloney. Minneapolis: Fortress, 1994.
Loveday, Alexander. 'Acts and Ancient Intellectual Biography.' Pages 31–64 in *The Book of Acts in Its Ancient Literary Setting*. Edited by Bruce W. Winter and Andrew D. Clarke. Grand Rapids: Eerdmans, 1993.
Lüdemann, Gerd. *Early Christianity according to the Traditions of Acts*. Minneapolis: Fortress, 1989.
Lyonnet, S. "La voie' dans les Actes des Apotres.' *Recherches de science religieuse* (1981): 149–64.
Lyons, George. *Pauline Autobiography*. Atlanta: Scholars Press, 1985.
MacMullen, Ramsay. 'Two Types of Conversion to Early Christianity.' *Vigilae christianae* 37 (1983): 174–92.
Malherbe, A. J. 'Not in a Corner: Early Christian Apologetic in Acts 26:26.' Pages 147–63 in *Paul and the Popular Philosophers*. Minneapolis: Fortress, 1989.
Manson, T. W. *Studies in the Gospels and Epistles*. Philadelphia: Westminster, 1962.

Marcus Minucius Felix. *The Octavius*. Translated by G. W. Clarke. New York: Newman, 1974.
Marshall, I. H. *The Gospel of Luke*. New International Greek Testament Commentary. Grand Rapids: Eerdmans, 1978.
———. *Luke: Historian and Theologian*. Grand Rapids: Zondervan, 1970.
Martyn, J. Louis. *The Gospel of John in History*. New York: Paulist, 1978.
Marx, Karl, and Friedrich Engels. *On Religion*. New York: Schocken, 1964.
McGowan, Andrew. 'Eating People: Accusations of Cannibalism against Christians in the Second Century.' *Journal for Early Christian Studies* 2 (1994): 413–41.
Meeks, Wayne A. 'The Man from Heaven in Johannine Sectarianism.' *Journal of Biblical Literature* 91 (1972): 44–72.
———. *The Origins of Christian Morality: The First Two Centuries*. New Haven: Yale University Press, 1993.
Mejer, Jorgen. *Diogenes Laertius and His Hellenistic Background*. Wiesbaden: Franz Steiner, 1978.
Mekler, Segofredus. *Academicorum Philosophorum Index Herculanensis*. Berlin: Weidmannos, 1902. Repr., 1958.
Michiels, R. 'La conception lucanienne de la conversion.' *Ephemerides theologicae lovaniensis* 41 (1965): 42–78.
Miles, G. B., and G. Trompf. 'Luke and Antiphon: The Theology of Acts 27–28 in the Light of Pagan Beliefs about Divine Retribution, Pollution, and Shipwreck.' *Harvard Theological Review* 69 (1976): 259–67.
Minear, Paul S. 'Luke's Use of the Birth Stories.' Pages 111–30 in *Studies in Luke-Acts*. Edited by L. E. Keck and J. L. Martyn. Nashville: Abingdon, 1966.
Misch, George. *A History of Autobiography in Antiquity*. 2 vols. Cambridge: Harvard University Press, 1951.
Momigliano, Arnaldo. *The Development of Greek Biography*. Cambridge: Harvard University Press, 1971.
Mommsen, Theodor, Paul Kruger, and Alan Watson. *The Digest of Justinian*. Philadelphia: University of Pennsylvania Press, 1985.
Moore, George F. *Judaism*. 3 vols. Cambridge: Harvard University Press, 1958.
Morford, M. P. O. *The Poet Lucan: Studies in Rhetorical Epic*. New York: Barnes and Noble, 1967.
Mulroy, David. *Horace's Odes and Epodes*. Ann Arbor: University of Michigan Press, 1994.
Murphy-O'Connor, Jerome. *St. Paul's Corinth*. Wilmington, Del.: Michael Glazier, 1983.
Musurillo, H. *The Acts of the Christian Martyrs*. Oxford: Clarendon, 1972.
Neyrey, Jerome H., ed. *The Social World of Luke-Acts: Models for Interpretation*. Peabody, Mass.: Hendrickson, 1991.
———. "Without Beginning of Days or End of Life' (Hebrews 7:3): Topos for a True Deity.' *Catholic Biblical Quarterly* 53 (1991): 439–55.
The Nicene and Post-Nicene Fathers. Series 1. Edited by Philip Schaff. 1886–1889. 14 Vols. Repr. Peabody, Mass.: Hendrickson, 1994.
Nock, A. D. *Conversion: The Old and the New in Religion from Alexander the Great to Augustine of Hippo*. Oxford: Clarendon Press, 1952.

Nolland, John. *Luke*. 3 vols. Word Biblical Commentary 35A, 35B, 35C. Dallas: Word, 1989-93.
O'Neill, J. C. *The Theology of Acts in Its Historical Setting*. London: SPCK, 1961.
Origen. *Contra Celsum*. Translated by Henry Chadwick. Cambridge: Cambridge University Press, 1953.
O'Toole, Robert F. *The Unity of Luke's Theology*. Wilmington, Del.: Michael Glazier, 1984.
Paget, James Carleton. 'Jewish Proselytism at the Time of Christian Origins: Chimera or Reality?' *Journal for the Study of the New Testament* 62 (1996): 65-103.
Parrinder, Geoffrey. *Son of Joseph: The Parentage of Jesus*. Edinburgh: T. & T. Clark, 1992.
Parsons, Mikeal. 'Reading Talbert: New Perspectives on Luke and Acts.' Pages 133-79 in *Cadbury, Know, and Talbert*. Edited by M. C. Parsons and J. B. Tyson. Society of Biblical Literature Centennial Publications. Atlanta: Scholars Press, 1992.
Pathrapankal, J. 'Christianity as a "Way" according to the Acts of the Apostles.' Pages 533-39 in *Les Actes des Apotres*. Edited by J. Kremer. Gembloux: J. Duculot, 1979.
Perrot, Charles. 'Les recits d'enfance dans la haggada antérieure au IIe siècle de notre ère: [OT personages and Jesus].' *Recherches de Science Religieuses* 55 (1967): 481-518.
Petersen, Norman R. *Literary Criticism for New Testament Critics*. Philadelphia: Fortress, 1978.
Praeder, Susan Marie. 'The Narrative Voyage: An Analysis and Interpretation of Acts 27-28.' Ph.D. diss., Graduate Theological Union, 1980.
Pseudo-Bonoventura. *Meditations on the Life of Christ*. Edited and translated by I. Ragusa and R. B. Greene. Princeton: Princeton University Press, 1961.
Rabil, A., Jr. *Erasmus and the New Testament*. Trinity University Monograph Series in Religion 1. San Antonio: Trinity University Press, 1972.
Rabinowitz, Peter J. *Before Reading: Narrative Conventions and the Politics of Interpretation*. Ithaca, N.Y.: Cornell University Press, 1987.
———. 'Truth in Fiction: A Reexamination of Audiences.' *Critical Inquiry* 4 (1977): 121-41.
———. 'Whirl Without End: Audience Oriented Criticism.' Pages 81-100 in *Contemporary Literary Theory*. Edited by G. Douglas Atkins. Amherst: University of Massachusetts Press, 1989.
Rackham, R. B. *The Acts of the Apostles*. Westminster Commentaries. 14th ed. London: Methuen, 1951.
Ramsay, William M. *The Bearing of Recent Discovery on the Trustworthiness of the New Testament*. London: Hodder and Stoughton, 1915.
———. *Was Christ Born at Bethlehem? A Study of the Credibility of St. Luke*. London: Hodder and Stoughton, 1905.
Ramsey, A. M. 'What Was the Ascension?' Pages 135-44 in *Historicity and Chronology in the New Testament*. Edited by D. E. Nineham. London: SPCK, 1965.

Reardon, B. P., ed. *Collected Ancient Greek Novels*. Berkeley: University of California Press, 1989.
Reicke, Bo. 'Jesus, Simeon, and Anna (Luke 2:21–40).' Pages 96–108 in *Saved By Hope*. Edited by J. I. Cook. Grand Rapids: Eerdmans, 1978.
Repo, E. *Der 'Weg' als Selbstbezeichnung des Urchristentums*. Helsinki: Suomalainen Tiedeakatemia, 1964.
Robbins, Vernon K. 'By Land and By Sea: The We-Passages and Ancient Sea Voyages.' Pages 215–42 in *Perspectives on Luke-Acts*. Edited by Charles H. Talbert. National Association of Baptist Professors of Religion Special Studies Series 5. Danville, Va.: Association of Baptist Professors of Religion, 1978.
Roloff, Jürgen. *Die Apostelgeschichte*. Das Neue Testament Deutsch 5. Göttingen: Vandenhoeck & Ruprecht, 1981.
Rummel, Erika. *Erasmus' Annotations on the New Testament: From Philologist to Theologian*. Erasmus Studies 8. Toronto: Toronto University Press, 1986.
Sanders, Jack T. *The Jews in Luke-Acts*. Philadelphia: Fortress, 1987.
———. 'The Parable of the Pounds and Lucan Anti-Semitism.' *Theological Studies* 42 (1981): 667.
———. 'Paul's Autobiographical Statements in Galatians 1–2.' *Journal of Biblical Literature* 85 (1966): 335.
Sanders, Jim Alvin. *Suffering as Divine Discipline in the Old Testament and Post-Biblical Judaism*. Rochester, N.Y.: Colgate Rochester Divinity School, 1955.
Schneider, Gerhard. *Die Apostelgeschichte*. 2 vols. Herders theologischer Kommentar zum Neuen Testament. Freiburg: Herder, 1980, 1982.
———. *Die Passion Jesu nach den Drei Älteren Evangelien*. Munich: Kösel, 1973.
Scholes, Robert, and Robert Kellog. *The Nature of Narrative*. New York: Oxford University Press, 1966.
Schrage, Wolfgang. *Suffering*. Nashville: Abingdon, 1980.
Schulz, S. 'Gottes Vorsehung bei Lukas.' *Zeitschrift für die neutestamentliche Wissenschaft und die Kunde der älteren Kirche* 54 (1963): 104–16.
Schweizer, Eduard. *Lordship and Discipleship*. Naperville: Allenson, 1960.
Scott, Walter. *Fragmenta Herculanensia*. Oxford: Clarendon Press, 1885.
Sherwin-White, A. N. *Roman Society and Roman Law in the New Testament*. Grand Rapids: Baker, 1978.
Shorr, Dorothy. 'The Iconographic Development of the Presentation in the Temple.' *Art Bulletin* 28 (1946): 30.
Shumate, Nancy. *Crisis and Conversion in Apuleius' Metamorphoses*. Ann Arbor: University of Michigan Press, 1996.
Silberman, L. H. 'Paul's Viper: Acts 28:3–6.' *Forum* 8 (1992): 247–54.
Slingerland, Dixon. 'The Jews in the Pauline Portion of Acts.' *Journal of the American Academy of Religion* 54 (1986): 305–21.
Smallwood, E. Mary. *The Jews under Roman Rule: From Pompey to Diocletian*. Leiden: Brill, 1976.
Squires, John T. *The Plan of God in Luke-Acts*. Cambridge: Cambridge University Press, 1993.
———. 'The Plan of God in Luke-Acts.' Ph.D. diss., Yale University, 1987.
Stambaugh, John E., and David L. Batch. *The New Testament in Its Social Environment*. Library of Early Christianity. Philadelphia: Westminster, 1986.

Stern, Menahem, ed. *Greek and Latin Authors on Jews and Judaism*. 3 vols. Jerusalem: Israel Academy of Sciences and Humanities, 1974–1984.
Sternberg, Meir. *The Poetics of Biblical Narrative*. Bloomington: Indiana University Press, 1987.
Streeter, B. H. *The Four Gospels: A Study of Origins, Treating of the Manuscript Tradition, Sources, Authorship, and Date*. New York: Macmillan, 1925.
Talbert, Charles H. 'Again: Paul's Visit to Jerusalem.' *Novum Testamentum* 9 (1967): 26–40.
———. 'The Concept of Immortals in Mediterranean Antiquity.' *Journal of Biblical Literature* 94 (1975): 419–36.
———. 'Discipleship in Luke-Acts.' Pages 62–75 in *Discipleship in the New Testament*. Edited by Fernando Segovia. Philadelphia: Fortress, 1985.
———. *Literary Patterns, Theological Themes, and the Genre of Luke-Acts*. Society of Biblical Literature Monograph Series 20. Missoula: Scholars Press, 1974.
———, ed. *Luke-Acts: New Perspectives from the Society of Biblical Literature Seminar*. New York: Crossroad, 1984.
———. 'Luke-Acts.' Pages 297–320 in *The New Testament and Its Modern Interpreters*. Edited by E. J. Epp and G. W. Macrae. Atlanta: Scholars Press, 1989.
———. *Luke and the Gnostics*. Nashville: Abingdon, 1966.
———. 'Oral and Independent or Literary and Interdependent? A Response to Albert B. Lord.' Pages 93–102 in *The Relationships among the Gospels: An Interdisciplinary Dialogue*. Edited by W. O. Walker, Jr. San Antonio: Trinity University Press, 1978.
———, ed. *Perspectives on Luke-Acts*. Edinburgh: T. & T. Clark, 1978.
———. 'Promise and Fulfillment in Lucan Theology.' Pages 91–102 in *Luke-Acts: New Perspectives from the Society of Biblical Literature Seminar*. Edited by Charles H. Talbert. New York: Crossroad, 1984.
———. *Reading Acts: A Literary and Theological Commentary on the Acts of the Apostles*. New York: Crossroad, 1997.
———. *Reading Corinthians: A Literary and Theological Commentary on 1 and 2 Corinthians*. New York: Crossroad, 1989.
———. *Reading Luke: A Literary and Theological Commentary on the Third Gospel*. New York: Crossroad, 1982. Rewritten ed., Macon, Ga.: Smyth & Helwys, 2002.
———. 'The Redaction Critical Quest for Luke the Theologian.' Pages 171–222 in vol. 1 of *Jesus and Man's Hope*. Edited by D. Y. Hadidian. 2 vols. Pittsburgh: Pittsburgh Theological Seminary, 1970.
———, ed. *Reimarus: Fragments*. Lives of Jesus Series. Philadelphia: Fortress, 1970.
———. Review of Francois Bovon, *L'Evangile selon Saint Luc 9:51–14:35*. *Biblica* 78 (1997): 425–28.
———. Review of Joel B. Green, *The Gospel of Luke*. *Biblica* 79 (1998): 579–82.
———. Review of John Nolland, *Luke*. *Critical Review of Books in Religion 1995*, 270–73.
———. Review of Joseph A. Fitzmyer, *Bible (NT), English: The Gospel According to Luke 10–24*. *Catholic Biblical Quarterly* 48 (1986): 336–38.
———. Review of Robert C. Tannehill, *The Narrative Unity of Luke-Acts: A Literary Interpretation*, vol. 1. *Biblica* 69 (1988): 135–38.

———. *What Is a Gospel? The Genre of the Canonical Gospels*. Philadelphia: Fortress, 1977.
Tannehill, Robert C. 'Israel in Luke-Acts.' *Journal of Biblical Literature* 104 (1985): 69–85.
———. *The Narrative Unity of Luke-Acts: A Literary Interpretation*. 2 vols. Philadelphia: Fortress, 1986–90.
Taylor, Vincent. *Behind the Third Gospel: A Study of the Proto-Luke Hypothesis*. Oxford: Oxford University Press, 1926.
———. *The Passion Narrative of St. Luke: A Critical and Historical Investigation*. Cambridge: Cambridge University Press, 1972.
Theophilus of Antioch. *Ad Autolycum*. Translated by R. M. Grant. Oxford: Clarendon, 1970.
Thimmes, Pamela. *Studies in the Biblical Sea-Storm Type-Scene*. San Francisco: Mellen, 1992.
Tompkins, Jane. *Reader-Response Criticism: From Formalism to Post-Structuralism*. Baltimore: Johns Hopkins University Press, 1980.
The Tosefta: *Neziqin*. Translated by Jacob Neusner. New York: KTAV, 1981.
Traversa, Augusta. *Index Stoicorum Herculanensis*. Genoa: Istituto di Filologia Classica, 1952.
Tremel, B. 'A propos d'Actes 20:7–12: Puissance du thaumaturge ou du témoin?' *Revue de théologie de Louvain* 112 (1980): 359–69.
Trites, Allison. 'The Prayer Motif in Luke-Acts.' Pages 168–86 in *Perspectives on Luke-Acts*. Edited by Charles H. Talbert. National Association of Baptist Professors of Religion Special Studies Series 5. Danville, Va.: Association of Baptist Professors of Religion, 1978.
Tyson, Joseph B. 'Source Criticism of the Gospel of Luke.' Pages 24–39 in *Perspectives on Luke-Acts*. Edited by Charles H. Talbert. National Association of Baptist Professors of Religion Special Studies Series 5. Danville, Va.: Association of Baptist Professors of Religion, 1978.
Underhill, Evelyn. *Mysticism*. New York: Meridian Books, 1974.
Veltman, Fred. 'The Defense Speeches of Paul in Acts.' Pages 243–56 in *Perspectives on Luke-Acts*. Edited by Charles H. Talbert. National Association of Baptist Professors of Religion Special Studies Series 5. Danville, Va.: Association of Baptist Professors of Religion, 1978.
Vielhauer, Philip. 'On the 'Paulinism' of Acts.' Pages 33–50 in *Studies in Luke-Acts*. Edited by L. E. Keck and J. L. Martyn. Nashville: Abingdon, 1966.
Wainwright, A. W. 'Luke and the Restoration of the Kingdom of Israel.' *Expository Times* 89 (1977): 76–79.
Wehrli, F. *Die Schule des Aristoteles*. 8 vols. Basel: Schwabe, 1967.
Wengst, Klaus. *Pax Romana: Anspruch und Wirklichkeit*. München: Chr. Kaiser Verlag, 1986.
Wilckens, Ulrich. 'Interpreting Luke-Acts in a Period of Existentialist Theology.' Pages 60–83 in *Studies in Luke-Acts*. Edited by L. E. Keck and J. L. Martyn. Nashville: Abingdon, 1966.
Wilson, S. G. *The Gentiles and the Gentile Mission in Luke-Acts*. Cambridge: Cambridge University Press, 1973.

Wink, Walter. 'Our Stories, Cosmic Stories, and the Biblical Story.' Pages 209–22 in *Sacred Stories: A Celebration of the Power of Stories to Transform and Heal*. Edited by Charles and Anne Simpkinson. San Francisco: Harper, 1993.

Wolfson, Harry A. *Philo: Foundations of Religious Philosophy in Judaism, Christianity, and Islam*. 2 vols. Cambridge, Mass.: Harvard University Press, 1948.

Wood, G. F. 'The Form and Composition of the Lucan Annunciation Narratives.' STD thes., Catholic University of America, 1962.

Yoder, John Howard. *The Politics of Jesus*. Grand Rapids: Eerdmans, 1972.

Zehnle, Richard. 'The Salvific Character of Jesus' Death in Lucan Soteriology.'

INDEX OF MODERN AUTHORS

Adler, Mortimer J., 60
Alexander, Loveday, 32
Alsup, J. E., 127
Athanasskis, Apostolos A., 40
Aune, David E., 57–63
Barrett, C. K., 199
Batch, David L., 143
Bauckham, Richard, 17–18
Bauer, W., 14–16
Baur, F. C., 9–10, 156
Beardsley, Monroe C., 17
Benko, Stephen, 209
Black, Robert Allen, 135
Borgen, Peder, 213
Bouttier, M., 102
Bouyer, Louis, 91
Bovon, Francois, 11, 102, 130
Brown, Raymond E., 65–66,, 76
Brox, Norbert, 110
Bruce, F. F., 150, 217
Bultmann, Rudolf, 10–11, 57–58, 60, 80, 79
Burridge, Richard A., 51, 54, 57–58, 81
Cadbury, Henry J., 11, 14, 183, 201, 210
Caird, G. B., 202
Camparetti, Domenico, 27
Campbell, T. H., 203–204
Cancik, Hubert, 50, 54
Cardauns, Burkhart, 55
Carter, Warren, 17
Cassidy, Richard, 115–117
Charlesworth, James H., 33, 36, 141, 146
Chesnutt, Randall D., 139
Childs, Brevard S., 13–14
Cohen, Shaye J. D., 148
Conzelmann, Hans, 10–11, 93, 108, 151

Cosgrove, Charles H., 17, 165
Cox, Patricia, 211
Danker, Frederick W., 91, 133
Daube, David, 113
Deissman, Adolf, 209
Delling, G., 94
Dexter, Miriam Robbins, 85
Dibelius, Martin, 14, 18, 210, 217
Dillon, John, 29
Donfried, Karl P., 202
Dorandi, Tiziano, 27–29
Doren, Charles van, 60–61
Doty, William G., 54
Downing, Christine, 85
Dreyfus, F., 14
Drury, John, 68, 72, 75
Duckworth, George E., 191, 193
Dupont, Jacques, 135, 136, 140, 143, 144, 146
During, Ingemar, 31
Durkheim, Emile, 79–80
Ellul, Jacques, 118
Enslin, Morton S., 205
Feuerbach, Ludwig, 79–80
Finn, Thomas M., 135–136, 138, 145
Fishel, H. A., 110
Fitzmyer, Joseph A., 11, 44, 126, 203
Fowler, F. G., 137
Fowler, H. G., 137
Frend, W. H. C., 110
Fuller, R. H., 91, 214
Gaiser, Konrad, 27
Gallagher, Eugene V., 144
Gapp, K. S., 202
Garrett, Susan R., 12
Gasque, Ward, 201
Gempf, Conrad, 181
George, Augustin, 107, 135
Gerstenberger, E. S., 98, 100
Gigante, Marcello, 27–29

Gill, W. J., 181
Goldin, Judah, 36
Goodacre, Mark S., 13
Goodenough, E. R., 69, 96
Goodman, Martin, 143, 147
Goulder, Michael D., 13, 194
Gowler, David B., 12
Grant, R. M., 179
Green, Joel B., 13
Griesbach, J. J., 9
Gustafson, James M., 103,
Guthrie, Kenneth Sylvan, 186–187
Haacker, Klaus, 203
Haenchen, Ernst, 108, 151, 156, 161, 212
Hanson, R. P. C., 199
Harnack, Adolf von, 8, 207–208
Harstine, Stanley D., 17
Hauerwas, Stanley, 113, 118
Hays, Richard B., 17
Heil, John Paul, 17
Hemer, Colin J., 197, 202, 211–212, 215
Hengel, Martin, 201
Hershbell, Jackson, 29
Hood, Rodney T., 69
Hornik, Heidi, 95
Horsley, Richard A., 89
Hubbard, Benjamin, 67
Iser, Wolfgang, 15–16
Jakobson, R., 12
James, M. R., 121, 184
Jauss, Hans Robert, 14–16
Jervell, Jacob, 44, 108, 162
Johnson, Luke Timothy, 44, 100, 150, 178, 195
Johnson, Roger A., 88
Jones, Donald L., 202
Jonge, Henk J. de, 69, 72, 92
Kaplan, Julius, 211
Karris, Robert, 109
Käsemann, Ernst, 15–16
Keck, Leander E., 69
Kee, H. C., 117
Kellog, Robert, 206
Knox, John, 205
Koester, Craig R., 18

Krentz, Edgar, 80
Kruger, Paul, 39
Kümmel, W. G., 203, 213
Ladouceur, David, 180
Laister, M. L., 3
Lake, Kirsopp, 203
Levine, L. I., 33
Lightfoot, J. B., 205
Lohfink, Norbert, 33
Lord, Albert B., 76
Lüdemann, Gerd, 208, 215, 216
Lyonnet, S., 102
Lyons, George, 205–206
MacMullen, Ramsay, 143
Malherbe, A. J., 149
Manson, J. W., 205
Marshall, I. H., 9, 11, 14, 105, 109, 124–125
Martyn, J. Louis, 14
Marx, Karl, 79–80
McGowan, Andrew, 156
McKnight, Scott, 147
Meeks, Wayne A., 80, 138, 143
Mejer, Jorgen, 30–31
Mekler, Segofredus, 27
Michiels, R., 135
Miles, Gary B., 65, 180
Minear, Paul S., 66
Misch, George, 205
Momigliano, Arnaldo, 31
Mommsen, Theodor, 39
Moore, George F., 171
Morford, M. P. O., 177, 182
Mulroy, David, 143
Munck, J., 147
Murphy-O'Connor, Jerome, 208–209
Musurillo, H., 114
Neibuhr, Reinhold, 88
Neyrey, Jerome H., 13, 83
Nock, A. D., 72, 77, 138, 140–141, 143
Nolland, John, 9, 11, 44
O'Neill, J. C., 162
Orrieux, C., 147
Paget, Carleton, 147
Parrinder, Geoffrey, 89
Parsons, Mikeal, 57, 95

Pathrapankal, J., 102
Perrot, Charles, 76
Petersen, Norman R., 12, 80
Praeder, Susan Marie, 177
Rabil, A., Jr., 4
Rabinowitz, Peter J., 14, 16, 43, 136
Rackham, R. B., 156
Ramsay, William M., 8–9, 18,
Ramsey, A. M., 205
Reardon, B. P., 85, 182
Reicke, Bo, 95
Reimarus, H. S., 6–7
Repo, E., 102
Robbins, Vernon K., 65
Rokea, D., 147
Roloff, Jürgen, 150
Rummel, Erika, 4
Sanders, Jack T., 161, 170, 206
Sanders, Jim Alvin, 100
Schliermacher, Friedrich, 79
Schmidt, K. L., 57
Schneider, Gerhard, 150, 172
Scholes, Robert, 206
Schrage, Wolfgang, 98, 100
Schulz, S., 165
Schweizer, Eduard, 100
Scott, Walter, 28
Sherwin-White, A. N., 200
Shorr, Dorothy, 95
Shumate, Nancy, 135, 139, 145
Silberman, L. H., 183
Slingerland, Dixon, 161
Smallwood, E. Mary, 198
Squires, John T., 122, 164, 188
Stählin, G., 92–93
Stambaugh, John E., 143
Sternberg, Meir, 191
Strauss, D. F., 8
Streeter, B. H., 8–9
Talbert, Charles H., 6, 12, 13, 49, 50, 57–63, 65, 67, 70, 73, 76, 81, 83, 91, 96, 99, 102–103, 105, 126, 129–132, 136, 149, 167, 170, 175, 179, 188, 193, 202, 213, 217
Tannehill, Robert C., 12, 131, 150, 164
Taylor, Vincent, 8–9
Thimmes, Pamela, 176
Tompkins, Jane, 81
Traversa, Augusta, 27
Tremel, B., 150
Trites, Allison A., 68, 97
Trompf, Garry, 65, 180
Tyson, Joseph B., 65
Underhill, Evelyn, 103
Veltman, Fred, 65
Vielhauer, Philip, 212
Wainwright, A. W., 109
Watson, Alan, 39
Wehrli, F., 32
Wengst, Klaus, 89
Wilckens, Ulrich, 213–214
Will, E., 147
Wilson, S. G., 108
Wimsatt, W. K., Jr., 17
Wink, Walter, 215–216
Wolff, C., 6
Wolfson, Harry A., 147
Wood, G. F., 67
Yoder, John Howard, 118
Zehnle, Richard, 105

INDEX OF SUBJECTS

ancient auditors, 19, 65, 70, 81, 82, 86, 115
angelophany, 67, 69, 75
antiheretical, 2
apology/apologetic, 1, 149, 151, 155, 158, 159
apostles, 39, 41, 45, 46, 48, 53, 132
atonement, 79, 100, 105
authorial audience, 15–18, 43, 47–49
authorial intent, 17, 81, 160
autobiography, 76, 205, 206
baptism, 3, 66, 68, 93, 96, 97, 104
biography, 28–32, 52, 55, 58–63, 70, 71, 73, 75, 81, 88
birth narratives, 65, 67, 80, 88, 89, 95
Calvinistic reading, 5–6
cannibalism, 156–159
canonical criticism, 13–14
characterization, 12
conspiracy, 151, 152, 154, 155
contemporary color, 198, 201
conversion, 106, 109, 113, 135–148
corporeality, 127, 128
correspondences, 65, 103, 193–194
covenant, 130, 172
death of Jesus, 7, 91, 97, 100, 102–103, 105, 106–107, 110, 114–115, 117, 130, 168
diachronic, 44, 80
divine plan, 101, 121–123, 164, 165, 168, 169, 182, 188–190
development(al), 92, 94–95, 97, 101, 103–104
enlightenment readings, 6–7
eschatology, 10, 50, 98, 109, 170
eucharist(ic), 121, 129–132
fate, 71, 74, 102
foreshadowing, 81, 191–193

genre, 51, 54, 57–58, 61, 63, 76, 88
gentile mission, 161, 169
gnostic, 1
gospel harmony, 2, 5, 13
grow(th), 92–93, 100–101
heresy, 1
historical sequence, 202–206
historicity, 7, 8–9, 14, 198–201
humanist readings, 5
ignorance, 168
immorality, 153–155, 157, 159
immortals, 58, 59, 73
implied author, 12
implied reader, 15
infanticide, 157–159
intentional fallacy, 17
justification, 5
Marcionite, 2
martyr(dom), 103, 105–107, 110, 112–115, 117
Marxist reading, 89
medieval exegesis, 3–4
miracles, 3, 143–144, 215–217
miraculous conception, 67, 70, 71, 73, 75, 91
misunderstanding, 168–170
Nestorians, 2
narrative criticism, 12–13
non-resistance, 115
nonviolent resistance, 115–116
obedience, 99, 100–101
origins, 161–169
pantheism, 85, 87
parousia, 10, 109
passion narrative, 9
perfect(ion), 92–94, 100
pioneer, 102, 128
portrait of Paul, 109, 212–215
prayer, 68, 93, 94, 96–98, 100
progress, 92–93, 101,

prophecy, 67, 68, 70–73, 75–76, 93, 105, 106, 111, 123, 124, 132, 165–169, 190, 192
readers' repertoire, 16
redaction criticism, 11, 18
redemption, 68, 95, 96
rejection, 97, 98, 101, 169, 170
religious language, 79. 80, 90
resurrection, 91, 101, 121–126, 129, 132, 194
revelation, 6–7, 74

storms, 177–181, 184–187, 195
semantic field, 46–48
semantic marker, 47
shipwreck, 187, 190, 194
snake bite, 182–184, 194
speeches, 130, 210–212
status reversal, 170–173
succession, 19–55
synchronic, 44, 80
temptation, 99, 140
violent resistance, 115

INDEX OF ANCIENT SOURCES

I. Old Testament

Genesis
- 3:6 — 99
- 15 — 130
- 15:18 — 44
- 21:27–62 — 44
- 26:28–62 — 44
- 27:4 — 133
- 31:44–62 — 44
- 36:33–39 — 21, 37
- 37:5–7 — 192
- 42:9 — 192
- 43:23, 28 — 192
- 44:11 — 192
- 48:15–16 — 133

Exodus
- 2:14 — 45
- 13:2 — 95
- 13:13 — 95
- 18:22 — 45
- 24:3–8 — 130

Leviticus
- 12:8 — 95

Numbers
- 3:47 — 95
- 17:23 — 22
- 18:16 — 95
- 20:2, 6 — 35
- 20:23–28 — 26, 35, 46, 53
- 26:1, 3 — 35
- 27:12–23 — 26, 33, 47, 48
- 35:30 — 127

Deuteronomy
- 1:37–38 — 26, 33
- 3:21–22, 28 — 26, 33
- 5:2–3 — 44
- 7:2 — 44
- 17:6–7 — 127
- 18:21–22 — 132
- 19:15 — 127, 132
- 28 — 166
- 29:14 — 214
- 31:2–6, 7–8, 14–15, 23 — 26, 33, 34
- 34:9 — 34, 47

Joshua
- 1:2–9 — 26, 34
- 1:16–18 — 34
- 3:7 — 34
- 4:14 — 34
- 5:28 — 34
- 9:6 — 44
- 24:25 — 44

Judges
- 2:2 — 44

1 Samuel
- 1–2 — 95
- 11:1–2 — 44
- 16–18 — 26, 35
- 20:29 — 44
- 28:8–14 — 128

2 Samuel
- 3:21 — 44
- 9:7, 9, 11 — 44
- 11 — 191
- 12 — 191
- 13 — 191

15:4	44, 45	17:7	167
16	192	17:23	167
16:21–22	192	17:38	44
18	192	25	167
19:16	26		
19:28	44	2 Chronicles	
		24:20–22	112

1 Kings

1	26, 50	Nehemiah	
1:13	21	9:26	112
1:35	21		
1–2	26	Psalms	
2:7	44	88:9	186
3:16–28	45	94:12	100
5:12	44	106	186
10:10, 14	112	119:71	100
15:8	21		
17:8–16	193	Isaiah	
17:17–24	193	6:9–10	162, 169
17:21–22	156	49:6	162, 169
18:14–15	192	53:7–8	105
18:19	44	53:12	105
18:45	193		
19:16	21, 23, 27, 36, 192, 193	Jeremiah	
		2:20	112
19:19	23	12:15	163
		15:18–19	100

2 Kings

1:15	193	Daniel	
2	27, 36	6:22	183
2:8	261		
2:9	24, 46	Amos	
2:13	24, 193	9:11–12	163
2:9, 16	24		
2:23–25	192	Jonah	
3:20	193	1:3–17	177
4:1–7	193		
4:18–37	193	Micah	
4:34	156	7:3	45

II. New Testament

Matthew

1:6	82	16:21	122
3:1–12	137	19:28–62	44
10:32–33	113	20:29–34	3
		23:31–39	112

INDEX OF ANCIENT SOURCES

26:28	105, 130	3:15	66
28:11–15	127	3:16–17	68
28:20	133	3:21–22	66, 68, 69, 93, 95, 96, 97
Mark		3:23–38	66, 69, 99
1:2–8	137	4:1–13	69, 70, 99, 102
8:31	122	4:16–21	93, 97
10:45	105	4:18–19	164, 189
12:1–12	112	4:21	164, 189
14:24	130	4:28–29	107
16:1	7	4:43	122, 164, 188
		5:1–11	3, 133
Luke		5:14	2
1–2	220	5:16	68
1:1	167	5:17–26	46, 49
1:2	43	5:29–32	105, 125, 129
1:5–7	82, 200	5:33–39	200
1:13	82, 189	6:12	68, 123, 124
1:16–17	66, 164, 189	6:13	48
1:18	82	6:19	46, 49
1:20	164, 189	6:20–26	129, 170, 171
1:24	82	7:5	107
1:29–32	164, 189	7:11–17	46, 49, 107, 126, 156, 200
1:32–33	66, 67, 164, 189	7:22	126
1:35	66, 67, 88, 164, 189	7:30	122, 164, 188
1:41–45	68, 70	7:36–50	125
1:46–50	5	8:1–3	46, 123, 127
1:51–53	129, 170	8:22–45	46, 126, 175, 186, 187, 188, 192, 193
1:57	82	9:9	97
1:67–79	67	9:11–17	129, 131
1:68	107	9:18	94
1:69	66	9:19	95
1:76	66	9:20	97
2:4	2, 66	9:22	97, 121, 122, 124, 127, 164, 168, 188, 189
2:7	95		
2:11	67		
2:22–24	94, 95	9:23	104
2:25–35	67, 70	9:28–29	68, 94, 95, 97, 98
2:28	1	9:31	126, 164, 189, 193
2:32	107	9:44	95, 99, 164, 168, 189
2:34	107		
2:36–38	1, 68	9:45	193
2:41–51	69, 70, 92, 95	9:51	122, 125, 164, 189, 193
2:49	66, 122, 164, 188		
2:52	93	9:57–58	1
3:1–14	66, 137, 200		

9:60	1	22:4	109
9:61–62	1	22:14–38	130
10:12	127	22:16–20	105
10:21	106	22:19–20	114, 129, 130, 131
10:29–37	170	22:22	164, 188
10:38–42	170	22:26	194
11:1	68	22:27	105, 123
11:2	106	22:28–30	43, 44, 45, 46, 52, 103, 106, 109
11:13	133		
11:37–54	116, 129, 170	22:32	68
12:1–12	2, 107	22:37	105, 122, 154, 188, 189
12:13–34	170		
12:50	193	22:39–46	22, 68, 69, 99, 102, 126, 150
13:10–17	116		
13:28–29	132	22:42	106, 114, 122, 149, 164, 188
13:31–35	94, 106, 107, 108, 116		
		22:49–51	99, 109, 117
13:32	99	22:54	49, 109, 194
13:33	112, 114, 122, 164, 188, 193	22:66	106
		22:69	25, 44, 106
14:1–24	116, 129, 132, 170	23:1–2	106, 107, 109, 194
15:1–2	105, 125	23:3	106
15:4, 8	1	23:4	105, 194
15:11–32	170	23:5	200
16:14–15	116	23:6	200
16:19–31	125, 126, 170	23:8	194
17:25	122, 164, 188	23:9	106
18:9–14	170	23:11	164
18:18–30	170	23:13	106, 109, 194
18:31–33	99, 121, 123, 164, 168, 189, 193	23:14–24	106
		23:26	102, 126
18:34	193	23:27–31	108
18:35–43	3	23:34	68, 106
19:1–10	105, 125	23:35–39	99
19:14	107	23:40–43	106, 114, 115, 125
19:28	102	23:45	106
19:39	107, 109	23:46	68, 106
19:41–44	108	23:49	123
19:45	49, 109, 116, 193	23:53	106
19:47	109, 117	23:55	123, 127
20:1, 19, 27	109	23:56	7
20:9–18	45, 108, 110	24:1–11	7, 105, 121, 122, 123, 124, 126, 127, 128, 164, 188
20:13–16	107		
21:9	122, 164, 188		
21:12–19	106, 114	24:12	121, 127
21:20–24	108, 109, 149, 164, 189	24:13–32	7, 121, 126
		24:20	107, 109

INDEX OF ANCIENT SOURCES 243

24:21	164, 189	2:23	106, 122, 124, 164, 168, 188
24:22–23	121, 127		
24:24	121	2:24	122
24:25–27	101, 106, 122, 164, 168, 188	2:32–33	122, 133
		2:34–36	44, 125, 126
24:30–31	105, 128, 129, 131	2:38	105, 125, 136, 143
24:34	122	2:41	105, 107, 163
24:36–49	7, 121, 126, 127, 128, 132	2:42–46	105, 107, 163
		2:47	107
24:41	128, 129, 131	3:1–10	46, 49
24:44	122, 123, 164, 188	3:15	45, 102, 122, 124
24:46	106, 168	3:17	45, 106, 168
24:47	105, 125, 164, 189	3:18	164, 168, 189
24:49–50	46, 132, 133	3:19	105, 136
24:51	7, 126	3:21	164, 188
		3:23	108, 110, 163
John		4:1–2	107, 109, 163
9:31	184	4:3	143
13:23	124	4:4	107, 163
17:11, 15	133	4:10	122, 125
18:15	124	4:12	125, 164, 188
19:26–27	124	4:17–18	107
19:35	124	4:25–28	114
20:1–18	127	4:27	97
20:6–7	127	4:28	122, 164
20:19	128	4:29–30	132
20:24–29	127, 128	4:38	188
21:1–11	3	5:14–17	107, 109, 163
21:7	124	5:15	46, 49
21:20–24	124	5:16	46, 49
		5:17	63, 107, 109
Acts		5:27, 30	106, 111
1:2	48, 126	5:31–32	45, 102, 105, 124, 125, 126, 132, 136, 144
1:4	45, 128, 129, 131, 132		
1:6	109	5:38–39	122, 164, 188
1:7	122, 164	6:1–6	22, 43, 47, 163
1:8	45, 46, 132, 133, 200, 201	6:7	107
		6:12	106, 109
1:9–11	46, 122, 124, 126	7:1	109
1:13–14	107	7:34	107
1:15–22	45	7:52	106, 112, 114
1:16	164, 188, 189	7:54	110
1:21	124, 164, 188	7:56	106
1:22	45, 124	7:58	107
2:3–4	68	7:59	106
2:17	46	7:60	106

8:1	106, 114, 201	13:36	122, 164, 188
8:4–5	162	13:38	105, 136
8:10	184	13:43	107
8:12–13	105	13:45	107, 163
8:14–15	45	13:46	108, 162, 164, 169, 189
8:32–33	105		
8:37–39	105	13:48	144
9:2	102	14:1	163
9:15	48	14:2	163
9:16	164, 188	14:4, 14	49
9:18	105	14:8–18	49, 135, 136
9:27–29	46, 48, 204	14:15–16	140
9:31	200, 201, 207	14:19	107
9:32–34	46, 49	14:22	47, 103
9:36–43	46, 156	14:23	23, 43, 47, 48, 52
10	68		
10:1	198	15	169, 204
10:5, 8	163, 164, 189	15:1–3	201
10:22	107, 164, 189	15:2	45, 46
10:32–33	163, 189	15:9	144
10:37	200	15:14	63, 144
10:38	97	15:15–18	107, 108, 163, 164, 189
10:39–40	122		
10:41	48, 128, 129, 131	16:4	46
10:42	164, 188	16:6–10	49
10:43	105, 125, 136	16:12	198
10:44	143	16:14	45, 144
10:47–48	105	16:15	105
11:1–2	45, 46	16:16–18	49, 192
11:18	144	16:17	102
11:19–21	106, 143, 162	17:1–9	117
11:22	45	17:3	164, 188
11:25–26	46	17:4	107
11:27–30	204	17:5–7	107, 163, 199
11:28	202	17:6	117, 198
12:19	200	17:10–11	163
12:20–23	202	17:13	107, 163
12:24	163	17:22–31	135, 136
12:25	202, 204	17:30	105
13:1–3	46, 49, 93, 162	17:31	122, 164, 189
13:4–12	135, 136, 198	18:2	202
13:17	107	18:5–6	107, 108, 162, 169
13:23	164, 189		
13:24	125	18:12–17	107, 117, 198, 203, 209
13:27	106, 164, 168, 189		
13:30	125	18:22	46, 204
13:32	122, 164, 189	18:25–26	102

19:5	105	27:9–12	176, 178, 180, 181
19:8–9	107	27:18	176, 178
19:9, 23	102	27:21–22	176
19:11–12	49	27:23–25	164, 179, 181, 189, 190, 192
19:13–20	192		
19:21	149, 181	27:24	164, 188
19:29–41	117, 199	27:31–32	178
19:35	198	27:33–36	105, 131, 179
20:2	149	28:1–10	175, 176, 181, 182, 184
20:3	107		
20:7–12	49, 105, 131, 149, 150, 151, 155, 156, 159	28:11–16	175, 176, 181, 187
		28:19	107
		28:25–28	108, 109, 162, 163, 164, 169, 189
20:17–35	48, 149		
20:20	149		
20:27	122, 149, 164, 188	Romans	
20:28	48	1–3	212
21:10–11	189	1:3–4	126
21:14	122, 164, 188	3:25	105
21:15–17	46, 204	4:24	122
21:20	107, 163	4:25	125
21:26	49	5:18–19	100
21:27–36	107, 199	6:3ff.	105
21:28	199	6:9	126
21:30–32	49, 117	8:34	125
21:31–37	198	9–11	109
22:4	102	11:20	109
22:14	122, 164, 188, 189	15:19	213
22:16	105	15:22–25	204
23:2	199	15:25–32	204
23:11	164, 181, 188, 190		
23:12–35	117, 185	1 Corinthians	
23:24, 26	198	4	98
23:31	201	1:13	207
24:2–3	185, 199	2:1–5	213
24:10, 17	107, 185	9:19–23	214
24:14, 22	185	10:6–9	99
24:24	185, 199	11:23–25	105, 130, 213
24:27	24, 43, 185, 198, 203	15	98, 129, 212, 213
		15:3–5	122, 126
25:1–27	185, 198, 199	15:3	105
26:4	185	15:14	207
26:16	48, 164, 189	15:15	122
26:18	105, 136, 140	15:17	207
26:23	125, 136, 140	15:42–50	126
26:24	107	15:51–52	214
27:1–8	175, 198	16:8–9	204

2 Corinthians
- 2:12 — 204
- 5:1–10 — 214
- 5:21 — 105
- 8–9 — 204
- 10:10 — 212, 213
- 11:7–9 — 204
- 11:32–33 — 207
- 12:10 — 204, 212
- 12:12 — 213

Galatians
- 1:11–12 — 48
- 1:13–14 — 204
- 1:15–17 — 204
- 1:18–19 — 204
- 1:20 — 205
- 1:21 — 204
- 1:22 — 207
- 2:1–10 — 204, 206, 207
- 2:11–16 — 212
- 2:19–21 — 214
- 3:1–5 — 213
- 4:4 — 214

Ephesians
- 1:20 — 122, 126
- 5:11–12 — 155

Philippians
- 1:12–14 — 117
- 1:19–26 — 214
- 2:6–11 — 125, 214
- 2:8 — 100
- 3 — 98
- 3:20–21 — 129
- 4:15–16 — 204

Colossians
- 3:1 — 126

1 Thessalonians
- 1:5 — 213
- 1:9–10 — 214
- 2:1–2 — 204
- 2:14 — 207
- 2:15 — 112

- 4:15 — 214

1 Timothy
- 3:16 — 125, 126
- 4:15 — 93
- 6:20 — 25, 40

2 Timothy
- 1:12 — 25, 40
- 2:2 — 23, 41
- 4:6–8 — 113

Titus
- 1:5 — 22

Hebrews
- 1:3 — 126
- 2:10 — 94, 100, 102, 128
- 4:14 — 125, 126
- 5:8–9 — 94, 100
- 7:3 — 83
- 7:25 — 125
- 8:1 — 125
- 8:12 — 125
- 10:12 — 125
- 11:36ff — 112
- 12:2 — 102, 128
- 13:20 — 126

James
- 5:16–18 — 184

1 Peter
- 1:3, 21 — 122, 126
- 1:7 — 100
- 3:21 — 126
- 3:22 — 126
- 4:1–2 — 100, 101
- 4:3–4 — 155

2 Peter
- 1:15 — 130

1 John
- 1:1–2 — 127
- 2:16 — 99
- 3:2 — 129

Jude
  12–13   155

III. Apocrypha, Pseudepigrapha, and Qumran

Apocrypha

Tobit
  12:19   128

Judith
  14   139
  14:10   144, 146

Wisdom of Solomon
  14:23–24   153, 157, 159

Sirach
  47:2   21
  50:19–20   133

1 Maccabees
  1:10–15, 41–50   147
  2:15–22   147
  2:50–68   211
  3:1   21
  6:14, 55   22

2 Maccabees
  6:18ff   112
  6:29   113
  7:2, 11   106
  7:4   112
  7:9   112
  7:37–38   112
  9:23   23
  14:26   23

4 Maccabees
  6:27–29   112
  7:15   100, 112
  9:18   112
  16:25   112
  17:22   112

2 Esdras
  9:26ff   68

Pseudepigrapha

Apocalypse of Abraham
  1–7   139, 145
  17:8–11   83

2 Baruch
  13:3–10   100
  21:1ff   68

3 Enoch
  48D.10   36, 37

Joseph and Asenath
  9:2   140
  13:11–12   140

Jubilees
  1:12   112
  6   172

Ps-Philo, L.A.B.
  25:3   21, 26, 34
  20:2–5

Testament of Job
  2–5   139, 145
  5:1   146
  27:4–5   146

Testament of Moses
  1:6–9   34

Testaments of the XII Patriarchs
T. Judah
9:3   156

IV. Josephus and Philo

Josephus
A.J.
1.3.4 § 83–87	24
1.4 § 85	22, 23
1.6.3 § 279–84	211
1.9.2 § 197	128
2.9.6 § 231	73
2.16.5 § 33	167
4.7.2 § 165	26, 35, 48
5.11.5 § 361–62	22, 23, 24, 26
6.8.1–6.10.2 § 156–196	35
7.14.2 § 337	23, 24, 26, 35
8.4.2 § 109–110	167
9.2.2 § 27–28	36
10.8.2–3 § 142	165, 189
10.11.7 § 278–81	167
13.2.2 § 45	23
13.10.6 § 297	21
13.16.1 § 407	22, 24
14.11.5 § 417	199
15.5.3 § 127–46	211
17.3.2 § 53	22, 23
17.6.2–4 § 149–67	106
18.1.1 § 4–10	200
18.2.2 § 32	21
18.3.1 § 261–309	116
18.6.9 § 219	23, 24, 26, 37, 46, 53
18.8 § 244–72	116
19.3–4 § 212–73	26
19.8.2 § 343–51	202
20.2.3–4 § 34–48	139, 143
20.2.5 § 51–53	202
20.5.1 § 97–98	20
20.5.2 § 100–104	200, 202
20.8.1–2 § 148–53	26
20.8.9 § 182	203

B.J.
1.19.4 § 373–79	211
1.23.2 § 451	22
1.30.7 § 600	22
1.33.3 § 651	112
1.33.7 § 664	22
2.1.1 § 2	22
2.2.5–7 § 31–38	22
2.8.1 § 118	200
2.9.3 § 184	116
2.10 § 184–198	116
2.14.4 § 284	66, 203
2.17.8 § 433	200
5.5.2 § 193–94	199
5.5.8 § 243–69	199
6.2.4 § 125–26	199
7.8.1 § 253	200

C.Ap.
1.8 § 41	110
2.8 § 89–102	157

Vita
1	73

Philo
Abr.
118	128

Decal.
9:33	172
11:46	172

Legat.
31.212	199

Leg.
3.159	92

Post.
132	92

Somn.
2.234–35	92

V. Rabbinic Writings

Abot R. Nat.
  1   36

Gen. Rab.
  82   113

Mek.
Bahodesh
  1   171

Tanh.
  26c   172

Mishnah
Abot
  1   36, 60
  5:21   95

Pesiq. Rab.
  30:4   171

Sipre
  §343   171

Talmud
  b. Abod. Zar. 18a   112
  b. Ber. 33a   183
  b. Ber. 61b   112
  y. Ber. 5.1   183
  y. Pes. 6.1.33a   42, 60

Tosefta
Sanh.
  8.3 [E]   183
Sotah
  8:6   172

VI. Early Christian Writings

Acts John
  70–75   183, 184
  106–110   131

Acts Pet.
  23   83
  24   83

Acts Thom.
  27, 49–50   131

Aristides
Apol.
  12   84

Arnobius
Disp. adv. nat.
  4.27   85

Athenagoras
Leg.
  3   158
  28.5   23
  37.2   23, 24

Augustine
Cons
  1.7.10   3, 33
  2.14.31   3

Bede
Hist.
  5.24   4

1 Clement
  42:4   22, 32, 39
  44:2   22, 23, 25, 32, 39, 49

Clement of Alexandria
Strom.
  1.1   33, 41
  4.9   1

Coptic Gos. Thom.
  17   128

Cyril of Alexandria
Com. Luke
  Homily 1   2

Homily 12	2	64	109
		110	113
Diogn.			
6.9	113	Lactantius	
7.7–8	113	*Epit.*	
		1.7.1	83
Ep. Apos.			
11–12	127	Mart. Pol.	
		1.1	113
Eusebius		4	113, 114
Hist. eccl.			
6.29.4	24	Minucius Felix	
Praep. ev.		*Oct.*	
4.22.3	21	8.4	154
11.14	21	9.6–7	154
14.5	25	9.5	158
14.9	24	30	159
Gos. Pet.		Origen	
35–42	121	*Cels.*	
		6.27	154, 158, 159
Hilary		8.66	111
Vit. Honorati			
8	40, 62	Orosius	
		7.6.15–16	203, 208
Ignatius			
Smyrn.		Paulinus	
3.1–2	127	*Vit. Ambr.*	
Trall.		46, 49	40
9.2	122		
		Preaching of Peter	
Irenaeus		1.2	26,
Haer.		Ep. Pet. Jac. 1	26
1.8.3–4	1		
1.20.2	1	Ps.-Clem.	
1.24.3–6	113	*Hom.*	
		Ep. Clem. Jac. 2	26, 39
Justin Martyr		14.7	131
1 Apol.		*Recogn.*	
26	155, 158, 159	1.42.1	163
2 Apol.		1.63	163
12	113, 158	1.64.2	163
Dial.		4	131
10	153, 159		
32	109	Tatian	
47.2	109	*Graec.*	
55	109	25	158

Tertullian		Theophilus of Antioch	
An.		*Autol.*	
5	128	3.4	153
Apol.		3.15	158
7.13–8.5	153, 158		
50	111, 113	Vit. Pach.	
Marc.		2	92
4.7–8	84, 128	28	93
4.43	2	43	93
Praescr.			
1	113		
Scorp.			
1	113		

VII. Greco-Roman Writings

Achilles Tatius		Chion of Heraclea	
3.15	157	4	179
Aeschylus		Cicero	
Ag.		*Cat.*	
647–66	179	1.1	151
		3.5–6	151
Anthologia Graeca		*De or.*	
7.290	182	2.15.63	28
		34.120	28
Apollonius Rhodius		*Ep. Brut.*	
Argon.		5.12	206
4.1228–47	179	*Leg.*	
		2.35	152
Appian		*Nat. d.*	
Hist. rom.		1.10.25–26	25
1.1.1	23, 24		
		Caesar	
Apuleius		*Bell. gall.*	
Metam.		1.40	211
11.7	166		
11.13	166	Dio Cassius	
		38.36–46	211
Aristotle		41.48.1	25
Soph. elench.		44.34.5	25
34.27–35	21, 23, 25	49.17.6	24
§ 183b		53.31.3	23, 25
		60.6.6	202, 208
Aulus Gellius		60.17.5–6	199
13.5	27, 29, 38		

Dio Chrysostom
Or.
1.57	145
7.2–7	179
11.124.6	22
37.5.2	23

Diodorus Siculus
1.23	86
4.2.1–4	85
4.9.1	85
4.71.1	85
15.60.4	24
17.117.4	37
17.117.17ff	26
18.1.4	22, 37
18.1.6	23, 24, 37
18.2.1	24, 37
20.5.1	157

Diogenes Laertius
Vit. phil.
1.6.2	22
2.3.1	22
2.46	21
2.47	21
2.85–86	21
3.16–18	146
4.3.16–18	144
5.62	25
5.68.5	22
7.36	21, 22
7.37	24, 25
9.68	179
9.110	26
10.16–22	131

Dionysius of Halicarnassus
Ant. rom.
1.53.4	24
1.77.2–1.78.4	86
4.34.3	24
5.56.1	28

Epictetus
Diatr.
1.4.1	92
1.4.4	92
1.4.18–21	92
1.29.56	111

Euripides
Bacch.
215–220	152

Tro.
77–86	179

Juvenal
8.231–35	152
12.1782	178

Herculanium Papyri
P. Herc. 164	38
P. Herc. 495	38
P. Herc. 558	38
P. Herc. 1018	22, 23, 24, 25, 28, 29, 38, 61
P. Herc. 1021	22, 23, 24, 25, 26, 28, 29, 38, 61
P. Herc. 1044	31, 61
P.Herc. 1508	38
P. Herc. 1780	38

Heliodorus
1.22	179
2.20	182
5.27	179

Herodotus
1.177	28
1.91	168
1.216	156
3.38	156
3.99	156
4.26	156
4.106	156
6.64	156
7.188–92	179

Historiae Augustae
Ant. Pius
1.1–7	73

INDEX OF ANCIENT SOURCES

Hadr.
  1.1–7   73

Homer
Od.
  4.499–511   179
  5.125–28   85
  5.291–453   179

Horace
Carm.
  1.22   183
  34   142

Iamblichus
Vit. Pyth.
  28   186
  36   25, 30

Isocrates
Aeginet.
  43   22

Justinian
Dig.
  1.2.2.1–34   39
  1.2.35–53   39
  1.2.37, 38, 39,   21
    44, 46
  1.2.36, 44   21
  1.2.37, 38   21
  1.2.40   22, 25
  1.2.48, 51, 53   21

Juvenal
Satr.
  8.231–35   152
  12.1782   178

Livy
  39.8   152, 157, 159

Lucan
Bell. civ.
  5.560–677   179
  9.319–47   179

Lucian
Alex.
  5   25, 26
  60   23, 26, 27, 37
Bis acc.
  17   137, 141
Hist. conscr.
  58   211
Merc. cond.
  1–2   178
Nigr.
  1–5   137
Pisc.
  31   111
Peregr.
  13   112
  43–44   179
Tox.
  19–21   178, 179
Ver. hist.
  1.5–6   178, 179

Lucretius
Rer. Nat.
  1.304   128

Marcus Aurelius
  11.3.2   112

Ovid
Metam.
  1.198–239   157
  3.259–318   85
  11.477–574   179
  14.125–28   85

Petronius
  114   178, 179

Phaedrus
Fab.
  4.23   178, 179

Philostratus
Vit. Apoll.
  1.4   73
  1.5   74

6.25	157	*Quaest. conv.*	
7.11, 20	157	4.6.2	153
8.5	157	*Rom.*	
8.31	141	2.5	73
		4.2	73
Plato		7.3–4	75
Apol.		*Thes.*	
39	111	2	73
		3	73
Pliny the Elder		6.4	73
Nat. hist.		7	75
2.47.125	181	36.3	73
30.4–5	42	*Virt. prof.*	
		75.1b-d	146
Pliny the Younger		*Vit. X orat.*	
Ep.		835C	21
1.16	210	850C	25
10.96	154		
		Polybius	
Plutarch		*Hist.*	
Alc.		1.4.1–2	165, 189
2.1	75	1.37	178, 179
Alex.		3.32	28
3.1–2	73	10.21.5–8	28
5.1	73	12.24–25	28, 211
Brut.			
1–2	73	Porphyry	
Caes.		*Vit. Pyth.*	
38.2–4	187	3	186
Def. orac.		29	186
434, 45d-f	141, 147	*Isag.*	
Demetr.		46.10	25
4.4	75		
Exil.		Quintus Curtius	
14	25	*Hist. Alex.*	
Fab.		1	73, 86
1	73	4.3.16–18	179
Is. Os.			
36	86, 88	The Elder Seneca	
Lyc.		*Controv.*	
1.4	73	7.1	180
Num.			
4	86	Seneca	
Oth.		*Ep.*	
15	211	6.1	146
Pyrrh.		24.15	111
1	73	24.25	112

INDEX OF ANCIENT SOURCES

52.8–9	110	Tacitus	
		Ann.	
Statius		2.23–24	178, 179
Silv.		15.62	22, 26
1.2.96–97	28	15.63	210
		Hist.	
Strabo		1.10	74
Nat. Hist.		1.18	74
15.1.56	157	1.22	74
		2.47	211
Suetonius		4.81	74
Aug.			
94	70, 74, 81, 86	Thucydides	
		1.22.1	210
Claud.		2.2.1	66
1–2	70		
25.4	202, 208	Vergil	
Dom.		*Aen.*	
14	74	5.14–43	179
Nero		7.652–53	191
1–6	71	11.587–94	191
Tit.		12.725–38	191
2	71		
5.2	71	Xenophon of Ephesus	
Vesp.		2.11	179
1–2	71	3.2	179
5	71	3.12	179

SUPPLEMENTS TO NOVUM TESTAMENTUM

ISSN 0167-9732

2. Strobel, A. *Untersuchungen zum eschatologischen Verzögerungsproblem auf Grund der spätjüdische-urchristlichen Geschichte von Habakuk 2,2 ff.* 1961. ISBN 90 04 01582 5
16. Pfitzner, V.C. *Paul and the Agon Motif.* 1967. ISBN 90 04 01596 5
27. Mussies, G. *The Morphology of Koine Greek As Used in the Apocalypse of St. John.* A Study in Bilingualism. 1971. ISBN 90 04 02656 8
28. Aune, D.E. *The Cultic Setting of Realized Eschatology in Early Christianity.* 1972. ISBN 90 04 03341 6
29. Unnik, W.C. van. *Sparsa Collecta.* The Collected Essays of W.C. van Unnik Part 1. Evangelia, Paulina, Acta. 1973. ISBN 90 04 03660 1
31. Unnik, W.C. van. *Sparsa Collecta.* The Collected Essays of W.C. van Unnik Part 3. Patristica, Gnostica, Liturgica. 1983. ISBN 90 04 06262 9
34. Hagner, D.A. *The Use of the Old and New Testaments in Clement of Rome.* 1973. ISBN 90 04 03636 9
37. Reiling, J. *Hermas and Christian Prophecy.* A Study of The Eleventh Mandate. 1973. ISBN 90 04 03771 3
43. Clavier, H. *Les variétés de la pensée biblique et le problème de son unité.* Esquisse d'une théologie de la Bible sur les textes originaux et dans leur contexte historique. 1976. ISBN 90 04 04465 5
47. Baarda, T., A.F.J. Klijn & W.C. van Unnik (eds.) *Miscellanea Neotestamentica.* I. Studia ad Novum Testamentum Praesertim Pertinentia a Sociis Sodalicii Batavi c.n. Studiosorum Novi Testamenti Conventus Anno MCMLXXVI Quintum Lustrum Feliciter Complentis Suscepta. 1978. ISBN 90 04 05685 8
48. Baarda, T., A.F.J. Klijn & W.C. van Unnik (eds.) *Miscellanea Neotestamentica.* II. 1978. ISBN 90 04 05686 6
50. Bousset, D.W. *Religionsgeschichtliche Studien.* Aufsätze zur Religionsgeschichte des hellenistischen Zeitalters. Hrsg. von A.F. Verheule. 1979. ISBN 90 04 05845 1
52. Garland, D.E. *The Intention of Matthew 23.* 1979. ISBN 90 04 05912 1
53. Moxnes, H. *Theology in Conflict.* Studies in Paul's Understanding of God in Romans. 1980. ISBN 90 04 06140 1
56. Skarsaune, O. *The Proof From Prophecy.* A Study in Justin Martyr's Proof-Text Tradition: Text-type, Provenance, Theological Profile. 1987. ISBN 90 04 07468 6
59. Wilkins, M.J. *The Concept of Disciple in Matthew's Gospel, as Reflected in the Use of the Term 'Mathetes'.* 1988. ISBN 90 04 08689 7
64. Sterling, G.E. *Historiography and Self-Definition.* Josephos, Luke-Acts and Apologetic Historiography. 1992. ISBN 90 04 09501 2
65. Botha, J.E. *Jesus and the Samaritan Woman.* A Speech Act Reading of John 4:1-42. 1991. ISBN 90 04 09505 5
66. Kuck, D.W. *Judgment and Community Conflict.* Paul's Use of Apologetic Judgment Language in 1 Corinthians 3:5-4:5. 1992. ISBN 90 04 09510 1
67. Schneider, G. *Jesusüberlieferung und Christologie.* Neutestamentliche Aufsätze 1970-1990. 1992. ISBN 90 04 09555 1
68. Seifrid, M.A. *Justification by Faith.* The Origin and Development of a Central Pauline Theme. 1992. ISBN 90 04 09521 7

69. Newman, C.C. *Paul's Glory-Christology*. Tradition and Rhetoric. 1992.
    ISBN 90 04 09463 6
70. Ireland, D.J. *Stewardship and the Kingdom of God*. An Historical, Exegetical, and Contextual Study of the Parable of the Unjust Steward in Luke 16: 1-13. 1992.
    ISBN 90 04 09600 0
71. Elliott, J.K. *The Language and Style of the Gospel of Mark*. An Edition of C.H. Turner's "Notes on Marcan Usage" together with other comparable studies. 1993.
    ISBN 90 04 09767 8
72. Chilton, B. *A Feast of Meanings*. Eucharistic Theologies from Jesus through Johannine Circles. 1994. ISBN 90 04 09949 2
73. Guthrie, G.H. *The Structure of Hebrews*. A Text-Linguistic Analysis. 1994.
    ISBN 90 04 09866 6
74. Bormann, L., K. Del Tredici & A. Standhartinger (eds.) *Religious Propaganda and Missionary Competition in the New Testament World*. Essays Honoring Dieter Georgi. 1994. ISBN 90 04 10049 0
75. Piper, R.A. (ed.) *The Gospel Behind the Gospels*. Current Studies on Q. 1995.
    ISBN 90 04 09737 6
76. Pedersen, S. (ed.) *New Directions in Biblical Theology*. Papers of the Aarhus Conference, 16-19 September 1992. 1994. ISBN 90 04 10120 9
77. Jefford, C.N. (ed.) *The* Didache *in Context*. Essays on Its Text, History and Transmission. 1995. ISBN 90 04 10045 8
78. Bormann, L. *Philippi – Stadt und Christengemeinde zur Zeit des Paulus*. 1995.
    ISBN 90 04 10232 9
79. Peterlin, D. *Paul's Letter to the Philippians in the Light of Disunity in the Church*. 1995.
    ISBN 90 04 10305 8
80. Jones, I.H. *The Matthean Parables*. A Literary and Historical Commentary. 1995.
    ISBN 90 04 10181 0
81. Glad, C.E. *Paul and Philodemus*. Adaptability in Epicurean and Early Christian Psychagogy. 1995 ISBN 90 04 10067 9
82. Fitzgerald, J.T. (ed.) *Friendship, Flattery, and Frankness of Speech*. Studies on Friend-ship in the New Testament World. 1996. ISBN 90 04 10454 2
83. Tilborg, S. van. *Reading John in Ephesus*. 1996. 90 04 10530 1
84. Holleman, J. *Resurrection and Parousia*. A Traditio-Historical Study of Paul's Eschatology in 1 Corinthians 15. 1996. ISBN 90 04 10597 2
85. Moritz, T. *A Profound Mystery*. The Use of the Old Testament in Ephesians. 1996.
    ISBN 90 04 10556 5
86. Borgen, P. *Philo of Alexandria - An Exegete for His Time*. 1997. ISBN 90 04 10388 0
87. Zwiep, A.W. *The Ascension of the Messiah in Lukan Christology*. 1997.
    ISBN 90 04 10897 1
88. Wilson, W.T. *The Hope of Glory*. Education and Exhortation in the Epistle to the Colossians. 1997. ISBN 90 04 10937 4
89. Peterson, W.L., J.S. Vos & H.J. de Jonge (eds.). *Sayings of Jesus: Canonical and Non-Canonical*. Essays in Honour of Tjitze Baarda. 1997. ISBN 90 04 10380 5
90. Malherbe, A.J., F.W. Norris & J.W. Thompson (eds.). *The Early Church in Its Context*. Essays in Honor of Everett Ferguson. 1998. ISBN 90 04 10832 7
91. Kirk, A. *The Composition of the Sayings Source*. Genre, Synchrony, and Wisdom Redaction in Q. 1998. ISBN 90 04 11085 2
92. Vorster, W.S. *Speaking of Jesus*. Essays on Biblical Language, Gospel Narrative and the Historical Jesus. Edited by J. E. Botha. 1999. ISBN 90 04 10779 7
93. Bauckham, R. *The Fate of Dead*. Studies on the Jewish and Christian Apocalypses. 1998. ISBN 90 04 11203 0

94. Standhartinger, A. *Studien zur Entstehungsgeschichte und Intention des Kolosserbriefs.* ISBN 90 04 11286 3
95. Oegema, G.S. *Für Israel und die Völker.* Studien zum alttestamentlich-jüdischen Hintergrund der paulinischen Theologie. 1999. ISBN 90 04 11297 9
96. Albl, M.C. *"And Scripture Cannot Be Broken".* The Form and Function of the Early Christian *Testimonia* Collections. 1999. ISBN 90 04 11417 3
97. Ellis, E.E. *Christ and the Future in New Testament History.* 1999. ISBN 90 04 11533 1
98. Chilton, B. & C.A. Evans, (eds.) *James the Just and Christian Origins.* 1999. ISBN 90 04 11550 1
99. Horrell, D.G. & C.M. Tuckett (eds.) *Christology, Controversy and Community.* New Testament Essays in Honour of David R. Catchpole. 2000. ISBN 90 04 11679 6
100. Jackson-McCabe, M.A. *Logos and Law in the Letter of James.* The Law of Nature, the Law of Moses and the Law of Freedom. 2001. ISBN 90 04 11994 9
101. Wagner, J.R. *Heralds of the Good News.* Isaiah and Paul "In Concert" in the Letter to the Romans 2002. ISBN 90 04 11691 5
102. Cousland, J.R.C. *The Crowds in the Gospel of Matthew.* 2002. ISBN 90 04 12177 3
103. Dunderberg, I., C. Tuckett and K. Syreeni. *Fair Play: Diversity and Conflicts in Early Christianity.* Essays in Honour of Heikki Räisänen. 2002. ISBN 90 04 12359 8
104. Mount, C. *Pauline Christianity.* Luke-Acts and the Legacy of Paul. 2002. ISBN 90 04 12472 1
105. Matthews, C.R. *Philip: Apostle and Evangelist.* Configurations of a Tradition. 2002. ISBN 90 04 12054 8
106. Aune, D.E., T. Seland & J.H. Ulrichsen (eds.) *Neotestamentica et Philonica.* Studies in Honor of Peder Borgen. 2002. ISBN 90 04 126104
107. Talbert, C.H. *Reading Luke-Acts in its Mediterranean Milieu.* 2003. ISBN 90 04 12964 2